SEYDER TKHINES

The title page of *Seyder Tkhines* printed in Amsterdam in 1689.

SEYDER TKHINES

The Forgotten Book of Common Prayer
for Jewish Women

Translated and edited,
with commentary by

DEVRA KAY

2004 • 5764

THE JEWISH PUBLICATION SOCIETY
Philadelphia

The Jewish Publication Society
2100 Arch Street, 2nd floor
Philadelphia, PA 19103

Design and Composition by Book Design Studio II

Manufactured in the United States of America

04 05 06 07 08 09 10   10 9 8 7 6 5 4 3 2 1

Library of Congress Cataloging-in-Publication Data

Seyder tkhines. English.
  Seyder tkhines : the forgotten book of common prayer for Jewish women / translated and edited with commentary by Devra Kay.—1st ed.
      p. cm.
  Includes English translation and discussion of Book of tkhines for a pregnant woman, a 17th century Yiddish and Hebrew manuscript in the Bodleian library.
  Includes bibliographical references and index.
  ISBN 0-8276-0773-3
  1. Tehinnot—Translations into English. 2. Judaism—Prayer-books and devotions—English. 3. Seyder tkhines. 4. Tehinnot—History and criticism. 5. Jewish women—Prayer-books and devotions—History and criticism. I. Kay, Devra. II. Book of tkhines for a pregnant woman. III. Title.
  BM675.T4Z554 2004
  296.4'5'082—dc22
                              2004005031

To Fay and Joe

The Jewish Publication Society is one of the most respected international Jewish cultural and educational institutions. In all of its endeavors, JPS seeks to preserve and enrich Jewish heritage.

The Society honors the members of its Giving Circles, whose generosity strengthens its ability to achieve its multifaceted mission:

CONTENTS

Contents

Acknowledgments

My grateful thanks to Professor Lewis Glinert for urging me to write this book and for all his help and encouragement. I also wish to thank Gabbie, Anthony and Gemma Asher, Rebecca, Eliahu and Ruchama, Rick Lecoat, Isabel Kosky, Ged Dixon, Cathryn Scott, Lee O'Rourke, Tom Goldsmith, Anne-Marie Douglas, and Amanda Epstein for their support, encouragement, inspiration, and unstinting help throughout the project. Special thanks must go to Doris Nicholson and her colleagues at the Bodleian Library and to Kayla Roberg at the London School of Jewish Studies Library for their generous assistance with texts. Then of course there is JPS. I could not have wished for more warmth, support, and experience than that provided by Ellen Frankel and Janet Liss and their colleagues. The book could not have been completed without them all.

Introduction

It was in Oxford in 1988 that I read the late, and much missed, Professor Chone Shmeruk's classic book on Yiddish literature in which he wrote that "the many-faceted *tkhines* literature in Yiddish has not been accorded a detailed and comprehensive study." I was delighted because I was in the middle of writing my doctoral thesis on that very subject. Some months later I met Professor Shmeruk in Jerusalem. He welcomed me with his customary shrug of the shoulders, wistful smile, head cocked to one side, arms beckoning, while he uttered what he considered to be a hilarious greeting: "Ah, *di tkhines yidene*!", which means "the *Tkhines* woman." This is a nickname that has remained with me. Unfortunately, the Yiddish word *yidene* possesses all the worst connotations of womanhood, including those of a harridan.

He was quick to tell me that I was not alone in my field of research. There was a woman in America who was also researching *tkhines*. I already knew this to be the case and, not long after, the person in question, Chava Weissler, arrived in Oxford for a few days. We met for lunch in college where we agreed that the field of *tkhines* was more than big enough for both of us to plow.

Tkhines are Yiddish prayers for women. The word *tkhine*, from the Hebrew, means "supplication" or "prayer." This book deals with *tkhines* from their earliest period, which starts in 1648, lasts for three generations, and ends where Chava Weissler begins. My main character, deservedly so, is the *Seyder Tkhines*, a standard prayer book written especially for women that was printed with the synagogue prayer book, and whose significance goes well beyond supplication and requests to God. It has no equal at any other time in history. It represents strange and fantastic times when both Jews and Christians became intoxicated with a belief in the imminent arrival of the Messiah. The man who first brought the *Seyder Tkhines* into print was the same man who persuaded Oliver Cromwell to readmit Jews into England with the argument that until Jews were scattered everywhere in exile, the Messiah would not come. It was also a period when Jewish women reached a peak of communal religious eminence that has never been equaled.

For various reasons, these *tkhines* have been shut away for so long that they have been wiped from the communal memory. This book seeks to restore them to their rightful place. It is hoped that the six authors whose work is featured here along with the *Seyder Tkhines* and other Yiddish literature of their day, may at last emerge from the silent stacks of university libraries where they have been confined for too long and begin to take their rightful place in world literary history. Now seems to be the time for *tkhines* to come into their own. Whether out of curiosity, duty, empathy, or dare I say tradition, it seems to have been left to two women to wipe away the dust of centuries.

Tkhines provide at least a lifetime of research, which is far too much material for one book. Unlike Yitskhok ben Elyokum of Posen, who boasted in the introduction to his Yiddish ethical book *Seyfer Lev Tov*, (Good heart)[1] that in his book could be found *gants yidishkayt* (the whole of the practice of Judaism), I cannot claim to have provided more than a modest introduction to this intriguing subject and to the works themselves in the hope that I and others will continue to exchange ideas and discoveries in pursuit of a greater understanding.

Devra Kay
London
February 2004

1. Published in Prague in 1620.

Pronunciation of Yiddish and Hebrew Words

The Yiddish words that appear in this book follow the international standard YIVO Yiddish pronunciation rules as they appear below:

Letter	Pronunciation	Letter	Pronunciation
a	as in "man," close to the Spanish "mañana"	m	as in "milk"
		n	as in "nut"
ay	as in "pie"	o	as in "pot"
b	as in "bat"	oy	as in "boy"
d	as in "dollar"	p	as in "pit"
e	as in "egg"	r	as in "ring," but
ey	as in "they"		guttural, as in French
g	as in "give"	s	as in "sun"
h	as in "head"	sh	as in "shine"
i	as in "pit" or "feel"	t	as in "town"
j	as in "jack"	ts	as in "wits"
k	as in "king"	tsh	as in "patch"
kh	as in "loch"	u	as in "put" or "fool"
l	as in "lemon"		

Hebrew words appear in the Ashkenazic pronunciation relevant to Yiddish speakers, and the same rules apply. In the case of names, I have, for the sake of consistency, transcribed them in Ashkenazic pronunciation with the exception of those that are generally well known in anglicized form. These I have reproduced in their familiar form.

PART ONE
COMMENTARY

1

Introducing Tkhines

The *Seyder Tkhines,*[1] which first appeared in print in Amsterdam in 1648, is a landmark in the history of women. It represents an age of religious, sexual, linguistic, and literary revolution within the Jewish community across Europe, an age when mysticism pervaded mainstream[2] Judaism. Yet this exceptional episode, along with its literature, has disappeared from the Jewish collective memory. Jews of this period believed themselves to be on the verge of a Messianic redemption that called for spiritual regeneration, heartfelt prayer, and repentance by the entire community, women as well as men. Each catastrophe experienced by the community, and these were many and cataclysmic, was seen as an affirmation of this belief. The urgency to get the community's "house in order" necessitated an unprecedented reform in the religious and cultural participation of women who traditionally had not played an essential role in communal prayer or learning in Orthodox Judaism. A new vernacular prayer literature for, and sometimes by, women was prolifically printed and widely circulated by a dynamic, pan-European Yiddish printing industry. These prayers, and in particular those entitled *tkhines,* are the subject of this book. Jewish women today who are seeking a precedent for women's prayer need look no further.

WOMEN, LITERACY, AND THE LANGUAGE OF PRAYER

Tkhines are a phenomenon of Ashkenazic Jewry that arose from the ninth century[3] in the German-speaking lands in the basins of the Rhine and the Danube. These Jews formed a community that was autonomous from the major Jewish settlements in the Middle East. They had a common culture that differed from the Christian community around them—even their language was different.

Three Jewish languages coexisted within the Ashkenazic community: Yiddish, Hebrew and Aramaic. Each had its own accepted function and status. The only spoken language was Yiddish, the Ashkenazic vernacular. Aramaic, which had been the vernacular in the Middle East from the time of the Babylonian exile in the seventh century B.C., was not spoken in Europe. It was learned only by an elite coterie of scholars for the study of the Talmud, and by yet more elite scholars of the central work of Jewish mysticism—the Kabbalah. The Hebrew language, known popularly in Yiddish as *Loshn koydesh* (Sacred tongue), was not spoken in Europe, but was the language of the Torah, Bible, and other sacred texts. Hebrew was also the established language of the Jewish prayer book known as the *Sider* (Modern Hebrew: "Siddur"). Yiddish, known also as *Mame loshn* (Mother tongue), developed from a fusion of Hebrew and Jewish Aramaic brought from the Middle East, which was then combined with what was the most sizeable constituent of Yiddish, medieval urban German dialects, and then, according to some scholars with the Jewish versions of Old French and Old Italian, known as *Laaz*. Jewish mass migrations across Europe, particularly in the eleventh and the fourteenth centuries, due to persecutions generated by the Crusades and the Black Death, were responsible for the gradual spread of Yiddish across territories as far afield as what are now Holland, Germany, parts of Denmark, Alsace and Switzerland in Western Europe, Italy in the Southwest, Hungary and the Czech Republic in Central Europe, and Lithuania, Latvia, Russia, Poland, and Rumania in the East. In all these places, the spoken language in the Jewish family and community was almost invariably Yiddish, and although Jews were often proficient in the local language for reasons of trade and other necessary communication, they could usually read only in the Hebrew alphabet.

4

While the Church conveyed its message visually by means of murals, statuary, stained glass, and altarpieces, Jews regarded any depiction of the human form as a "graven image" and did not permit visual art in synagogues. Their religious knowledge came from books, and unlike their Christian neighbors, the Jewish community was highly literate. Girls were taught the Hebrew alphabet, either at elementary school (*kheyder*) along with boys, or privately at home. For boys from poor families, communities set up non fee-paying elementary schools (*Talmud-Toyre*) in preparation for further education.

Boys were expected to be able to read Hebrew well enough to enable them to use the Hebrew prayer book. Opportunities existed for the most able boys to extend their education beyond the rudimentary level by attending seminaries (*yeshives*) where they were able to study up to rabbinic level. Such advanced education was not extended to women. Although women achieved a basic literacy in the Hebrew alphabet in which both Hebrew and Yiddish are written, they were generally literate only in Yiddish, the vernacular. Men, on the other hand, were encouraged to attain proficiency in Hebrew, the traditional language of prayer and literature. At the time of the heyday of the Yiddish literature presented in this book, Yiddish was spoken and read by millions of Ashkenazim across Europe.

The established language of the Ashkenazic prayer book in the sixteenth century, as with Jewish prayer books in other times and places, was Hebrew. Jewish prayer was male dominated. The attendance of a quorum of ten adult males, a minyen, was obligatory for the three daily synagogue services, as it is today. Women are not permitted to participate in the minyen. Women are exempt from time-bound and location-bound prayer and are therefore not obliged to attend the synagogue services. They are, however, obliged to pray once a day.[4]

The *Seyder Tkhines* was a new, standard prayer book of daily and occasional prayers for women, which was printed repeatedly between 1648 and about 1720, in various centers across Europe. Unlike the *Sider*, it was composed in Yiddish, the language that women would better be able to read and understand. The *Seyder Tkhines* never attained the status of the *Sider*, and never challenged it, but for more than seventy years it was endowed with the remarkable prestige of being printed, in its entirety, inside many editions of the *Sider*. It offered a liturgy of prayer for women to say once a day as an alternative to, but based upon, the Hebrew liturgy. These prayers, together with

5

others that were specific to women's needs, had no precedents in the history of Jewish prayer.[5]

The printing and circulation of prescribed vernacular prayers for women, and often authored by women, were not only permitted, but also encouraged. This was revolutionary and unparalleled in all respects. Motivation for this encouragement may have stemmed just as much from a profit motive on the part of Yiddish printers, as from a spiritual one, as women were the predominant readership of Yiddish books. It was repeatedly emphasized in introductions to the Yiddish books of the time that Hebrew prayer was the "higher" form of Jewish prayer.[6] However, in the following lines from the introduction of the seventeenth-century Yiddish ethical work *Seyfer Lev Tov* (Good heart), its author, Yitskhok ben Elyokum of Posen,[7] states that it is of little value to say a prayer without understanding it:

> A little prayer that one understands and prays [recites] with that little bit of spiritual intensity, is a thousand times better than a prayer that is not understood or that has no spiritual intensity.[8]

In the introduction to the earliest printed Yiddish translation of the Pentateuch,[9] it is stated that the book is for "women and young women who can after all generally read Yiddish." This suggests not only that women were, for the most part, literate, but that they were usually literate in Yiddish. The author of the preface to the earliest known edition of the *Seyder Tkhines*,[10] refers to "the holy language (Hebrew) which women do not generally understand," indicating that Hebrew was not the language in which women were generally proficient. The introduction to an atypical *tkhine* published in Prague in 1718 contains the information that the work is adapted from Hebrew for women to say in synagogue and states rather charmingly:

> As soon as a person enters the synagogue she must immediately bow and say *Ma Toyvu*,[11] then bow low, sit down and start to say this *tkhine*, which must be said with deep concentration[12] for I have plucked a rose from the Holy Tongue and made it Yiddish so that all pious women may honor beloved God.

There is evidence to suggest that although some women were able to recite prayers in Hebrew, they still may have chosen to recite them in Yiddish:

And many pious women will particularly wish to say this [prayer] in Hebrew. Therefore, we have also printed it in Hebrew so each may choose
to say it as they please.[13]

Yiddish is seen here as the language chosen by women for prayer,
not as a necessity for the uneducated. The phrase "also printed it in
Hebrew" unexpectedly places Hebrew in a secondary role. The passage implies that Yiddish would be the automatic language for
women's prayer, and that those who wished to do so, could read the
prayers in Hebrew. Women are given the choice of language in which
to pray; but the vital thing is that they pray.

In 1648, Yiddish was the language selected for the *Seyder Tkhines*,
the new standard prayer book that was not a translation, had no precedents, and was tailor made for women with the sanction of the religious authorities. It continued to be printed and reprinted for the
next seventy years, until its relevance ceased to exist.

CLASSIFICATION OF TKHINES

An attempt to classify *tkhines* was made by Chava Weissler in her book
Voices of the Matriarchs (1998). She divided them into those that
were printed from 1648 until around the 1720s, which she calls "Western European," and those that began in the middle decades of the eighteenth century and continued into the nineteenth, which she called
"Eastern European."

To categorize *tkhines* geographically is problematic. Although the
earlier *tkhines* were published in Amsterdam and in various towns in
Germany, they were also published in Prague, which although further west than some of the later eastern European centers of printing, is indisputably located in Central Europe. Weissler herself
includes Prague in both the western and eastern categories, and
writes elsewhere:

Prague is in between Western and Eastern Europe and *Seyder Tkhines* by
Mattithias Sobotki [1718] has some of the Eastern European as well as of
the Western European *tkhines*.[14]

Virtually all of the extant religious songs or *lider* that were written
by women were published in Prague. One of the authors, Toybe Pan,
claimed to be writing her song in a literary style that she called "*tkhine*

loshn" (tkhine language). Thus, the majority of early works related to *tkhines* written by women were not published in Western Europe at all. The *Seyder Tkhines* published in Prague was in an identical form to those published in Amsterdam and German towns, and it appears that the genre was firmly enough established in Prague to have had its own recognizable literary language.

Another center of Yiddish printing that cannot be regarded as Western European is Dyhernfurth, near Breslau in Silesia, which, although ruled by the Hapsburgs in the seventeenth century, became part of Poland in 1945. Its Jewish press, established in the 1680s, supplied Yiddish books to both Poland and Germany, including a *Seyder Tkhines* that appeared in 1705 in a joint Polish-German rite *Sider*. Therefore, when it is applied to where texts were printed as well as where they were circulated, the term "Western European" is inaccurate.

A further problem with a division into west and east is that there were no clear-cut geographical boundaries for the Ashkenazic community, and there was a mass migration of Jews across Europe at this time. From 1648, large numbers of Jews fled from the atrocities of the Cossack massacres, led by Bogdan Chmielnicki, and it is estimated that at least 100,000 Jews were murdered in Poland and the Ukraine over a two-year period. Entire Jewish communities were wiped out, and many of the Jews who managed to escape, migrated westward and settled in towns such as Amsterdam and Prague. Among those displaced, were some of the printers and technicians from Jewish printing houses. They took up their trade in their new locations and practiced their skills alongside the resident printers, thus producing a hybrid, mutually influential, trans-European printing industry that provided the best of east and west. The influx of new immigrants necessitated the printing of liturgical and other religious books to replace those left behind. Those who survived the massacres, but remained in the East, also needed to replenish the books that had been destroyed in the turmoil. From its earliest days, the *Seyder Tkhines* appeared within *Sidorim* used for both German and Polish rites.

The earliest known edition of the *Seyder Tkhines*, which was printed in the year the massacres began, testifies to an intermingling of Eastern and Western traditions. For example, a *Seyder Tkhines* was printed in Amsterdam in Western Europe by Yoysef ben Naftali of

Koskowola who, as his name indicates, hailed from Poland in the East. A prayer book entitled *Minhagim: Rites for all seasons in Poland, Ruthenia, Lithuania, Bohemia, Moravia and Germany* by Aisik Tyrnan, which was printed in Amsterdam in 1635, was clearly intended for Jews from all over Europe, both east and west. This is typical, and emphasizes the difficulty of clearly dividing the Western and Eastern European Jewish populations. Another example of this phenomenon can be seen from the life and publications of the seventeenth-century scholar and rabbi Nathan Note Hanover. Born in Volhyni, he lived in Zaslave before he was forced to flee during the Chmielnicki massacres of 1648. He lived in Prague and Amsterdam, and then studied Kabbalah in Venice. He was later rabbi of Jassy in Moldavia and is believed to have died in Venice. His homiletic work on the Feast of Tabernacles, *Ta'ame Sukkah*, was published in Amsterdam in 1652, and his book containing a vivid account of the Chmielnicki massacres, entitled *Yeven Metzulah* (Abyss of despair), was published in Venice in 1653. Another of his books, a Hebrew-German-Italian-Latin dictionary was published in Prague in 1660, and a second edition of the same book, with added French, was published in Amsterdam in 1701. His book of mystical prayers and religious customs, *Sha'arey Tsion* (Gates of Zion), was published in 1662 in Prague. From the life of one man, and the many places his books were published (all for the same intended readership), it is clear that the geographical criteria of Eastern European and Western European does not really apply. During this period, Jews across Europe had more in common with one another than with their Christian neighbors, and the same Yiddish books were being printed during the same time period, in completely different countries.

I have divided my analysis of *tkhines* and related prayers into Phase 1 and Phase 2, which offer historical rather than geographical divisions. Weissler's field of interest is Phase 2; mine is Phase 1. As is clearly reflected in the prayers themselves, Phase 1, when the *Seyder Tkhines* first appeared in print, is a very different period from Phase 2, in terms of the readership, the authorship, and, in particular, the historical relevance of *tkhines*. This book deals solely with Phase 1 (that is, from 1648 until about 1720), and does not look, in any detail, beyond the middle of the early decades of the eighteenth century.

THE TEXTS

The prayers and religious songs that have been translated in this book from their original Yiddish are all from Phase 1 and date back more than three centuries. Today, their existence, their significance in the lives of women, and the names of those women who wrote some of them, have disappeared like "smoke in the wind."[15] They lie forgotten and neglected in the libraries of academic institutions to which only scholars have access. These texts are not easily accessible to the modern reader of Yiddish, as the language is a specific literary form of Yiddish that was archaic in its own time, easily distinguishable from the spoken language. While the living language had been transformed with the addition of a large Slavic component following Jewish migrations east across Europe,[16] the literary language remained in an earlier form that was predominantly Germanic[17] and owed much of its vocabulary to early Yiddish Bible translations.[18] Equally remote is the appearance of the unfamiliar cursive Hebrew characters, a style known as *mashket*, used in early Yiddish printing to differentiate Yiddish from Hebrew texts. *Mashket* is unlike the familiar bold, square, Assyrian Hebrew characters of the Torah scroll that are found in Hebrew prayer books and also differs from the typefaces used by modern Hebrew printers. It resembles Rashi script in some respects,[19] but also differs from it. Yet when the technical difficulties are overcome, the language is energetic and earnest.

The literature reveals an insecure society that lived in the shadow of persecution, but never lost its optimistic spirit and belief in imminent redemption. This is expressed in the voices of female narrators or by female authors for a mainly female readership. The Yiddish prayers and religious songs bear little resemblance to the more sophisticated works being produced contemporaneously in Christian Europe.[20] Rather, they look back to medieval forms for a model. They are part of a popular, communal literature and there is little emphasis on the author as an individual voice.[21] But due to their historical uniqueness, the literature speaks out to a modern readership from the remoteness of a past that often proves to be startlingly unexpected.

Of the works translated, it is the *Seyder Tkhines* that is most significant.[22] It has generally been believed that *tkhines* were written by women.[23] However, even though the *Seyder Tkhines* is the standard prayer book for women in the voice of a female narrator, it is anonymous. Part 2 of this book provides translations of related single prayers by women, some called *tkhine*, some *tfile*,[24] and some *lid*,[25] which were printed at the end of the seventeenth and early eighteenth century. During this period, women were producing new prayers, songs, and sermons, for both men and women.[26] Together with the translations of the printed texts, I have included the first ever printing of a manuscript dating from the seventeenth century: a unique collection of *tkhines* for a particular pregnant woman.[27]

From what follows, I hope that the names of some of the leading women of early Yiddish literature: Beyle Hurvits; Khane Kats; Toybe Pan; Rokhl, daughter of Mordkhe Soyfer; Sheyndele, wife of Gershen ben Shmuel; Royzl Fishls; and Rivke Tiktiner, along with the *tkhines*, *tfiles*, and *lider* recited and sung by Ashkenazic women across Europe for three generations, may at last emerge and take their rightful place in world literary history.

Ñotes

1. *Seyder Tkhines* means "Sequence of Supplications." *Tkhine* (pl. *tkhines*) comes from the Hebrew *tehinnah* (pl. *tehinnoth*) meaning "supplication" or "prayer."
2. At this early juncture the use of the terms "mainstream" and "orthodox" should be clarified when applied at the time of the *Seyder Tkhines*. They refer here to the whole Ashkenazic community. Today, when Judaism is fragmented into many different denominations, "mainstream" and "orthodox" have particular meanings, and refer to a recognizable section of the faith. Until the eighteenth century, however, there was no clear division between orthodox and non-orthodox, religious and secular. Jews led an all-embracing Jewish life. In the period when the *Seyder Tkhines* was printed, Jews across the world, whether rich or poor, educated or uneducated, were more in tune with one another than ever in their shared expectation of the Messiah.
3. Weinreich 1973:I, 338.
4. Berakhot 3:3 (from the Mishnah, the code of Jewish law that dates mainly from the middle of the first century to the second decade of the third century B.C.E.).
5. Ibid.
6. Yoysef bar Yokor's introduction to the earliest Yiddish prayer book translation, Ichenhausen, 1544.
7. Prague, 1620.
8. Yitskhok ben Elyokum of Posen, 1681:7-8.
9. Mikhl Odem, Constance, 1544. Another translation was printed in the same year: Paulus Æmilius, Augsburg.
10. Amsterdam 1648.
11. The Hebrew prayer that appears in both the *Sider* and many editions of the *Seyder Tkhines* that is said on entering the synagogue.
12. The word *kavone* is used.
13. Introduction to prayer book entitled *Menoyre* printed in Frankfurt an der Oder, seventeenth century.
14. *Voices of the Matriarchs*, 1998:20.
15. A line from the daily prayers in the *Seyder Tkhines*.
16. Known as Eastern Yiddish.
17. Known as Western Yiddish.
18. Leibowitz 1931.
19. The script in which commentaries on the Bible and the Talmud by Rashi (Rabbi Shlomo Yitzchaki, 1040-1105) are printed.
20. The *Tkhines* are contemporaneous with Donne, Milton, Congreve, Aphra Behn, Ludamilia Elisabeth Grimmelshausen, Bedrich Bridel, Adam Michna Otradovic, etc.
21. See Chapter 4 on defining *tkhines*, about the personal and communal aspects of *tkhines*.
22. See Part 2: "The *Seyder Tkhines*" and Chapters 3, 4, and 5.

23. E.g., Niger 1913: 131–138.
24. Prayer.
25. *Lid*, pl. *lider*, meaning song (s).
26. See Chapter 2 on Yiddish printing.
27. See Part 2, "Book of *Tkhines* for a Pregnant Woman," for the translation and Chapter 6 for a discussion of the manuscript.

2
CHAPTER

Profit and Prayer: Women and a Unique Pan-European Printing Industry

The advent of Yiddish printing began in earnest in Europe in the 1540s, enabling publication and circulation of cheaply produced, vernacular books for a mass Jewish audience of both men and women. Its success was due, in part, to the uniquely high level of literacy in the Ashkenazic community. There were other distinctive aspects to the Yiddish printing industry.

It profoundly affected the religious and cultural lives of Jewish women. They were not only a major part of its readership, but they were also involved in both the creative and practical processes of publishing. They became printers, translators, editors, adaptors of existing literary works, copyists, and even typesetters, and at the height of their prestige, they composed new prayers, sermons, and religious songs for both men and women.

As authors, Jewish women held equal status with their male counterparts. Their writings were not like those of the individual voices of the few privately educated Christian women writing in Europe[1] in what has been described as "a time when few women read, wrote, or passed on their thoughts in print."[2] Rather, they were at the forefront of a new communal literature and became involved in providing women's prayer and religious and cultural education.

It has been claimed that Yiddish literature was "perhaps unique among world literatures as until recent times it existed for the female reader, not for the male."[3] Although this is not strictly true, there are very few Yiddish books printed from the middle of the sixteenth century to the middle of the eighteenth century that were solely for men. The targeted readership is usually stated on the title pages,[4] and it is clear that with very few exceptions, books were either for both men and women, or solely for women. The fact that female readership was catered to and courted by printers is demonstrated by the following typical examples from books of that time: Yoysef bar Yokor writes in the earliest Yiddish translation of the *Sider* (Ichenhausen 1544), "Come here you pious women, here you will see a delightful thing"; the title page of a Yiddish translation of the Psalms[5] is addressed to "you pious women"; and the title page found most often in contemporaneous Yiddish books of all kinds is addressed to *"frume vayber un meydlekh"* (pious women and girls).

In early Yiddish printing we also find the beginnings of modern publishing. Affordable books were printed for profit and circulated to many thousands of readers internationally. The content and vernacular language of Yiddish books reflects that they were printed for everyone, not just for a scholarly or wealthy elite.

Jewish printers had to face insecure economic and political conditions in Central and Eastern Europe as a result of wars, frequent expulsions, raids, and fire. They also had to contend with the constant denial or revoking of their printing licenses. As Jews fled from their homes in Eastern Europe in the wake of the Chmielnicki massacres (1648–1649) and settled in Western Europe, they left behind everything, including their books and libraries. There was an urgent need for the reprinting of books of all kinds, including copies of the Talmud and rabbinic literature. Many presses sprang up in Germany, such as those in Sulzbach, Wilmersdorf, and Fürth am Main. Presses were also established by the Ashkenazic printers of Amsterdam in Dyhernfurth, Dessau, and Halle. Often, when Jewish printers had their licenses revoked, they were forced to continue printing unofficially under the auspices of a Christian printer. When Jews were banned from owning businesses in large towns, they had to close down their presses and set up again in some nearby location, or be incorporated into a Christian printing house. In spite of all these setbacks, from the middle of the sixteenth century, the Yiddish printing trade continued to expand and flourish, with the same popular works being printed and sold across Europe.

MOTIVATIONS FOR PRINTING
Spiritual sterility

Warnings of a deterioration and dilution of the spiritual and religious life of the community are expressed in the introductions to various religious and moral books. The author of the Yiddish ethical work *Lev Tov* complains that "now in our generations, in our countries, in our communities," Jews are no longer conversant with the ritual of synagogue.[6] He specifically points to the Ashkenazic community of his own day and protests that when they are in synagogue, men indulge in "idle talk" and ignorantly sit when they are supposed to stand during the *Amide* prayer.[7] *Lev Tov* details the correct procedure for the synagogue service, including when to sit down and stand up and at what point of the service "amen" should be said. Yitskhok Sulkes, in his introduction to a Yiddish translation of The *Song of Songs*,[8] complains that men are no longer solemn enough in synagogue, but show off by trying to demonstrate who can pray fastest or who has the best and loudest singing voice. In his ethical work *Derekh hayosher leoylem habe* (The path of righteousness to the world to come),[9] the mystic and scholar, Yekhiel Mikhl Epshteyn, gives detailed rules on the ritual and practice of prayer and on proper behavior for both men and women. In the long introduction to another work by Epshteyn, his Yiddish prayer book translation,[10] he emphasizes the importance of carrying out commandments as they are written in the Shulḥan Arukh (Prepared table)[11] and in other authoritative books, to prevent the commandments from becoming void and unacceptable to God. Epshteyn was a great advocate of Yiddish prayer and emphasized the importance of prayer being fully understood. Fears are expressed in the ethical work *Brantshpigl* [12] that men are as unlearned as women and are therefore unable to instruct their children on matters that are essential to the continuance of Jewish religion and culture.[13]

17

According to those producing and supervising the content of Yiddish books at that time, religious life was not being strictly observed and was becoming weakened, neglected, or possibly even forgotten by Jews in exile from the Holy Land. Through the forces of pan-European Yiddish printing and distribution, a medium was in place to reach the whole Ashkenazic community in order to influence and educate it in religious and spiritual matters.

The profit motive

The impetus to produce Yiddish ethical and prayer literature was not only spiritual; it also involved a profit-making motive. The new mass readership provided a mass market. The use of commercial advertising in a sacred book was a new development that became widespread from the beginning of Yiddish printing in the mid–sixteenth century. An unashamed, unsubtle combination of commercialism and piety existed, a feature that usually appeared on a book's title page.[14] Examples can be seen from the title pages translated in Part 2 ("Single Prayers and Songs in *Tkhine* Language"), such as Rokhl's penitential *tkhine* from which the following extract is taken:

> These beautiful *tkhines* were created
> For pious women and girls,
> For a sum that you will not consider
> To be too expensive.
> It is a good price for you to pay
> To pass through to the next world,
> And this *tkhine* is well worth the money.

In his Pentateuch translation, Yehude Leyb ben Moyshe Naftali Bresh writes:

> All you girls should not hesitate to sell your own dress or all your things to obtain the money with which to buy this [Pentateuch].[15]

On the title page of a penitential prayer by Beyle Hurvits, whose work is also translated in Part 2,[16] the reader is assured that the purchase of the prayer will result in spiritual gain:

> So beloved women,
> Don't begrudge a tiny sum of money

When with this prayer and the shofar[17]
You will gain instant merit.

The advertisements usually end in a hope, an assurance, or even a guarantee that a trifling financial investment will result in the arrival of the Messiah and eternal Paradise. The most frequently used advertisement contains the end rhyme of "*loyfn*" (to run) and "*koyfn*" (to buy). Women are urged to hurry out and buy books of prayer and religious edification. The fact that all these appeals are made directly to women indicates that these women must have chosen and bought books for themselves.

Men, however, were also targeted. In a Yiddish translation of a *Sider* published in Halle in 1710, which also contains a *Seyder Tkhines*, there is a movingly expressed colophon[18] written in rhyme by an eleven-year-old girl who declares that she is the typesetter of the book. This is evidence of the existence of female typesetters as well as being an example of the "prayer and profit" phenomenon.

> *From beginning to end*
> *Of this beautiful new prayer book*
> *I, Gele, daughter of Moyshe the printer*
> *And Madam Freyde, daughter of Yisroel Kats of blessed*
>   *memory*
> *Have set all the letters with my own hand.*
> *I who was born one of ten children*
> *Am a maiden less than twelve years old.*
> *But do not be shocked that I must work*
> *For we daughters of Israel*
> *Sit long in exile.*
> *One year ends and another begins,*
> *But the Messiah does not come.*
> *Year after year*
> *We cry out to God and implore Him*
> *But our prayers do not seem to reach their destination.*
> *And I must stay silent*
> *For I and my father's house*
> *Cannot speak too openly*
> *As it is with all Jews.*
> *As the verse says:*

> *Those who have known the destruction of Jerusalem*
> *And have suffered in bitter exile*
> *Will know great joy again*
> *With the coming of the Messiah.*
> *Amen and so may it be.*
> *Beloved Sirs, buy this prayer for a small sum of money*
> *For there can be no greater delight in the world*
> *Than to please God, blessed be He, as much as you can.*

Another example of "profit and prayer" advertising occurs in various editions of the ethical work *Lev Tov*. This is the book in which the author claims he includes the whole of the practice of Judaism. He is no less restrained in his anticipation of his readership: "All you men and women, and all who were made by the Creator." In the 1679 edition he continues: "Get this for you, your wife and child." The earlier 1670 edition published in Amsterdam says "Buy" instead of "Get." Both say: "You will earn your place in the next world, you and all daughters and sons."

In spite of the profit motive, printers did express what appears to be a genuine desire to cater to those moral and religious needs, previously overlooked, of the new, religiously uneducated mass readership, among whom these printers counted themselves. To identify themselves with their readers, the printers often emphasized that they, too, were in need of learning. Yitskhok Sulkes, the translator of The Song of Songs mentioned above, admits:

> I hardly know how to recite the blessing for bread, therefore, I should be ashamed to take on such things [as writing books], but they are needed for ordinary people.

Men lacking in religious education had never before participated in the religious direction of the Jewish community. Theirs was a new cultural influence on prayer and ethics, and the difference in approach was obvious.

APPEARANCE OF YIDDISH BOOKS AND THE SEYDER TKHINES

Yiddish books printed during the sixteenth to eighteenth centuries were generally very different in appearance from the sacred books and prayer books printed at that time in Hebrew. Because of the great religious, moral, and historical significance of Hebrew books, their appearance reflected their sanctity, and great care was taken in their preparation. Yiddish books were cheaply produced and cheap to buy. They were the paperbacks of their day. Sometimes the text appears slightly askew on the page or unevenly inked and there are frequent type errors. Yiddish books did not challenge the sacred texts in appearance. They could be abandoned when Jews were forced from their homes at a moment's notice, as so often occurred. The sacred Hebrew scrolls, Bibles, and prayer books would have priority and, if possible, would be taken by displaced Jews to their next communal place of settlement. Taking into account the disposable nature of Yiddish books, it is remarkable that so many have survived from that period, suggesting that an even greater quantity must have originally existed. We only know of the existence of certain books from references made to them in other books from the period that are extant.

The *Seyder Tkhines* was an exception to the poorer quality of Yiddish books. This is because it was usually printed inside the Hebrew *Sider*. The few editions of the *Seyder Tkhines* that were printed alone are of the quality expected of Yiddish books. However, most *Seyder Tkhines*, or at least those that have survived to this day, are inside *Sidorim* (plural of *Sider*) and are therefore endowed with the stature of the appearance that was usually reserved for a Hebrew prayer book. They would also have been more expensive than other Yiddish books as a consequence. Some of the *Sidorim* that contain *Seyder Tkhines* are very grand. Many have gilded page edges[19] and others gold-embossed leather covers that have not faded with time.[20] One particularly handsome edition has thick, parchment-like marbled pages that are a deep blue in the *Sider* and a slightly lighter blue in the *Seyder Tkhines*, which is located in its usual place at the end of the *Sider*. The page edges are crinkled and silver.[21] The page edges of another are marbled blue.[22] In general, *Seyder Tkhines* had a more impressive appearance than most other Yiddish books and were imbued with a status that was, if not as sacred as the Hebrew prayer book, then at least semi-sacred.

EDUCATING RIVKE

Let us call the female reader of early Yiddish literature Rivke, the Yiddish form of Rebecca. It is the name of one of the matriarchs,[23] the wife of Isaac and mother of Jacob and Esau, repeatedly referred to in the *tkhines*. It is also the name of the best-known Yiddish authoress of the period, Rivke Tiktiner, whose religious song is translated in Part 2, and a commonly used female name in Yiddish-speaking Europe. Let us compare Rivke with the protagonist in Willy Russell's 1980 play, "Educating Rita." Like Rita, Rivke is a woman who has received no more than a very basic education and is exposed for the first time to the power of literature. The difference between the two women is that Rita, who enrolled in an Open University course, chooses to change her life through education and the personal development it will inspire. Rivke's new opportunity for education, however, was offered to all women, for the benefit of the community. Rivke was educated so that she could fulfill her traditional role as Jewish wife and mother, as well as ensure that her religious, moral, and prayer responsibilities were fully enacted. But the new books available to Rivke that were so full of ideas and information would certainly have increased her awareness and fostered her personal development.

The *Seyder Tkhines*, together with other new Yiddish prayers and religious songs, evolved out of a century of rich sources of various forms of printed religious and ethical works and translations from Hebrew that were available to women for the first time, and which expanded their knowledge and heightened their spiritual and cultural life. Women had access for the first time to a mutually supportive network of information presented in different ways. This was not education at a scholarly level, but the Yiddish *tkhines* and *lider* assumed a certain level of knowledge from their readers. Most women might have been considered uneducated in comparison to the men who received a higher level of education, but the women who recited these prayers and sang the religious songs required biblical, midrashic, and even halakhic[24] knowledge, and this was provided by the different genres of Yiddish literature that are discussed below.

WOMEN'S COMMANDMENTS

The intention of Yiddish printers to cater to women is evident from the earliest printed sources. Of all the laws and regulations in Judaism, there are three commandments that are specifically for women. They are *khale* (the setting aside of a portion of the dough used for making Sabbath bread as a symbolic priestly offering, in the custom of the ancient Temple in Jerusalem), *nide* (laws concerning menstruation and purity), and *hadlokes haner* (the lighting of ritual candles for Sabbath and festivals). The three commandments are collectively known by the acronym *KhaNoH* (Hannah). In the Mishnah, the incorrect observance of these commandments is deemed fatal:

> Women die in childbirth due to three transgressions: because they are not careful concerning *nide, khale* and *hadlokes haner*.[25]

The second known Yiddish book ever to be printed was a book exclusively for women entitled *Azhoras Noshim* (Warnings to women) by Dovid Hakoyen, which informs and instructs women on the observance of these three women's commandments.[26] Similar works to *Azhoras Noshim*, usually entitled *Mitsves noshim* or *Mitsves hanoshim* (Women's commandments), were printed during the sixteenth and seventeenth centuries in Krakow, Venice, Basle, Hanau, Prague, and Dessau. Books on women's commandments existed in manuscript at least as long ago as the fifteenth century, but these early versions met with strong rabbinic opposition. In the sixteenth century, the Maharil,[27] in a formal answer to a written question from a Reb Khayim, judges such books to be superfluous to existing Hebrew rabbinic texts:

> I must reply to my esteemed and beloved R. Haim. . . . I was greatly amazed that it should have occurred to you to compose a work in Yiddish as you plan. And we already regret those who have preceded you, since any layman who knows how to read Rashi's commentary or a festival prayer book . . . will glance at the works of great rabbis . . . and make practical legal rulings from such works: and now you have come to add all this . . . for the ignorant and for women . . . in order to instruct them on the basis of your Yiddish work in matters of menstrual laws and stains . . . even though we see many works dealing with laws of ritual prohibitions, menstrual laws, and Sabbath bread . . . .[28]

In fact, anyone who would have been able to read Rashi's commentary as the Maharil recommends, would almost certainly have been an educated male. This letter reveals a fear that popularization of legal sources might lead to misinterpretation by the unlearned, which would result in incorrect behaviour. The Maharil added in his letter that women needed only informal, oral teaching to assure the correct observance of their religious duties.

The connection of *nide* to women is obvious. Regarding candle lighting, Maimonides gives the following reason for this being a woman's obligation:

> And women are commanded this more than men since they are at home and they do the housework.[29]

An earlier rabbinic source explains that women's commandments stem from the sin of Eve:

> And why was the precept of menstruation given to her? Because she shed the blood of Adam [by causing death], therefore the precept of menstruation was given to her. And why was the precept of *khale* given to her? Because she corrupted Adam, who was the *khale* of the world (Num. 14:1), therefore the precept of *khale* was given to her. And why was the precept of Sabbath lights given to her? Because she extinguished the soul of Adam, therefore was the precept of the Sabbath lights given to her.[30]

So by fulfilling their three special commandments, women constantly atone for Eve's Edenic sin. The "merit" of women is referred to throughout Yiddish prayer as resulting from their fulfillment of these commandments. This idea corresponds with the underlying mystical belief of the time that woman was responsible for destroying the paradisal state but could now contribute to its restoration.

The printing of these books gave women the opportunity to make their own decisions on matters relevant to them. The extent of the authority of women is, however, still limited. Final responsibility for difficult decisions rests with a rabbi or her husband: "And she should ask her husband whatever she does not know.[31] If any doubts arise in these matters, they should be brought before a rabbi."[32]

The religious prestige of women was, however, considerably enhanced in spite of the limitations on total jurisdiction over their own matters. They could make their own judgments, consulting their husband or a rabbi only as a last resort. And the very production of these books suggests that women were viewed as an important audience and market for the new Yiddish printers.

Yiddish translations of Hebrew books

There has been a tradition since ancient times of Bible translations from Hebrew for those who do not easily understand the original. The best known is probably the Targum,[33] which was translated by Onkelos into the vernacular of the time, Aramaic, following the destruction of the Second Temple. From the earliest days of Yiddish printing, translations of the Bible, the *Sider*, and other Hebrew religious works were published. Many of the title pages of these works are addressed to women as the intended readership.

One book that is known to have been a particular favorite of women, though it was originally intended for both men and women, was the *Ts'ene Ur'ene*, known universally as the *Tsene-rene* or the *Taytsh Khumesh* (Yiddish Bible) by Yankev ben Yitskhok Ashkenazi of Yanov. It first appeared in the early seventeenth century and is a free-flowing Yiddish translation of and exegesis upon the Pentateuch, together with weekly and festival readings from the Prophets, interlaced with homiletic material. This work is sometimes referred to as the "Women's Bible" because of its predominantly female readership in modern times, but when it was first published, the author claimed in his introduction that he had produced it "in order to enable men and women to find a balm for their souls and to understand the words of the living God in simple language." Its name derives from a passage in The Song of Songs: "Come out you women, and see" (3:11). The book was granted recognition by some of the most prominent Torah scholars of the age, including the Taz,[34] who decreed that a reading of the *Tsene-rene* constituted a fulfillment of the "translation" requirement: "Those who are incapable [of comprehending Onkelos or Rashi] should surely read a Torah commentary that is available nowadays in Yiddish, such as *Tsene-rene*."[35] From its first known edition printed in Basel in 1622[36] until 1785, sixty-four editions of the *Tsene-rene* were published.

Not all Yiddish translations specify the intended gender of their readership, as for example, the translation of The Song of Songs by Yitskhok Sulkes (1579) and the Book of Proverbs by Mordkhe ben Yankev Toplits (1582); but it seems clear that the sacred texts, prayers, psalms, and so on were being made accessible and available to women.

Conduct manuals

Newly composed manuals instructing the whole community, men and women, on how to lead an exemplary moral and religious Jewish life, were printed in the seventeenth century and were immensely popular. In their day, these books must have resembled today's popular "lifestyle" books and magazines that advise on relationships, social etiquette, and moral dilemmas. The number of editions certainly seems to indicate that both men and women were eager for, and receptive to, religious and ethical education when it was presented in a popular form in the vernacular language. Among the best known and most popular are *Seyfer Brantshpigl* (Burning mirror) by Moyshe Henokhs Yerushalmi (1596) and *Sefer Lev Tov* (Good heart) by Yitskhok ben Eliakum of Posen (1620), popularly known by the shortened titles *Brantshpigl* and *Lev Tov*.

As the title of *Brantshpigl* suggests, the reader is urged to look deep into the mirror of his or her soul and to emerge reformed. The author claims that his mirror is not one of poor quality that tones down images; it is a burning mirror that accentuates the ugliness of spots and defects. He expresses the hope that the readers will recognize the ugliness of their transgressions and will take care not to repeat them. Instructions for women include how a wife should encourage her husband to do good, how housewives should treat their servants, how to train young children, how to rejoice at a wedding, how to comfort a mourner, advice on marital relations, and the blessings that women are obliged to say over Sabbath and festival candles (*hadlokes haner*) and how to say them. It also gives advice on menstruation (*nide*): "Our sages write that a woman who is bleeding should not on that day enter the synagogue or pray there."

In another section, the social manners of the times are revealed. Young married women are chastised for their extravagant clothes and unseemly manners. They are accused of dressing in silks and velvets and bedecking themselves in jewels in order to attract the attention of single men, thus depriving unmarried girls. The author bewails the lack of modesty in women, their arrogance and their interference in the conversation of men. An example from *Lev Tov* of practical advice for a man concerns the ethics of milking a cow on the Sabbath, and the implications of allowing a non-Jew to do the milking.

The author of *Lev Tov* graphically depicts the tortures of hell intended for sinners and frequently reminds the reader of death and its terrors. This approach must have suited the spirit and taste of the time because between 1620 and 1695, at least twelve known editions of *Lev Tov* were printed in Amsterdam, Krakow, Dyhernfurth, Frankfurt am Main, Frankfurt an der Oder, Prague, Sulzbach, and Wilmersdorf, and at least seven known editions of *Brantshpigl* in Basel, Frankfurt am Main, Hanau, Krakow, and Prague.

Although these books are for men and women, the differences between the genders is emphasized time and time again. In *Brantshpigl* it is stressed that man must not see himself reflected in the mirror of his wife, suggesting that men and women have different and separate roles to fulfill. It also reminds readers that the Torah instructs that a man must not dress in women's clothing. This insistence on separation between the roles of men and women is paralleled by the *Seyder Tkhines* and its inclusion inside the *Sider* to form a double prayer book, one part predominantly for men, the other entirely for women, with their own separate title pages, languages, content, styles, and typeface. The sexes were now side by side, but the demarcation of their roles was clearly defined.

Literature as entertainment

It seems fair to assume that the books that went into many editions and were printed in different locations, were popular and in demand. Popularity, however, was not always the main consideration for publication, as some books that proved to be great favorites were discouraged, while others were banned by Jewish censorship and taken out of circulation.[37]

With profit ever on their minds, the printers imported a cultural intruder into Yiddish literature: the epic romance, based on European Christian literature. Jewish women were exposed to the concepts of Christian courtly love and chivalric knights who were devoted to the ladies they championed. One of the most popular examples of such a book, *Bovo-d'Antona*, known as the *Bovo-bukh* (1541), was adapted from the Middle Italian *Buovo d'Antona* and the Middle English *Bevis of Hampton*. It is the skilled literary work in ottava rima poetic form[38] of the same Elijah Levita who produced a Yiddish translation of the Book of Psalms.[39] This demonstrates the overlap that existed of

27

printed Yiddish secular and religious works at the time, which pushed out new boundaries in Jewish publishing. Other European epics were translated and adapted into Yiddish in manuscript form, including the Arthurian legend, which appeared in print. Overtly Christian references were altered to suit a Jewish readership, with "Christmas" becoming "winter," "Easter" becoming "spring," and so on.

The rabbinic authorities soon attempted to discourage, if not repress, literature that provided entertainment without any suitable religious message. More suitable epics were printed that could be both romantic and didactic. They, too, were taken from earlier Yiddish manuscripts and had as their heroes biblical characters, as in the *Shmuel-bukh* (Book of Samuel) and the *Mlokhim-bukh*,[40] a reworking of the Book of Kings into a courtly romance. The second editions of these two books (Krakow 1578 and Krakow 1582, respectively) address their title pages to "pious women and girls," showing that they were aimed at a female readership. Many Yiddish religious books openly discouraged women from reading "undesirable" books. Mikhl Odem (1544), Yitskhok Sulkes (1579), and Corneleo Adelkind (printer of Levita's Psalm translation, 1545) all admonish the women and girls who read epic romances, naming in particular the Yiddish versions of the German *Der schönen Glück*, *Dietrich von Bern*, and the *Hildebrandslied* (The beautiful Glück, Dietrich of Bern, and Song of Hildebrand). They recommend that their own Yiddish translations of Jewish religious works are more appropriate Sabbath reading for women.

Book introductions did not only strongly discourage Christian-based literature; they also made Jewish stories sound so enticing that they would appear more attractive than their Christian counterparts. For example, in "A beautiful new song about the *Megile*"[41] (Book of Esther)—a work relating to the story in rhyme about the Jewish heroine Queen Esther—the author claims to tell of the great miracle performed by "such a pious, virtuous girl."[42] The author boasts in the introduction that his work is so amusing that none will need to read what he calls *galkhes sforim*, a term for non-Jewish books, but "should always keep Jewish books before their eyes."[43] The term *galkhes* came to be used to signify non-Jewish script (the Latin alphabet) or a non-Jewish language.[44] Perhaps its meaning was extended to cover Yiddish books adapted from non-Jewish sources. It is very unlikely to have been the case that Jews read Christian books very widely, as Jewish literacy was based in the Hebrew alphabet, and knowledge of Latin letters would not have been widespread.[45]

The Yiddish translation of the New Testament (Krakow 1540–1541) is a good example of this. In the mid–sixteenth century, the Christian Reformation aroused much interest in the study of the classics and Hebrew became one of the languages to be learned and studied. Because Yiddish, too, was written in the Hebrew alphabet, it became a curiosity among some scholars. At this time, there was a spate of religious conversions both to and from Judaism. Some of the printers of Yiddish books were Christian converts to Judaism, while others were Jewish converts to Christianity. By the seventeenth century, in spite of conversion to Judaism being strictly prohibited, secret conversions from Christianity took place because of the eagerness for the anticipated redemption of the Jews. Against this background, the New Testament was published in Yiddish by Paul Helic, a convert from Judaism to Christianity, in an attempt to reach a Jewish audience at its widest level, in familiar language. The Krakow Jewish community banned all his books after the first edition of his New Testament was printed. No further editions of Helic's translation have come to light, but its existence confirms that Helic considered it necessary to translate, or at least transcribe, Christian texts into Yiddish in order to render them accessible to the Jewish community.

Fear of religious and cultural "invasion" or influence from the Christian community may, in part, have been expressed by printers to satisfy the censorship of the Jewish ruling bodies. Yet the same printers who expressed concern for the spiritual welfare of the community in their introductions were producing not only religious and moral books, but also the epic romances that were much maligned by them. Corneleo Adelkind published the Yiddish Psalm translation by Elijah Levita in which he admonished the epic romances.[46] He also expressed his desire to provide religious books for everyone and a hope that the money received from the sale of the Psalms translation would enable him to print a translation of Proverbs, as soon as possible, for everybody's spiritual advantage. Yet we find that four years earlier in Isny, the same Adelkind printed the most popular epic romance of all, the *Bovo-bukh*,[47] with the same Elijah Levita, this time as author/adaptor.

In the rhyming introduction to a Psalms translation by Moyshe Shtend printed in Krakow in 1586, it is claimed that the Psalms have been adapted "in the rhyme and melody of the *Shmuel-bukh*" (line

13). It appears that this connection is used in an attempt to give the Psalm translation the same popular appeal as that of Yiddish entertainment literature.

For a short period, until it was brought under control to the satisfaction of rabbinic censorship, commercialism and religious propaganda were undefined and lines had not yet been drawn. Meanwhile, women enjoyed the secular romances while they lasted.

This network of mutually supportive forms of Yiddish literature made it possible for women to attain a new level of knowledge. What they read in the Bible translations could be found reinforced in story-like form in the *Tsene-rene* and yet again in the more literary courtly romances of the *Shmuel-bukh* and the *Mlokhim-bukh*. There were also translations of festival prayer books that provided biblical stories in their readings. Laws on women's commandments and how to fulfil them in practical terms would have been set out in *Mitsves Noshim*. The conduct manuals would have provided instruction on the relevant moral issues, and new prayers were provided to recite on the occasion when the commandments were performed. Everything linked up to cover every aspect of religious and moral obligations, and to fortify the learning process.

The impact of this literature must have been remarkable. The new Yiddish books were full of information on religious and ethical matters, advice on lifestyle, while some even introduced women to an idealized world outside of the community in the form of entertainment. Women could choose and buy these books for themselves, and their intellectual and cultural development extended to the provision of their own standard prayer book. They enjoyed unprecedented communal participation and enhanced their spiritual status.

But while Rita was on a personal journey of discovery, Rivke's personal growth was carefully controlled and restricted by the very books that educated her. The education on offer to Rivke had wider implications than personal growth. It was aimed at all women, for the benefit of the community. For the first time, women were reading the same books and saying the same prayers, and their eagerness for them is clear from the number of editions printed. There must have been a common bond that drew them closer and provided them with a collective experience that had always been available to men.

Notes

1. E.g., Ludamilia Elisabeth and Sibylle Schwarz (Germany); Maria Tesselschade (Netherlands).
2. Susan L. Clarke in *Women Writers of the Seventeenth Century* (eds. Katharina M. Wilson and Frank J. Warnke), Athens, Georgia, 1989.
3. Niger 1913:100.
4. See Glossary.
5. Elijah Levita, Venice 1544.
6. Yitskhok ben Elyokum, Prague, 1602: Introduction.
7. The main prayer of the thrice-daily synagogue service.
8. Krakow 1579.
9. Frankfurt am Main 1704.
10. Frankfurt am Main 1697.
11. The *Shulḥan Arukh* is the sixteenth-century legal code written by Joseph Karo, which serves as an authoritative guide to Jewish law.
12. Moyshe Henokhs Yerushalmi, Krakow, 1596.
13. See Moyshe Henokhs Yerushalmi, 1620: Introduction.
14. See Glossary for explanation of title pages.
15. Cremona, Germany, 1560.
16. At least three editions of Beyle Hurvits's penitential prayer (translated here in Part 2, "Single Prayers and Songs in *Tkhine* Language") were printed in Prague, one around 1705 and one in 1718, of which at least three copies have survived.
17. A ram's horn blown like a musical wind instrument in synagogue as a call to repentance.
18. See Glossary.
19. E.g., Frankfurt am Main, 1696, Sulzbach 1712.
20. E.g., Amsterdam 1703–1704, 1711, 1714.
21. Amsterdam 1715.
22. Dyhernfurth 1705.
23. Sarah, Rebecca, Rachel, and Leah (referred to in Yiddish in the *tkhines* as Sore, Rivke, Rokhl, and Leye.
24. The word *halakhah* is usually translated as "Jewish Law," although a more literal translation might be "the path that one walks." The word is derived from the Hebrew root *Hey-Lamed-Kof*, meaning to go, to walk, or to travel. *Halakhah* are rules and practices that affect every aspect of Jewish life, including the 613 commandments
25. Mishnah Shabbat, Ch. 2.
26. Dovid Hakoyen, Krakow 1535 or 1538. See Rosenfeld 1987:121.
27. Maharil (acronym for Moseynu haRav Yankev, Leyvi). Yankev ben Moyshe La-leyvi Moelin (b. 1365, Mainz, Germnay; d. Worms, Germany 1427) was regarded as a leading halakhic authority of his time, especially in regard to customs and

synagogue ritual. His teachings were collected in *Minhagey Maharil* (Sabbionetta 1556), by his pupil Zalman of St. Goar.

28. Satz, Jerusalem 1997: 92-97; Segal, Jerusalem 1986: 39.
29. Maimonides, *Mishneh Torah* (twelfth century compilation of *halakhah* or Jewish law by Maimonides): Laws of Sabbath: ch. 5, law 3; Segal 1986, 37.
30. Genesis Rabbah 17:8.
31. Dovid Hakoyen 1535 or 1538.
32. Krakow 1552, Segal 1986:41.
33. The Targum was the Five Books of Moses translated into Aramaic by Onkelos, a convert to Judaism, at the beginning of the Christian era, when Hebrew had ceased to be the spoken language of the Jewish people and Aramaic took its place as their vernacular.
34. Dovid ben Shmuel Haleyvi (1586-1667), known as the Taz, who was rabbi of Posen and then of Ostraha in Poland.
35. Taz, seventeenth century, *Orakh Khayim*: 265:2.
36. According to its title page, this is not the earliest edition. It also refers to three earlier editions: one in Lublin and two in Krakow, which were all out of print by 1610. The first edition may have been that of Prague in 1608, with a reprint in 1610 (Stark Zakon 1983, xii).
37. See section on Arn ben Smuel of Hergeshausen in Chapter 4 on *defining tkhines*.
38. Ottava rima, a stanza of eight iambic lines, containing three rhymes, invariably arranged as a b a b a b c c, is an Italian invention that dates back to the poetry of the fourteenth century. Boccaccio employed it for the *Teseide*, which he wrote in Florence in 1340, and for the *Filostrato*, which he wrote in Naples some seven years later.
39. Shmeruk 1986:16.
40. Moyshe Esrim veArbe, first known printing (Augsburg) 1543.
41. Lit. scroll. Usually refers to the Book of Esther.
42. Efrayim bar Yehude Haleyvi, Amsterdam, 1650-55.
43. The word *galkhes* denotes "Christian priestly" and derives from the word *galekh* (a derogatory Jewish term for a Christian priest), which itself stems from the root of the verb "to shave" and indicates the tonsure on the head of a monk or priest.
44. Weinreich 1973, 1:99, 272.
45. Ibid. 1973, 1:195.
46. See above.
47. The term "*bobe-mayse*" which today is widely believed to mean "old wives tale" (literally "grandmother's story") stemming from the Slavic word "bobe" (grandmother), in fact stems from the *Bovo-bukh*, which was a tale of adventure and romance. In the Yiddish alphabet (*alef beys*) the letters *beys* (b) and *veys* (v) have the same outline, so *Bovo* became *Bobo*. The *Bovo-bukh* continued to be published in an altered version into the twentieth century under the title *Bovemayse*.

3
CHAPTER

The Seyder Tkhines: A Book for a Messianic Age

An analysis of the *Seyder Tkhines* could fill an entire book. The three chapters I have devoted to it merely scratch the surface of a rich seam of available evidence. In this chapter, I will attempt to set the book in its historical context; in Chapter 4, I proffer some definitions; and in Chapter 5, I claim that the *Seyder Tkhines* provided a new Yiddish daily prayer liturgy for Ashkenazic women, as an alternative to the male-dominated Hebrew service.[1] The *Seyder Tkhines* was at the very heart of the concerns of the closely knit, interactive, pan-European Ashkenazic community whose subsequent fragmentation and transformation were paralleled in the fate of the book itself.[2] It was produced at a time of social, political, and religious turmoil in Europe, for a community that was about to experience the most widespread messianic movement in Jewish history. It not only reflects that period, but was also both a harbinger and a survivor of it. Literature usually reflects or anticipates the age in which it is written, and the *Seyder Tkhines* is no exception.

In Amsterdam, in 1648, an anonymous Yiddish prayer book entitled *Tkhines* appeared in print for the first time. Subsequent editions of the same book were occasionally entitled *Taytshe Tkhines* (Yiddish *tkhines*),[3] but usually *Seyder Tkhines,* the title by which it must generally have been known. It is this book that demonstrates, more than any other, that the prayer life of women in the Ashkenazic community had undergone a significant change. It was a newly composed prayer book for women in the voice of a female worshipper, and from its first appearance, the *Seyder Tkhines* was a fixed liturgy. Unlike the *Sider*,[4] the Hebrew synagogue prayer book whose eclectic contents slowly evolved over centuries to meet the changing needs of its readers, the *Seyder Tkhines* was composed as one cohesive work intended for a particular readership, that of Ashkenazic women in the seventeenth century. Sometimes it appeared as a book on its own,[5] although from its earliest days it was usually published in its entirety as a supplement to various editions of the Hebrew *Sider*. Some *sidorim*[6] offer a parallel Yiddish translation,[7] and others appear in Hebrew alone.[8] It is the only collection of *tkhines* that was printed regularly in its complete form in the *Sider*, and although many editions of the *Sider* were published without a *Seyder Tkhines*, there were only a few editions of the *Seyder Tkhines* that were not published inside a *Sider*. Most of the *Seyder Tkhines* editions that did appear alone were published in Prague.

I have found no evidence to suggest that any edition of the *Seyder Tkhines* was printed prior to 1648 or existed in an earlier manuscript form. The 1648 *Seyder Tkhines* contains an introduction explaining why the book was printed, which is not found in any other edition I have seen,[9] which provides further evidence to support the belief that this was the introductory printing of a new work. With academic caution, therefore, the 1648 edition of the *Seyder Tkhines* might be viewed as the first. If this is indeed so, the year could not be of greater historical significance.

THE YEAR OF THE MESSIAH

Prediction

The year 1648 corresponds to 5408 in the Hebrew calendar, one of the years in which Jewish kabbalists had predicted the first coming of the Messiah.[10] Using the mystical system of *gematria*, which attributes numerical values to the letters of the Hebrew alphabet and equates the value of words or phrases, the phrase from the Zohar, *"keyts hayomim"* (the end of days), was calculated as 5408, the year of redemption for the Jews and the subsequent end of the world and the beginning of the new messianic era. The expectation of the imminent arrival of the Messiah was not confined to the Jewish world; the Christian world had reached a similar conclusion. In his book *Du Rappel des Juifs*, published at an unknown place in 1643, Isaac de la Peyrere, a French Calvinist of Marrano[11] extraction, synthesized Christian and Jewish messianism by claiming that the imminent Messiah would be Christ on his second coming, and that the Jews would at last acknowledge Christ.[12] He chiefly emphasized that the redemption of the Jews must be physical and political as well as spiritual, and their gathering in Jerusalem and the Holy Land was the prerequisite and instrument for the salvation of all mankind. The Christian millenarian Pierre de la Fons predicted 1648 as the date when the Christian Messiah would return to bring salvation to his people, the "New Israel," the people of England. The fact that this redemption failed to occur did not dampen the hope of the believers. The time was right for Jews to be readmitted to the "New Jerusalem," and, like the Jewish kabbalists, the Christian millenarians set the next year of salvation as 1666.

Right on cue, in the apocalyptic climate of 1648, Shabbetai Tsvi, a Jew born in Smyrna, Turkey, declared that he was the Messiah and predicted 1666 as the year of the redemption. The Shabbatean movement, as it came to be known, was in place for the preparation of the expected redemption.

THE END OF THE THIRTY YEARS WAR AND THE CHMIELNICKI MASSACRES

In 1648, the Thirty Years War ended, leaving a devastated Europe in its wake. In the same year, the Cossacks, under the leadership of Bogdan Chmielnicki, rose up against Polish rule in the Ukraine in protest at the role of the Jews as intermediaries for the absentee Polish landowners. Jews had lived in Poland since the tenth century, and by the seventeenth century they numbered about half a million. In the years 1648 and 1649, more than 100,000 Jews were murdered and 300 Jewish communities were wiped out in the Chmielnicki massacres, the worst atrocities occurring in the spring and summer of 1648. Those who managed to escape fled from Eastern Europe into Western Europe.[13]

Many kabbalists believed that "before the time of the Messiah, there shall be war and suffering,"[14] and the Chmielnicki massacres seemed to support such a prediction.

Jews needed to attach some meaning and purpose to their sufferings. They sought comfort in the belief that beyond the catastrophes and humiliations they experienced at Christian hands lay imminent redemption and release.

The authoritative scholar of Jewish mysticism, Gershom Scholem, did not believe that the massacres in Eastern Europe were the spur of the messianic movement because Jews, everywhere, were affected by the spread of mysticism, in places where they prospered, as well as in places where persecution was rife.[15] Scholem reasoned that there were "the same reactions in ruined Poland and flourishing Constantinople, Salonika, Leghorn, Amsterdam and Hamburg."[16] Indeed, the Iberian exiles of the Spanish Inquisition, now in the Ottoman Empire, Italy, and Amsterdam, were experiencing relative prosperity, and the freedom and citizenship rights granted them in Amsterdam led to a kind of renaissance in both religious liberalism and utopianism. The Sephardic Jews of Amsterdam were fully aware of the devastation in Poland and the Ukraine and witnessed the arrival and settlement of a new immigrant Ashkenazic community of refugees, fleeing from the atrocities, which was poorer and less skilled than its own. The Sephardim had arrived as refugees themselves from Spain in 1492 and from Portugal in 1498 because of the expulsions by the Roman Catholic monarchs, and from the torture and burning of Jews who refused conversion to Christianity. The Jews of Amsterdam were no strangers to persecution and human misery, and Jewish books were printed in the seventeenth century as a tribute to these sufferings by those who viewed them as a stimulus to redemption.[17] The growth in mysticism captured the imagination and affected the lives of Jews across the world, and "never before had there been a movement that swept the whole House of Israel."[18]

KABBALAH: FROM ELITISM TO POPULAR APPEAL

Kabbalah had always been the preserve of men over the age of forty who were learned scholars with a knowledge of Aramaic and the ability to embrace its impenetrable mysteries. In 1492 Spain, for example, kabbalists were a small group of esoterics who had no intention of spreading their ideas outside of their own circle. They were not messianist centered, but concerned themselves with the origins of the world, rather than its end. They sought to go back to the original unity that existed before the first sin. Their messianist ideas of redemption were fueled by the catastrophe of the expulsion and the belief that the end was near. Two writings on this subject were the anonymous *Sefer Hameshiv* on Torah and *Kaf Haketoret* on the Psalms. Both works force an apocalyptic meaning into their texts. In *Kaf Haketoret*, the Psalms were weapons to be used in the final battle that would destroy all forces of evil in the world.

In the seventeenth century, kabbalism was simplified and made accessible to the masses in the name of Isaac Luria, who was the inspiration for the popular messianic movement that appealed to Jews everywhere. His teachings developed in Safed in Galilee in the Holy Land during the sixteenth century, and came to dominate global Jewish religiosity in the seventeenth century. It was a movement that appealed to both Sephardim and Ashkenazim, rich and poor, learned and unlearned.

THE SAFED INFLUENCE

In the sixteenth century, Safed became a flourishing center of Judaism, attracting Jews from the Diaspora, including many Spanish exiles. A number of kabbalists settled there, one of whom was Isaac Luria. Born in Jerusalem to German parents, Luria, also known as the "Ari" (Lion) because of the initials of the phrase *haeloki Rabbi Yitskhok* (the divine Rabbi Isaac), spent the last six years of his life in Safed. In 1572, at the age of thirty-eight, he died there in an epidemic. During his last years, he taught Kabbalah orally, writing down virtually nothing. Yet even today, he remains a legendary figure and his ideas are encapsulated in what is known as Lurianic Kabbalah. The intricacies of Lurianic Kabbalah are best explained by the great scholars of Jewish mysticism.[19] They are not essential for an understanding of Luria's influence on the general messianic movement.

By the time Luria died in 1572, his reputation as a saintly man of God had been established, but his teachings had not spread. He had been known to live a pure existence, engaging in self-flogging, ablutions, and penance. Luria came to believe that he was the Messiah, but most of what we now have of his system of thought was recorded, with inevitable subjectivity, by his disciples and others after his death. Often Luria's message was intentionally modified. For example, an Italian Kabbalist, Israel Sarug, who combined Luria's ideas with neoplatonism, spread Lurianic kabbalism in Italy, Holland, Germany, and Poland. He is said to have falsely claimed that he studied with Luria and to have used writings that he stole from Khayim Vital, a genuine student of Luria, as the source of his own works. Vital assumed himself to be Luria's natural successor, though he was not accepted by some of Luria's followers. He recorded Luria's teachings, which he wished to restrict to a group of learned kabbalists. He therefore taught them only to twelve students who promised never to divulge them. He, too, thought that he was the Messiah, but he died in 1620, some years short of the predicted redemption. It is mainly through Vital's work *Eyts Khayim* (Tree of life) that we are aware of Luria's system of thought. Others, too, wished to document Luria's ideas, which were first recorded in manuscript form and then printed after 1630. Another of Luria's students, Joseph ibn Tabul, committed the teachings to print. He taught those who had not studied under Luria directly. Together, they believed they could conjure up the spirits of deceased rabbis. One of the spirits to whom they *spoke,* convinced them that he was the Messiah and that he would soon appear to redeem the Jews. In 1648, a book on Lurianic Kabbalah by the German kabbalist of the first half of the seventeenth century, Naphtali ben Jacob Bacharach of Frankfurt, entitled *Emek haMelekh* (Valley of the king) influenced kabbalists from many countries and was widely quoted by them.[20] However, these books in Hebrew that recorded complicated kabbalistic concepts were not for the unlearned masses, and Luria's teachings were also spread through preaching, through the seminaries, and through the many pious groups that had spread across Europe.

It was not the complex concepts of Lurianic Kabbalah that were spread to the masses, but rather the inspiration of Luria's name, personality, exemplary behavior, and the miracles he is said to have performed, together with a clear, simplified message that could be easily understood and applied. This was practical Kabbalah, in the sense that it served a purpose and demanded that each Jew play his or her part. At its heart was the basic idea of imminent redemption that could be hastened by personal acts, piety, heartfelt prayer, and repentance. The message that began in sixteenth-century Safed spread far and wide. It pervaded every corner of Jewish life, and began to dominate Jewish religiosity in the seventeenth century.

The ritual, liturgical, and other practical innovations of the Safed kabbalists became public property. Examples of this can be seen in the *Seyder Tkhines*. For example, the *tkhines* to be said at the graveside of saintly men and women, asking for intercession on behalf of the living, testify to a custom that became widespread in the seventeenth century. Luria is said to have revealed to his disciples the locations of the graves of rabbis that he claimed to have discovered through spiritual revelations. He taught methods of communication with the souls of saintly men. Luria's glorification of the Sabbath, suffused in holy light as the foretaste of Paradise, is another concept found in the *Seyder Tkhines*. The theme found in the *Seyder Tkhines* of the unification of the "bride" and "bridegroom" of Sabbath echoes his concept that there are both male and female sides of God[21] depicted as bride and bridegroom, which have been separated and must be reunited before order can be restored to the universe and redemption can occur. A third concept, and one with which Jews could readily identify, was that of exile. There was a new doctrine of exile of the souls that paralleled the exiles from Spain and Portugal and, more recently, the refugees from Poland and the Ukraine. Exile came to be regarded not merely as a test of faith or a punishment of sins, but as a mission. The purpose of this mission was to restore the world to a pre-Edenic perfection.[22] By 1648, only one generation after its dissemination had begun, Lurianic Kabbalah had established an almost unchallenged supremacy and was the "generally accepted form of Jewish theology of the time."[23]

SHABBETAI TSVI[24]

The man who declared himself Messiah in 1648, Shabbetai Tsvi, displayed signs of brilliance at an early age. He received a traditional education, but left his seminary to live a life of abstinence and solitude. He also began studying the Kabbalah. Some historians have speculated that he suffered from bipolar syndrome, known more generally as manic-depressive disorder. He imposed the severest mortifications on himself, including bathing in the sea in winter and undertaking prolonged fasts. His behavior was erratic, and though he seems to have possessed great charm and charisma, he would carry out highly eccentric acts that were a deliberate and outrageous flouting of Jewish law. As figurehead of the movement that was nourished on the ideas of Lurianic Kabbalah, Shabbetai Tsvi introduced his own rules. He adapted and mutated kabbalistic concepts and Jewish law and added to them, advocating a form of Judaism that was often unrecognizable and extreme. For example, he publicly pronounced the forbidden four-letter name of God and took part in a bizarre marriage ceremony between himself and a Torah scroll under a *khupe* (wedding canopy). He decreed certain fasts as days of celebration, ate food that is forbidden under Jewish law, and worked on the Sabbath, the day of rest. He devised the blessing: "Blessed art Thou, O Lord our God, King of the universe, who permits the forbidden." He also vowed to absolve Jewish women of the curse of Eve's sin and encouraged them to read from the Torah, the preserve of men. His followers accepted his behavior, but early on it led to his excommunication and expulsion by the Jews of Smyrna. He moved to Salonika and then, in 1663, to Jerusalem, where he was received with great excitement. There he gathered around himself the people who would later become the active leaders of his messianic movement. The following year, Shabbatai left Jerusalem for Egypt where he met Nathan of Gaza, a kabbalist who was born in Jerusalem in 1643 or 1644. Nathan had a vision in which God revealed to him the coming of the Messiah, which spurred him to go out and heal the souls of those who had sinned, requiring them to fast and do penance. Shabbatai came to him seeking guidance and healing, but instead of a cure, Nathan declared that Shabbatai was in fact the Messiah. While Shabbatai had wavered over whether he was or was not the Messiah, declaring himself to be so on some occasions, while being less sure on others, he now had another voice to support his beliefs. Nathan publicized the arrival of the Messiah and by 1665, a wave of religious fervor and zeal swept through the Jewish communities of Europe. At the height of the messianic expectation, 1665 to 1666, many supporters wore a green ribbon, the color that represented Shabbatai Tsvi, vowing repentance and striving for moral perfection. Most of the leading rabbis joined in. In 1665, Yair Khayim Bacharach (1638–1702), the seventeenth-century German rabbi renowned for his learning, began to meet daily with a circle of Shabbatean enthusiasts to help hasten the day of redemption.[25] For approximately six to eight months, virtually all the Jewish governing boards and assemblies were swept up in the messianic fervor. In 1666, in Amsterdam, the printer David de Castro Tartas, produced some small prayer books dated "Year 1" of the new Shabbatean era that included an engraving of Shabbetai Tsvi as King Messiah. In the same year, in preparation for the redemption, Shabbatai announced that he was going to Constantinople to demand that the sultan give up his throne to him. When his ship docked at the Turkish port, however, he was arrested and imprisoned. There he was given the choice of conversion to Islam or death by execution. He chose conversion. The effect on his followers was devastating. Many had gone as far as to sell their homes in Europe in a frenzied attempt to get to the Holy Land in readiness for the redemption. In 1670, the leaders of the Council of Lands, the Jewish authority that governed the Jews of Poland and had a wider, if undefined, primacy within general Ashkenazic community, belatedly condemned Shabbetai Tsvi and his mystical following. Its ban was regarded as authoritative far beyond the confines of Poland.[26] But while many rejected him entirely and tried to rebuild their lives, others did not desert him, and even followed him into apostasy. They held on to the belief in Shabbetai Tsvi as the Messiah, and even after his death in 1676, fervently hoped for his resurrection and return.

Books popularizing kabbalism and Luria's ideas continued to be published for some years after Shabbetai Tsvi's death, as did the *Seyder Tkhines*, which was published even more intensely during the first two decades of the eighteenth century. New books were provided for the general readership, as well for the highly educated. These included a Yiddish translation of the Zohar, known popularly as the *Taytsh Zohar* (Yiddish Zohar), by Tsvi ben Jeramil, which was published for the first time in 1711;[27] a Zohar containing writings by Luria and Vital in Amsterdam of 1719; an edition of the Zohar published with what were purported to be Luria's notes, in Venice in 1663; a *tkhine* in Luria's name that appeared in the mystical work *Sha'are Tsion* (Gates of Zion) by Nathan Note Hanover in Prague in 1662; and a Yiddish translation of the same book published in Prague in 1708. In the face of prohibition and in spite of the failure of Shabbetai Tsvi to fulfil his proclamation of 1648, the publication of these books indicates that the messianic dream continued to be encouraged, to some extent, even after his death. Perhaps this is because mysticism had become ingrained in prayer and practice, and the new age that was to offer alternative aims and ideals had not yet been established.

THE PRINTER OF THE EARLIEST SEYDER TKHINES

The man who was in charge of the printing house that published the first *Seyder Tkhines* in 1648 died in the same year. The printer of the *Seyder Tkhines* has previously been identified as Yoysef ben Naftali of Konskovola,[28] which is the name found in the colophon at the very end of the 1648 Amsterdam edition. However, it is most likely that his role was that of a hands-on printer who set the type and carried out the practical production of the book. Evidence indicates a more exciting story concerning the publisher. It seems that the *Seyder Tkhines* was launched by the publishing house of Menasseh ben Israel (1604–1657), one of the great historical figures of the age. Menasseh was a Sephardic rabbi, a multi-lingual scholar, a Kabbalist who believed firmly in the prevailing messianic movement, and a man who played an important role in international politics. He also founded Jewish publishing in Amsterdam in 1629 and in 1644 brought out *Mizmor letodah* (Psalm of thanks), the first Yiddish book to be published in Amsterdam. He published scholarly books in languages as diverse as Hebrew, Latin, and Spanish. Some of the works, a number of which were his own, were translated into Yiddish and Dutch.[29]

Menasseh's involvement in the prevailing messianic movement is evident. In his Spanish work of 1650, entitled *Esperança de Israel* (Hope of Israel),[30] Menasseh promises imminent release for Jews from humiliation and oppression, seeing signs of pending redemption in the very persecution of his people. In particular, he glorifies martyrs who in Spain, Portugal, and Spanish America had been burned alive at the stake for their Jewish beliefs by the Inquisition:

> *Otra razon, y para nos otros de grande fundamento, es ver muestra preseverancia entre tantos males, y assi juzgamos, ue para grandes bienes nos tienes el Señor guardado.*[31] (And seeing our perseverance amid such great hardships, we judge that the Almighty has preserved us for great rewards to come.)

Menasseh's words contradict Gershom Scholem's theory that in the seventeenth century the prosperous Sephardic Jews of Amsterdam would not have been as deeply affected by Jewish suffering as the Ashkenazim in Poland, and were not seeking the comfort of a deeper significance for it. Menasseh reflects the widespread belief in imminent redemption of the Jewish people:

> *Pero avn que no podemos feñalar pontualmente el tempo de nuestra redencion, juzgamos que està muy cerca"* (Although we cannot specify the exact moment of our redemption, we consider that it is very close).[32]

The Messiah was also expected in England in 1648, the year in which Oliver Cromwell put on trial and sentenced to death Charles I, whose execution took place at the end of January 1649. The next year of expectation, 1666, was preceded in England by the anticipated disasters of a crippling outbreak of plague in 1665 that claimed many lives, followed by the Great Fire of London in 1666. Earlier, in 1651, Menasseh traveled to England and it was largely in response to his petition, written in English, that Cromwell readmitted Jews into England in 1656. Menasseh was able to appeal in his argument to the powerful force of the messianic vision that had captivated Christian as well as Jewish Europe. I have quoted below the whole intriguing paragraph from Menasseh ben Israel to Oliver Cromwell:[33]

> My second motive is, because the opinion of many Christians and mine do concur herein, that we both believe that the restoring time of our nation into their native country is very near at hand; I believing more particularly, that this restoration cannot be, before these words of Daniel, chapter 13, verse 7, be first accomplished, when he says, and when the dispersion of the holy people shall be completed, signifying therewith that before all be fulfilled the people of God must be first dispersed into all places and countries of the world. Now we know, how our nation at the present is spread all about and has its seat and dwelling in the most flourishing parts of all the kingdoms and countries of the world, as well in America, as in the other three parts thereof, except only in this considerable and mighty island. And therefore this remains only in my judgment, before the MESSIAH[34] come and restore our Nation, that the first we must have our seat here likewise.

Cromwell was convinced by Mennaseh's argument, which indicates his own deep conviction in the messianic expectation.

I was first alerted to the fact the *Seyder Tkhines* might have been introduced to the world by the prestigious printing house of Menasseh ben Israel, with the messianic movement in mind, because of certain features on the title page. First, the space where the name of the printer would be expected to appear is entirely blank. More will be said of this below. Second, in Jewish books, the date usually appears on the title page in letters of the Hebrew alphabet, the numerical values of which are added together and then added to the number 1240. But in the *Seyder Tkhines*, there are the added words before the date "*Yoyvel ha* 1648" (Jubilee/Commemoration of 1648). I began to wonder why this was a commemoration of the year rather than just the straightforward recording of it. The English word "jubilee," which derives from the Biblical word "yoyvel," usually celebrates a fiftieth anniversary, and fifty years earlier, in 1598, the Jews built their first synagogue in Amsterdam. I discovered that there is another book published in the same year, 1648, entitled *Seyfer HaEmunot vehaDeot* (Beliefs and ideas) by Saadiah Gaon (c.1000 C.E.), translated from the original Arabic into Hebrew by Judah ibn Tibbon, which bears the identical phrase, "*Yoyvel ha* 1648." It was published by the printing house of Menasseh ben Israel. All the remaining features on the title page, the wording, the format, and position on the page of the date and place of publication, as well as the style and size of lettering and the numerical value for the year expressed in Hebrew letters, are the same. The title page is decorated with a woodcut of a classical arch supported by columns, which is similar, but not identical to, the title page of the *Seyder Tkhines*. There are, however, two extant books, published in 1635 and 1636 respectively by Menasseh ben Israel, which feature identical woodcuts of the classical arch with an eagle at its pinnacle, which appear in the *Seyder Tkhines*. The 1635 book is entitled *Minhagim: Rites for all seasons in Poland, Ruthenia, Lithuania, Bohemia, Moravia and Germany* by Aisik Tyrnan.[35] The second book is of daily readings from the Bible, the Mishnah, and the Talmud.[36] I have not found this design used by any other printer.

It would appear, therefore, that the first edition of the *Seyder Tkhines* was not printed by one of the new breed of less than scholarly printers, like so many other Yiddish religious and ethical books and prayer books of the time. This new vernacular prayer book exclusively for women was considered worthy enough to be introduced among the scholarly works in Latin, Hebrew, and other languages, by a publishing house whose Yiddish publications made up only a tiny percentage of its output. The association of the *Seyder Tkhines* with Menasseh ben Israel and his printing house establishes its prestige and links it to the messianic movement. On the title page, the printer writes that the purpose of reciting the *tkhines* is to gain entry to the Holy Land through the coming of the Messiah.

A mystery pervades the title page of the *Seyder Tkhines*. It has been mentioned above that where the printer's name would usually appear, there is a blank space. Yet the title page of Saadia Gaon's work, also published in 1648, bears the name of Menasseh's older son, Joseph, as printer. Joseph's name appears on all books that were published in the printing house from 1646 until his death in 1648, the two years in which he was in charge of the press under the aegis of his father. It may be that Joseph died after the publication of Saadia Gaon's book, but before the publication of the *Seyder Tkhines*, and therefore a blank was left either as a mark of respect or to show that there was no one officially in charge of the printing house at that particular moment. It was at this juncture in history, in a remarkable year, that the *Seyder Tkhines* made its first appearance.

Ñotes

1. See Kay 1993: 49-96.
2. See Chapter 8.
3. E.g., Amsterdam 1649, 1667; [Frankfurt am Main] 1708.
4. Weissler 1998:19.
5. E.g., Amsterdam 1648; Prague 1718.
6. Plural of *Sider*.
7. E.g., Dyhernfurth 1705, Halle 1710, Amsterdam 1715.
8. E.g., Frankfurt am Main 1696; Sulzbach 1712.
9. I have examined almost forty editions of the *Seyder Tkhines*.
10. Or Hachama (Ramak) Sh. (2)10.
11. Jews who were baptized at the time of the Inquisition and their descendants, but who often continued covertly to practice Judaism.
12. More on this subject can be found in Popkin 1990.
13. A contemporary eyewitness account is to be found in *Yeven Metzulah, The Abyss of Despair* by Nathan Nate Hanover, published in Venice in 1652.
14. Ezek. 28:16.
15. Scholem 1973:2.
16. Ibid.
17. For example, Menasseh ben Israel's Latin *De Resurrectione Mortuorum Libri III*, Amsterdam, 1636 and the Spanish version, *De las Resurrection de los Muertos, Libros III* in the same year. (A second edition of the Latin was published in Groningen in 1676).
18. Scholem 1973: 2.
19. For a detailed explanation of the complexities of Lurianic Kabbalah a good starting point is by the established authority, Gershom Sholem in Scholem: 1973: 244-286.
20. Scholem 1965: 394-95.
21. The female side of God is known as the *Shkhine*.
22. Scholem, 1973: 45.
23. Ibid., 23.
24. For a full account of the life and Messianic movement of Shabbetai Tsvi, see Ibid., 1973.
25. Israel 1985: 210.
26. Ibid., 188.
27. Place unknown.
28. Weissler 1998: 17.
29. A rhymed Yiddish version of biblical stories from Genesis to Exodus 22 and four scrolls: The Song of Songs, Ruth, Ecclesiastes, and Esther.
30. Translated and printed in Dutch in 1666, Yiddish in 1691, and Hebrew in 1698.
31. Menasseh ben Israel, 1650: XVII: LXVI: 101-102.
32. Ibid., 95.

33. I have modernized the English language and spelling to a degree.
34. This word was printed entirely in capital letters unlike any other.
35. The title indicates the wide geographical area to which the books from Menasseh's publishing house were circulated across Western and Eastern Europe.
36. These books published by Menasseh ben Israel are in a collection at the University Library, Amsterdam.

Seyder Tkhines: Definitions

A STANDARD PRAYER BOOK

The *Seyder Tkhines* began life as a standard prayer book. There is a fixed core that contains thirty-seven *tkhines* divided into five sections: (1) those to be recited daily; (2) those to be recited on the Sabbath (related to two of the three women's commandments of *khale* and candle lighting); (3) those related to the third women's commandment of *nide* which includes purification, pregnancy, and childbirth; (4) those for recitation on fast days; and (5) those to be recited on the burial ground, some of which are for the festivals of New Year and the Day of Atonement.

It might be expected that certain differences would exist from edition to edition in a book that was published numerous times, for three generations, by different printers, in different towns, and which ultimately appear in *sidorim* of different rites. However, any differences are very slight and infrequent. I have examined about forty editions of the *Seyder Tkhines* that span the entire historical period and geographical area of Phase 1, and I have found that the content of specific prayers remains the same. The only difference is in the occasional addition of one or more prayers. These might be extra Yiddish prayers at the end of the book, sometimes for pregnancy and childbirth,[1] or as a daily prayer.[2] There are also examples of one or two additional familiar Hebrew prayers, the significance of which is discussed later in the chapter. In the Amsterdam 1649 edition, which is from a different publisher than the Amsterdam 1648 edition, some prayers relating to the women's commandments, fast days, and the burial ground have been omitted, but in all other editions the core collection is complete. So these established a content and form from the first edition that continued to serve its purpose for a period of about seventy years, during which it was continuously printed.[3]

The existence of this standardized, prescriptive prayer for women is at odds with the generally accepted notion that women's prayer, unlike men's, is individual, private, and spontaneous. This notion was established from the first record of a Jewish woman making a request directly to God, which is located in the Book of Samuel.[4] It would have been familiar to women in the seventeenth century from contemporary Yiddish sources, including Bible translations, the *Shmuel-bukh*, and the *Tsene-rene*.[5] It is the story of the barren Hannah praying in the Temple for a child. She stands apart, away from the Temple service, and there is no record of what she says. Her lips move silently and she weeps. Her sincerity is evident and her prayer is answered. There are features of Hannah's prayer that appear to have influenced the *Seyder Tkhines*. Reference is made to Hannah in the daily *tkhines* and also in the particular *tkhine* that, like Hannah's own prayer, is a request for a child. In the Book of Samuel, Hannah's prayer is accompanied by weeping:

And she prayed to the Lord weeping all the while.[6]

This is paralleled in the *tkhines* when the female worshipper asks God to accept her prayer and her tears as he accepted the prayer of Hannah:

> *God Almighty,*
> *Accept my prayer,*
> *And take my tears in Your vessel*
> *Like the tears of Hannah,*
> *Whose prayer You granted*
> *When You allowed her to speak to You*
> *Through the Prophet,*
> *And brought her happiness.*

Hannah's prayer is depicted as personal, private, and heartfelt:

And Hannah was praying in her heart; only her lips moved but her voice could not be heard. So Eli[7] thought she was drunk.[8] Yet Hannah protests: "I have drunk no wine or other strong drink, but I have been pouring out my soul before the Lord."[9]

The female worshipper in the *tkhines* is similarly depicted as praying "with all my heart" and is instructed in the rubrics to recite each *tkhine* "with *kavone*," or deep concentration.

Eli's mistaken belief that Hannah was drunk indicates that she was not praying in a conventionally recognizable manner. In fact, later in the first Book of Samuel, it is assumed that a prophet or priest is required as an intermediary for private supplication, which is also reflected in the lines noted above from the *tkhines*.[10] Although we know that Hannah prayed for a child, the exact contents of her prayer are unknown and unrecorded because this is a spontaneous prayer between her and God. Only the method of recitation and the reasons for supplication can be compared to the *Seyder Tkhines*, together with the implied underlying principle that a pious woman who prays to God with sincere devotion will achieve an effective result. Hannah's supplication sets a precedent, from the earliest times, for women's prayer as private, spontaneous, and separate from the male-orientated communal service.

Through the ages, Jewish women's prayer has been viewed in this way, in contrast to men's prayer, which is formulated, collective and bound by time and place. In the seventeenth century, contemporaneous with the *Seyder Tkhines*, the Polish Rabbi Abraham Gombiner (c. 1637–1683), who escaped the Chmielnicki massacres in 1648 after the death of his parents, cites Maimonides when he explains in the book for which he is best known, *Mogeyn Avrahom* (Shield of Abraham) that "women have been accustomed not to pray in a set manner."[11] A late twentieth-century view of seventeenth-century prayer proffers the same theory that "a division developed between 'women's prayer' which was private and individual in content and time, and 'men's prayer' which was in codified formulas and scheduled at certain times of the day . . . yet women's prayers remained essentially private, personal and spontaneous supplications."[12]

The *Seyder Tkhines* was different in that it provided a standard book of prescribed prayers exclusively for women where none existed before and none have since on the same scale. Far from being spontaneous and personal, words couched in the first person were being put into the mouths of women whose prayer then lost its significance to their own private and personal needs in favor of communal needs. But the *tkhines* must have been acceptable and relevant to the readers or they would not otherwise have bought or recited them. The popularity and standing of the *Seyder Tkhines* is evident by the sheer number of extant editions and copies of editions that were printed and distributed across Europe. These alone attest to around forty editions between 1648 and 1723, and the large number that have survived suggests that an even greater number must have existed. No other Yiddish prayer book of the period goes beyond three or four editions, and most appear in single editions only. Therefore the *Seyder Tkhines*, with its unique inclusion in the synagogue prayer book, would have been the established, standard Yiddish prayer book for women throughout the Ashkenazic community.

TIME AND PLACE

Time

Although women are exempt from time-bound prayers, the *tkhines* in the *Seyder Tkhines* were not simply "recited when the woman wished,"[13] as has been claimed. They were certainly voluntary, in the sense that there was no obligation to read or recite them. However, for those who did recite them, the *tkhines* were not intended for random moments when spiritual comfort or inspiration were sought. They were linked to specific times that, though they did not coincide with the male-orientated morning, afternoon, and evening synagogue services, were related to time-bound religious obligations. The requirement for women to pray once a day was continually stressed in new Yiddish books, and it is clearly stated on the title page of the 1648 *Seyder Tkhines* that the daily *tkhines* were to be said every day of their lives, first thing in the morning, "after waking, dressing, hand washing and acknowledging God." The phrase "acknowledging God" may refer to the Hebrew *Moyde ani* (How good) prayer that is said immediately on waking, before carrying out the first required daily commandment of hand washing:

> I gratefully thank You, living and eternal King, for You have compassionately restored my soul within me. Your faithfulness is abundant.

Because it is time bound, it is a prayer from which women would normally be exempt; however, it appears as an additional prayer in its original Hebrew at the beginning of many editions of the *Seyder Tkhines*, preceding the fixed core of *tkhines*.

The prevailing custom of women saying their daily prayers first thing in the morning is further confirmed by a commentary contemporary with the *Seyder Tkhines* stating that "immediately in the morning, around the time of washing, [women] say some kind of request and according to scriptural law that is sufficient. And it is possible that the rabbis also did not obligate them for more than that."[14]

The Sabbath *tkhines* are also time bound. Sabbath candles had to be lit before dusk on Friday night, because once darkness arrived, heralding the beginning of Sabbath, it would be prohibited to kindle a flame. Similarly, *khale* had to be freshly baked and ready to eat before the commencement of Sabbath, during which cooking is prohibited. Fast day *tkhines* relate to specific dates in the Jewish calendar, and one *tkhine* was to be said at a particular point during the afternoon synagogue service on all fast days. Even some of the burial ground *tkhines* were said on specific High Holy Days. Those prayers relating to *nide* were bound by the monthly menstrual cycle and by other measured time spans, either physical or religious, related to childbirth. Perhaps the only prayers that could have been said at any time were some of the burial ground prayers, although they might have been linked to fast days, as there was a prevailing custom for visiting graves at that time to ask the dead for intercession.[15] Just as the words of the prayers were prescribed, so were the times when they were to be recited.

Place

Although it has been claimed that the *tkhines* were recited "most typically at home,"[16] very few appear to have been specified for that purpose. The few *tkhines* that were said in the home were those for candle lighting, dividing and baking *khale*, dressing in white before visiting the *mikve*, prior to giving birth (unless the child is being delivered elsewhere), and upon leaving the childbed. Although there were some specified prayer locations, such as the burial ground and the *mikve*,[17] and some *tkhines* were recited in synagogue, the locations of others remain unspecified and open to speculation. That the *Seyder Tkhines* frequently appears bound into the *Sider* links it with the synagogue. Women are not officially obligated to pray in any particular location, and there is no requirement for any set text to be said at any specified time; their domestic obligations take priority.[18]

We know, however, that women would have attended synagogue on some occasions, from the following lines that appear in the *Seyder Tkhines*:

> *And give us houses that are near to the synagogue*
> *And not far from the study house*
> *So that I, and my husband and children*
> *Shall be able to come quickly*
> *To worship Your holy name.*[19]

It is significant that many editions of the *Seyder Tkhines* contain the Hebrew prayer *Ma Toyvu* (How good).[20] This is said upon entering the synagogue and always appears in the *Sider*. In the *Seyder Tkhines*, *Ma Toyvu* is accompanied by a prayer to be said on leaving the synagogue. These prayers appear in their original Hebrew but have Yiddish rubrics to instruct when they should be recited. They appear in the *Seyder Tkhines* that are included inside the *Sider*, as well as in those that are printed alone. Therefore, when the *Seyder Tkhines* is printed inside a *Sider*, the *Ma Toyvu* appears in both books. It is clear from the inclusion of these prayers that some parts of the *Seyder Tkhines* were intended for recitation in synagogue, and that the only two categories to which the prayers for entering and leaving the synagogue could have applied are those for fast days and for daily recitation. One fast day *tkhine* was definitely to be said in synagogue, indicating that women would have attended synagogue in the afternoon on fast days. This prayer is a short form of the *tkhine* that is said every day, which suggests that women may have prayed twice on fast days. Perhaps some other fast day *tkhines* were also said in synagogue, but there is no specific indication of this and some might possibly have been said either at home or on the burial ground. It seems unlikely that the prayers for entering and leaving the synagogue would have been included merely for the sake of one *tkhine*. Therefore, the only other candidates to whom synagogue recitation can be applied are the daily *tkhines*, and it seems likely that they would have been said either in synagogue or at home. There are certain days every month, during and immediately following menstruation, when a woman is forbidden to enter the synagogue and would be obliged to pray at home in order to fulfill her daily obligations. Women could either have read the *tkhines* in their separate part of the synagogue on their own, or as part of a group of women. There are features in the religious songs written by women that indicate the likelihood of communal prayer and singing led by a *firzoger*, or female prayer leader. It was perhaps because the *Seyder Tkhines* was a standard work and reflected prevailing customs that made it unnecessary to specify many of the locations for the recitation of the different *tkhines*. Clues may be found in the small number of atypical *tkhines* where unfamiliarity necessitates more specific instructions. A double-sided page containing two single Yiddish *tkhines* at the end of a *Sider*,[21] one to be said every day and the other when going to bed at night, offers a clue that daily Yiddish *tkhines* would have been recited in synagogue. The page begins with the rubric: "A prayer for when one comes into synagogue." There is no *Ma Toyvu*, and this rubric refers to the Yiddish *tkhines* that follow. Since it is unlikely that the worshipper would have slept in synagogue at night, the daily *tkhine* must have been intended for recitation in synagogue.

As far as reciting *tkhines* in synagogue on Sabbath is concerned, in a *Seyder Tkhines* published in 1672 in Frankfurt am Main, there are prayers for entering and leaving the synagogue, together with an additional prayer, the *Av Harakhamim*, said in Ashkenazic synagogue services on Sabbath morning. It is preceded by a rubric noting that it should be said "when the *Seyfer Torah* is taken out of the Ark for the reading." There is also evidence from an atypical *tkhine* collection, of which only one edition is known, that women attended synagogue and read their *tkhines* on the New Year and the Day of Atonement. It contains the instruction that a particular *tkhine* should be said "on New Year and the Day of Atonement when the *Seyfer Toyre* has been taken out of the Ark." This is confirmed in the *Seyder Tkhines* in which there is a *tkhine* to be recited at the burial ground "after synagogue on the eves of New Year and the Day of Atonement." It seems evident that *tkhines* would have been read in the synagogue on a daily basis, on the Sabbath, on the two major festivals, and on fast days. For the first time, women could pray in synagogue, from their own communal prayer books, in a language they could easily understand.

PUBLIC VS. PRIVATE

Another unexpected feature of the *Seyder Tkhines* is that its content is communal, rather than private and individual, as has previously been believed. It has been claimed that "the pages of the *Sider* are typically phrased in the plural . . . *tkhines* were almost always phrased in the singular."[22] However, this is only half the story. The synagogue service is inherently communal because of the requirement that there must be a *minyen* in order for it to take place. Nachmanides[23] contradicted the view of Rashi that prayer in a minyen is a *mitsve*[24] that men should actively seek out, by claiming that it was not, in fact, an individual *mitsve*, but that if a minyen is available, then the ten men should pray as a congregation rather than as ten individuals.[25] When women gather together for prayer, however, they are regarded as praying as a group of individuals, as there is no requirement for a minyen.[26] In the *Seyder Tkhines*, there are pleas in the first person on behalf of the worshipper that give the impression of being intensely personal, but these personal pleas are accompanied by pleas for either "all Jewish women" or the Jewish people as a whole. This is evident even in *tkhines* concerned with intimate matters such as menstruation or sexual relations, as in the following lines, which endow them with a communal, as well as a personal, quality:

> *I observe Your Commandment*
> *As every woman under Israel*
> *Should observe the Commandments.*[27]

Throughout the *tkhines*, the use of "I" is combined with the use of "us" as in the *tkhine* to be said every day:

> *And be merciful to me,*
> *And to my husband*
> *And my children*
> *And all my household*
> *And all your children, Israel,*
> *And bring us good luck*
> *And help us in all we do.*

She continues later in the *tkhine*:

> *Lord of all the world*
> *May I, and mine,*

And those who do not belong to me
Have their share of this world
And the world to come.
Protect us from all the evil in the world
And protect us from an untimely death . . .

The *tkhines* are expressions of personal pleas that are extended to the wider community. In Judaism, unlike Christianity, redemption is communal, public, and in this world. All Jews must be brought to the same place, Jerusalem, and redeemed collectively and simultaneously.[28] This differs from the Christian concept of the individual redemption of the deserving in the next world. Therefore, Jewish prayer, particularly in a time of messianic expectation, would have to be communal, and the *tkhines* reflect this.

DOMESTIC VS. DIVINE

This collection of prayers[29] is firmly rooted in domestic and family life . . . thus, [the *Seyder Tkhines*] tells a tale of domestic religion, of sanctifying hearth and home . . . by reciting *tkhines* women could also sanctify the ordinary events of home life, baking bread, preparing the Sabbath.[30] . . . Women could sanctify the most ordinary household chores.[31]

In fact, unlike the later Phase 2 *tkhines* that provide prayers for the making of potato kugel (potato pudding) or memorial candles, there are no *tkhines* for ordinary, everyday tasks in the *Seyder Tkhines*. Those matters relating to the home are also related to the religious rituals of the women's commandments. The prayers for *khale* relate to the special Sabbath dough and its connection to ancient Temple rites. There are no *tkhines* for baking bread for everyday consumption or for any other cooking. The *tkhines* for lighting candles relate only to the Sabbath or festival candles that are kindled to fulfill the Commandment, and are part of the religious obligations of the female worshipper. There are no *tkhines* for lighting candles to provide the house with light on a weekday, and the *tkhines* for Sabbath or festival candles would not be appropriate for such a purpose. The very presence of a potato kugel is enough to indicate that we could not be reading the *Seyder Tkhines*. Neither are there *tkhines* to be said over the usual household chores such as sweeping the floor, cleaning the furniture, or doing the laundry. The *Seyder Tkhines* confines itself to religious matters. It therefore differs from the larger anthology, the *Seyder Tkhines u-vakoshes*, which came into print, in a changed world, 120 years later, and which contained prayers for all sorts of occasions, including everyday events. While it was an obvious ancestor, the eighteenth-century book was intended for a different purpose and readership.[32] Revolutionary concepts such as Torah learning for women or the existence of women Kabbalists, quoted by Weissler from individual Phase 2 *tkhines* written by women, would also not have any place in the *Seyder Tkhines*. In the *Seyder Tkhines* we find traditional, established religious values in a revolutionary context.

THE WOMAN OF THE TKHINES
Wife and mother

But who is the woman of the *tkhines* who prays to God as her personal "God, my God" and in whose voice the *tkhines* are recited? The title page is addressed to *"frume vayber un meydlekh"* (pious women and girls). In spite of the inclusion of the word "girls," the *tkhines* is geared toward the wife and mother, so that girls would become aware of their future roles and the values associated with them early in their lives. The word *vayb* (wife) is used for "woman" throughout the *Seyder Tkhines*. The woman of the *tkhines* is a married woman who prays that her sons will be talmudic scholars and that her daughters will marry talmudic scholars. She prays on behalf of "my husband, my children, and my household" as well as on behalf of all Jewish women and the whole Jewish people. In practical terms, she asks that her home may be near the synagogue and learning house, so that the family can be geographically close to prayer and study. She asks that the family will have sufficient money to support itself, but no more, and believes in the giving of charity. She acknowledges responsibility for carrying out her own commandments and is aware of how her husband and children should conduct themselves. The *tkhines* are instructive, but in a subtle manner, not as a sermon or an obvious form of education. Information is put into the mouth of the worshipper as if her level of knowledge is assumed. She is not scholarly, but shows a familiarity with biblical, midrashic, halakhic, and kabbalistic references, and this knowledge appears unwitting, uttered in an apparently natural outpouring.

Sexual relations

The woman of the *tkhines* does not regard chastity as a desired sign of fidelity to God, like contemporary Catholic exemplars, who often chose to remain chaste even in marriage. She regards sexual relations with her husband as a spiritual highlight and prays for a successful outcome resulting in pregnancy. The *tkhines* for *nide* reveal the attitude toward sex that she would be expected to have. The sexual act is portrayed as harmonious, blessed, and blissful, suffused in a light of spiritual perfection. She refers to the event as "When I come to my husband." He must wait for her approach. In Jewish law, there must be no physical contact whatsoever between husband and wife during menstruation and for seven days thereafter. After menstruation, women must inspect themselves twice daily for seven days to ensure that the blood flow has entirely ceased. At the end of the "clean days," a woman should immerse herself in the *mikve* and recite a brief Hebrew blessing, after which she may resume physical contact and sexual relations with her husband.[33] *Tkhines* are provided for this occasion in the *Seyder Tkhines*.

The lady of the *tkhines* requests:

> May I be pure when I come to unite to my husband in great light . . . to bring my husband to blessedness/bliss/fulfillment[34] in the keeping of Your Commandment . . .

In these lines, she comes to her husband at the appropriate time in order to "unite to" him. A few lines later, she speaks of her husband "uniting to me." This suggests a mutual, willing act in which neither partner is dominant. There is a sense that the experience is pleasurable because of its inherent spiritual nature. There is nothing routine about it and there is no reticence on her part, only the expectation of an opportunity for her and her husband to fulfill God's commandment together in the heavenly, blessed light. She takes the responsibility to "bring my husband in bliss to keep your Commandment." She asks God to ensure that the event will be untainted by any impurity, including unseemly thoughts from herself or her husband. The repetition of the image of radiance and great light emphasizes a moment of heightened beauty that has a strong spiritual dimension. It is her hope that this perfect climax will result in the perfect result, the delivery of seed by an angel sent by God for a pure conception.

"I, maid, daughter, your maid"

It is interesting to see how the woman of the *tkhines* refers to herself throughout the prayers. Prior to passages of supplication in which a list of requests are made, she prostrates herself and prays as "*ikh meyd tokhter dayner meyd.*" The words mean "I, maid, daughter, your maid," though there is no punctuation to help with the translation. The word "*dayner*" could also be translated in the genitive, making the translation instead, "I, maid, daughter of your maid," and in some later *tkhines* from Phase 2, the phrase is interpreted in this way. Spaces are left to insert the name, and the mother's name, of the worshipper, thus expressing lineage through the female line. Traditionally, however, a woman is known as her father's daughter, as in the names of the authoresses of religious songs translated in Part 2 of this book, e.g., Rivke bas (daughter of) Meyer, Rokhl bas Mordkhe (Mordecai), and there is no suggestion of spaces being left for names to be inserted in any edition of the *Seyder Tkhines*. The adjective "*dayner*" is used throughout the *Seyder Tkhines* to simply mean "your," so it seems likely that the phrase was intended to mean "I, maid, daughter, your maid." A further confusion in interpreting this far from simple phrase arises: Does the word "maid" refer to a chaste girl or to a servant? It is possible that the married woman and mother sees her relationship with God as purely spiritual and divorced from her worldly self. However, the idea of a chaste maiden is at odds with the rest of the text and it is more likely that "maid" refers to a servant. This becomes evident when the worshipper says some lines later, "Here I stand, a poor woman, before You . . . I ask You as a Father and King." There are also the following lines in the *tkhine* to be said every day:

> And You created people on earth
> To be Your servants at all times.

This depiction of the *tkhine* worshipper as servant and child closely resembles a term found in one of the most awesome annual

Hebrew canonical prayers, entitled *Hayoym haras oylom* (Today is the birth of the world). This is recited in the additional service for the New Year festival, which begins a concentrated period of penitence that ends ten days later on the Day of Atonement. The prayer immediately precedes the sounding of the shofar,[35] and proffers a request to God for inscription into the Book of Life for the coming year. During this prayer, the worshippers refer to themselves as God's children and servants:

> Today all creatures of the world stand under judgment, whether as children [of God] or as servants. If as children, be merciful with us as the mercy of a father for children. If as servants, our eyes depend on You, until You are gracious to us and release our verdict as light, Awesome and Holy One.

These Hebrew terms "servants" and "children" closely parallel the feminized version found in the *Seyder Tkhines* ("maid" and "daughter") and may reveal the nature of the relationship between the woman of the *tkhines* and God that was envisaged by the author. The first time this phrase appears in the daily *tkhines*, a request follows that parallels that of the Hebrew liturgy, asking God to inscribe the worshipper in the Book of Life.

The relationship between the woman of the *tkhines* and God is on the one hand an inherent, loving, familial connection of a father who supports a child for whose very existence He is responsible. The other is one of formal accountability of a servant and the duty of support and protection by a master. Both relationships demand a sense of mutual obligation. The father must protect, while the King, who is referred to elsewhere as Master and Lord, must treat servants as he would his own family:

> *Have you remembered*
> *That you must treat a maid or servant correctly?*
> *You must not drive them from your table*
> *To wash up or clean up*
> *While something is still in their dish.*
>
> *Also you must not plague them too much,*
> *Then you will not need to beat them.*
> *They must live happily with you,*
> *Which is why you pay them good wages.*[36]

The reference to "Father and King" echoes the Hebrew prayer *Ovinu Malkeynu* (Our Father, Our King).[37] These parallels suggest that the contents of the daily *tkhines* liturgy is derived in part from some of the most sacred prayers in the Hebrew prayer service, and that the tenets of these prayers are reiterated daily in the *Seyder Tkhines*.

"A pauper at the door of a rich man"

In another guise, the woman of the *tkhines* likens herself to "a pauper at the door of a rich man." Thus, her worldly wealth is immaterial. The idea of the superior spiritual worth of a pauper appears in a contemporary Yiddish religious song entitled "Delightful song of death,"[38] which emphasizes that God favors the poor and that entry to Paradise cannot be bought:

> *God loves the poor man very much.*
> *He gives him no silver or gold.*
> *He does not wish to give him money*
> *So he may attain eternal life.*

The image of the pauper at a rich man's door also implies that God is compelled to answer the woman's prayers, just as a rich man is obliged to be charitable to the poor:

> *When a poor man comes to you for help*
> *In his prayer shawl or tunic,*
> *Or his wife in her Sabbath hat,*
> *Do not be impatient or irritated*
> *Or turn them away.*[39]

There is a communal obligation to the poor that the *tkhines* worshipper acknowledges, and rather impertinently reminds God, by implication, that He must follow the rules that He imposes on His people.

Superstition

The woman in the *tkhines* is superstitious. Her fear of evil spirits and demons who might hinder her prayers and delay redemption, strengthens her determination to strive for goodness. The presence of devils, evil spirits, and people who can generate evil, are expressed in requests for God's protection in the daily *tkhines*. This extends to requests in the *tkhine* that is said every day for protection of the prayers themselves from evil influences:

> *Allow my prayers to reach You*
> *Without the interference of devils,*
> *Or evil spirits who hinder prayers.*

Such subject matter does not appear in the Hebrew prayer book. She is very much aware of the evil that is attributed to women due to the sin of Eve, and she acknowledges it. Demons, including the female Lilith and Igres,[40] are fended off in a prayer for kindling Sabbath candles that also welcomes the mystical queen and bride of the Sabbath. There is an underlying certainty that by fulfilling her commandments, and through prayer and repentance, the woman of the *tkhines* can banish the dangers of lurking evil. Women are not only a force for good, but also represent the highest level of virtue. Like "all pious women," she is depicted as a direct descendant of the four matriarchs and other female biblical examplars from whom she seeks inspiration. She constantly refers to these biblical women as she recites her *tkhines*. Through prayer and repentance she hopes to gain eternal life in the world to come for herself, her family, and the whole Jewish people, and to restore the cosmos to its paradisal state, which predated Eve's sin.

Insecurity in exile

The *tkhines* also reflect the experience of Jewish suffering in "bitter, hard exile from the Holy Land," and the day-to-day fears of deprivation and tyranny. The woman of the *tkhines* asks for God's protection from worldly dangers:

> *And protect us from an untimely death,*
> *And from captivity,*
> *And hunger and thirst,*
> *And corruption and evil decrees.*[41]

She reflects the concerns of her exiled community, which lives in constant fear of a cruel and inhospitable regime while striving to keep its religious customs intact, in readiness for a return to its homeland.

The power of nature

The woman of the *tkhines* voices requests in awed recognition of God's power and control over what seems to her to be the uncontrollable power of nature. The following lines that precede one such request depict the female worshipper in devout prostration:

> *Therefore Lord of all the world,*
> *I spread open the palms of my hands*
> *And bend to You and bow down before You*
> *With all my heart . . .*[42]

She makes the following request for protection:

> *Protect us from water and fire,*
> *And from evil winds, thunder, and lightning*
> *That may strike us*
> *Awake or sleeping,*
> *In our homes or on the streets,*
> *And protect us from all great terror,*
> *From great floods or from storms,*
> *When suddenly water comes*
> *From below or from above.*
> *And protect us from all evil encounters*
> *Wherever we walk or stand,*
> *So we may worship Your Name with joy.*

The woman of the *tkhines* is portrayed as being constantly insecure. She expects natural disaster to strike at any time. Fear of flood, fire, and storm could justifiably be considered as contemporary, practical concerns, recalling biblical images as well. Accidental fire was also a real threat during this period of history. In 1590, for example, a fire in the Jewish community of Posen (Poland) killed seventy-six Jews, and eighty Torah scrolls were destroyed. The Jewish section of the town had to be abandoned for two years, only to be destroyed again by fire in 1613. However, the degree of fear and terror expressed in the *tkhine* is not just restricted to fire, and it conveys an exaggerated, if not irrational, fear of the mysteries of nature.

Intercession

The presence of a whole section of *tkhines* to be said at the burial ground that contains requests for intercession indicates a preoccupation with the dead that stems from Kabbalism, a mystical tradition usually discouraged in Judaism. It is the custom to locate Jewish cemeteries away from the living, and Jews generally visit graves annually between the festivals of the New Year and the Day of Atonement. In the *Seyder Tkhines*, as well as in the burial ground *tkhines*, the Hebrew *Av Harakhamim* (Father of mercy) prayer is instructed to be said at the graveside,[43] and the prayer itself is sometimes included at the end of the *Seyder Tkhines*.[44]

There were Yiddish books printed in the seventeenth century entitled *Mayne Loshn* (literally "response language"), which contained prayers called *tkhines* that were especially for recitation on the burial ground, but were not the same as those in the *Seyder Tkhines*.[45] Three different versions of *Mayne Loshn* are known to have been printed, and the existence of these difference sources of burial ground prayers verifies the custom of regular grave visiting. One of the rubrics in *Mayne Loshn* offers an insight into the manner in which burial ground *tkhines* were recited:

> One does not say all the *tkhines* beside one grave. The *tkhines* are said at various places: at one section of graves, one section of *tkhines* is said; and at another place, another section, so that one may pray at many graves. But do not say *tkhines* while walking around, as some people do. No deep concentration (*kavone*) can be derived when one walks around like that. Therefore, we have divided up the *tkhines* so they may be said for all of the dead at each section, so that it may be possible to say *tkhines* at many places.[46]

Angels acting as intermediaries between the worshipper and God also appear as a common theme in the *tkhines*. Intercession has always been a bone of contention among Jewish scholars and teachers. It has been postulated that Maimonides's opposition to worship through an intermediary in his *Thirteen Principles of Faith* was a "conscious rejection of the Christian doctrine of Incarnation and prayers to and through Jesus."[47] There is no reference to angels in the Mishnah.[48] In talmudic literature,[49] the Palestinian Talmud opposes prayer through an intermediary in favor of direct prayer to God: "Whosoever shall call on the name of God will be delivered."[50] This was reinforced with opposition to vernacular prayer, as found in the *tkhines*, when it was claimed in the Babylonian Talmud that "he who prays in the Aramaic language (i.e., the vernacular) will not be helped by the ministering angels for the ministering angels do not know Aramaic."[51] Such opposition indicates that the custom must have existed for prayers to be directed to God via the angels, in the vernacular, some eleven centuries before this popular motif was revived in the *Seyder Tkhines*.

It is difficult to know where to separate the fast day *tkhines* from those to be said on the burial ground, because it was a contemporary custom to visit burial grounds on public fast days, to offer prayers at the graves of the departed, and to ask for intercession,[52] especially on the ninth of Av[53] and in the month of Elul.[54] Therefore, it is possible that with the positioning of the fast day *tkhines* immediately preceding those for the burial ground, at least some of these prayers would have been said at the burial ground, although there is no mention in the rubrics that this is the case. But the custom of seeking intercession must have been established and accepted for it to be included in the *Seyder Tkhines*. The woman of the *tkhines* asks both the dead and the angels for intercession. She clearly believes in the power of intercession, and beseeches them to mediate on her behalf as she prostrates herself on the graves of saintly men and women, or on the grave of a deceased husband.

FILLING GAPS IN THE HEBREW LITURGY

There were gaps in Hebrew liturgy that coincided with the concerns of the new audience of women readers. About a third of the *Seyder Tkhines* is devoted to previously unwritten prayers for occasions when the three women's commandments were performed. This material is not found in the Hebrew prayer book in which brief blessings are provided. The *tkhines* are newly composed additions to these brief blessings.

The Yiddish books of *mayne loshn* filled another gap in Hebrew liturgy with the rise in interest in visiting graves for intercession. It was a case of supply and demand. But these books were not standard works, and there were only three known editions, all different, and published some years apart (in 1615, 1627, and around 1688). The *Seyder Tkhines* provided prayers within the standard women's prayer book for a purpose that would not have been necessary at other times in history. The *Sider* had always been responsive to the needs of its users, and prayers were added to it as they became appropriate over time. Similarly prayers could be discarded when they lost their relevance. Prayers for the burial ground do not appear to have entered the Hebrew liturgy with the exception of the *Kaddish*, the prayer for mourning that is recited by a man in the presence of a minyen, as well as a prayer to be said when visiting the burial ground after thirty days absence. The latter appears as the first burial ground *tkhine* in the *Seyder Tkhines* translated into Yiddish. The rest are new material.[55]

MOTIVATIONS FOR A STANDARD YIDDISH PRAYER BOOK FOR WOMEN

The *Seyder Tkhines* that was printed in 1648 in Amsterdam is of particular interest because of its unique, twenty-four-line introduction, which gives the only known declaration of the aims of the *Seyder Tkhines*. Most significantly, the *Seyder Tkhines* fulfills the essential duty of making prayer comprehensible to women, as is evident from the following lines:

> When a woman who does not understand a prayer desires one to read it to her so that she can understand, one is obliged to read it so that she may understand it, in order that the prayer will come from the heart.

This obligation of men to translate and explain prayer to women was extended with the provision of the *tkhines* that enabled women to understand their prayers without any help from men. By the very existence of the *Seyder Tkhines*, it was clearly deemed essential that women fulfill their prayer obligations. It was no longer enough for men to pray as part of the communal service and thus pray on behalf of women. The *Seyder Tkhines* empowers women to pray not only for themselves, but to pray directly to God for the well-being of their husbands, families, and their people. Not only do they pray for the redemption of their people, but also the very act of praying is part of that redemption.

Ñotes

1. E.g., 1699 Prague, Halle 1710, Sulzbach 1712.
2. E.g., Amsterdam 1649, Halle 1710.
3. See Bibliography of primary sources for places and dates of publication.
4. 1 Sam. 10–19.
5. See Chapter 2.
6. 1 Sam. 10.
7. The Temple Priest.
8. 1 Sam. 13.
9. 1 Sam. 15.
10. 1 Sam. 12:19, 23.
11. Gombiner 1692: 106:2; Biale 1984:20.
12. Biale 1984:20.
13. Weissler 1998:8. Chava Weissler's book *Voices of the Matriarchs* deals mainly with Phase 2 *tkhines*.
14. Abraham Gumbiner: Magen Avraham, Commentary on Maimonides, Shulḥan Arukh, Orah Khayim: 106:2; Biale 1984: 19.
15. See section on intercession later in this chapter.
16. Weissler 1998:8.
17. Ritual bath visited by a woman for monthly ritual cleansing from the "impurities" of menstruation, and after a designated time following childbirth.
18. Nevertheless, according to the Mishnah (160–200 C.E.) women do have an obligation to recite *tfile* (prayer) once a day (M. Berakhot 3:3) (Maimonides: *Mishneh Torah, hilkhot tefillah* 1:1; Biale 1984, 20).
19. *Tkhine* to be recited on Tuesdays.
20. E.g., Frankfurt am Main 1696, Prague c.1710.
21. Wilmersdorf 1721, in a German/Polish rite *sider*. This is the only known printing I have found of these two *tkhines*.
22. Weissler 1998: 8.
23. Nachmanides, known as the Ramban, the acrostic of his full name (Rabbi Moshe ben Nachman) (1194–1270).
24. Religious obligation.
25. Rashi on Pesahim 46a; Nachmanides, *Milhamot Ha-Shem, Megillah* 5a.
26. Meiselman 1978: 140.
27. From "This *tkhine* is to be said when women dress themselves in white."
28. Sholem: "Toward an understanding of the Messianic idea in Judaism," in *The Messianic Idea in Judaism and Other Essays on Jewish Spirituality* (New York, 1995) Schocken Books (first edition 1971), p. 1.
29. Referring to the *Seyder Tkhines*.
30. Weissler 1998: 9.
31. Ibid., 34.
32. See Chapter 8.

33. Lev. 15:19–24; 18–19.
34. To convey the meaning in translation, all these alternatives are possible.
35. Ram's horn.
36. See "Song" by Yankev ben Elyohu in Part 2: "Single Prayers and Songs in Tkhine Language."
37. Recited throughout the Ten Days of Penitence, except on Sabbath, and at the end of the morning service on the Jewish New Year (*Rosh Hashona*). This prayer is a confession of sins and concludes with a plea for God's acceptance of the supplications of the community.
38. *A hipsh, nay toytn lid* by Yankev ben Elyohu. Prague, seventeenth century.
39. Ibid.
40. Meir Arama, *Sefer Meir T'hillot*, 91b; Nathan Nata Pora, Tuv haAretz, 19
41. *Tkhine* to be said on Sunday.
42. *Tkhine* to be said on Monday.
43. *Av Harakhamim* is usually said in Ashkenazic synagogue services on Sabbath mornings in memory of the martyrs of the Crusades. It was composed during the First Crusade and left on the reader's desk in the synagogue at Worms by its unknown author. The prayer is a mixture of tender recollection of martyred victims and bitter renunciation of those who perpetrated the massacre.
44. E.g., Frankfurt am Main 1672.
45. See Kay 1993:83.
46. Elieyzer Soyfer ben Leyb, c.1688, place of publication unknown.
47. Jacobs 1964: 172.
48. Completed by the end of the second century.
49. Fifth century.
50. Jer. er. ix: 13a.
51. Sabb. 12b.
52. Ta'an 16a, 23b, Sot. 34b, Maimonides: Yad, Ta'anit 4:18.
53. Ramo 1570, 559: 10, 581–4.
54. There is no mention of this custom in the Mishnah, but the Talmud takes it for granted that people visit the graveyard on a public fast so that the souls of the departed might intercede on behalf of the living.
55. The *Mayne Loshn* is still printed in Yiddish today. *Tkhines* for the burial ground are no longer included in the modern version of the *Seyder Tkhines*. Therefore, the *Mayne Loshn* that developed as a parallel form of the burial ground prayers in the *Seyder Tkhines* and became a separate, specialized liturgy, has survived from seventeenth-century literature for a small, marginalized readership.

5

Side by Side by Seyder

PHYSICAL SEPARATION

The social and religious roles of men and women in the seventeenth century were clearly and separately defined, as seen from the popular Yiddish ethical books of the time that instructed the community on correct forms of behavior, such as *Lev Tov* and *Brantshpigl*. The women's commandment of *nide* dictated that although husband and wife shared the same home, they were to have no physical contact during and immediately following menstruation.[1] Men and women prayed in the same synagogue, but always in different sections. Men prayed in the main body of the synagogue with access to the Ark and the Torah scrolls that were kept therein. The scrolls were removed for reading by men only. Women prayed either in their own separate room from which the main service could be heard,[2] or they sat segregated in a gallery that was usually screened off by almost opaque grilles. In the only known firsthand account of Jewish life by a woman from those times, its author, Glikl of Hameln, writes of the synagogue in Metz as having an upper balcony that could be reached by a staircase, as well as a lower gallery that was five or six steps higher than the ground level. Both were for women only.[3] She also writes of the separate women's part of the synagogue in Hanover: "You must know that to reach the men's synagogue, one had to pass through the women's section."[4] Men and women had different prayer obligations and their prayer language was different as well.

For three generations, this bound-together, yet side-by-side, existence of men and women was reflected in a unique prayer book. This volume contained the *Sider* (also known as the *Seyder Tfile* [Order/sequence of prayer]), the ancient Hebrew book for communal synagogue prayer convened and led by men, together with the newly composed Yiddish prayer book solely for women, the *Seyder Tkhines*. Though it was one book, the *Seyder Tfile* and *Seyder Tkhines*, were produced separately, often by different printers, and then bound together. Each book appeared in the appropriate print associated with its language, the Yiddish *Seyder Tkhines* in *mashket*, the Hebrew portion in square characters. The Yiddish prayer book often had a separate title page that was different in decorative design from the Hebrew prayers. These two separate prayer books existed comfortably together within the same cover.

TWO GENDERS: TWO SIDES OF GOD

The word *Shkhine* derives from the Hebrew root meaning, "to dwell," as in Exodus: "They will make Me a sanctuary and I shall dwell among them."[5] The ancient rabbis attributed to *Shkhine* the meaning of the Divine Presence of God, which was believed to have been present in the Temple in Jerusalem. But in kabbalistic tradition,[6] *Shkhine* came to mean the female element within God, so that God had both male and female sides.[7] In Lurianic Kabbalah, it was deemed essential to reunite the male Godhead with His exiled "bride," the female side of God, in order to restore the order of the cosmos to the paradisal state that predated Eve's sin. The two were alienated for most of the time, uniting only once a week on the Sabbath. This concept is found in the *tkhine* to be recited after kindling the Sabbath candles:

> . . .On Your holy Sabbath,
> Which we are bound to honor
> And keep in all things,
> Like a king his queen
> Or a bridegroom his bride,
> Because in the words of our sages:
> The Sabbath is queen and bride.

In an age in which the exile of the Jews was a terrible and constant reality, the idea of the exile of the "bride of God" gained great importance. Rather than being a metaphor, it became a genuine symbol for what was seen by kabbalists as the "broken" state of things. The two prayer books, side by side, imply a prevailing belief that the religious observance and prayer of men alone would be inadequate to ensure the arrival of the Messiah. Women would have to play their part. By observing all their commandments meticulously, repenting their sins and praying with deep conviction, women were given the opportunity to absolve themselves of the sin of Eve, and, in fact, would need to do so in order for the "bridegroom" to be reunited with "his bride."

The notion that anything that was male could only be complete when accompanied by its female counterpart is highlighted in the *Seyder Tkhines* in a feature that is absent from Hebrew liturgy. For each male mentioned, there is the inclusion of a parallel female counterpart. The matriarchs, Sarah, Rebecca, Rachel, and Leah, are included as female counterparts to the three patriarchs, Abraham, Isaac, and Jacob. Even where more general terms are found in the Hebrew liturgy such as "pious men" or "saintly men," in the *Seyder Tkhines* we find "pious men and pious women" or "saintly men and saintly women," as in the following typical lines from the daily *tkhines*:

> *And let us benefit from the merit*
> *Of Abraham, Isaac, and Jacob,*
> *Moses, Aaron, David, Solomon,*
> *Sarah, Rebecca, Rachel, Leah,*
> *Hannah, Abigail,*
> *And other saintly men and saintly women.*
> *And pious men and pious women.*

The named women do not replace the usual male examplars; they co-exist with equal status.

STYLE

I cannot agree with the recent claim that the *Seyder Tkhines* was "almost entirely unrelated to the prayers of [Hebrew] liturgy."[8] Evidence shows that the *Seyder Tkhines* provided a new Yiddish daily liturgy for Ashkenazic women that served as an alternative to the Hebrew liturgy, but was based upon it. Its author demonstrates a convention that was much used in Yiddish prayer of the time. Hebrew prayer was taken as a starting point and adapted into Yiddish, but the content was considerably extended to include additional supplications and other material. The Yiddish version varied in length and content from the original, while corresponding to it in certain parts. This method was used in the daily liturgy of the *Seyder Tkhines*, and its style has been termed *tkhine loshn* or *tkhine* language. It is exemplified in its simplest form in the Yiddish adaptation of the Hebrew *Ma Toyvu* prayer that appears in a booklet printed in Amsterdam under the name of Khane Kats, a translation of which can be found in Part 2, "Single Prayers and Songs in *Tkhine* Language."

Modern Yiddish authors and scholars alike have sensed the existence of a special language associated with *tkhines*. In Mendele Moykher Sforim's[9] classic nineteenth-century story *Fishke der Krumer* (Fishke the lame), the first-person narrator exclaims: "*Almekhtiger Got!—zog ikh mit a gebet af tkhine loshn* (Almighty God!—say I, praying in *tkhine* language.)."[10] The Yiddish literary scholar, Israel Tsinberg, refers to a "specific classic *tkhine* style."[11] The concept of *tkhine loshn* is at least three hundred years old. In the seventeenth century, the authoress Toybe Pan coined the term when she claimed that her work was "a song newly composed in *tkhine loshn*."[12] She was aware that she was writing in a special style that was instantly recognizable. In his *History of the Yiddish Language*, the linguist Max Weinreich refers to the language in which *tkhines* are written as *loshn halb koydesh*" (semi-sacred language),[13] suggesting that it fits somewhere between *loshn koydesh* (sacred tongue, i.e., Hebrew) and *Mame loshn* (Mother tongue, i.e., everyday Yiddish). He claims that through *tkhines*, Yiddish reached its highest status, because it became a language of prayer.[14] It was in this identifiable, elevated form of Yiddish, which differed from the spoken Yiddish of the time, that the daily *tkhine* liturgy was written.

AN ALTERNATIVE DAILY LITURGY FOR WOMEN

A Comparison of the daily Hebrew synagogue liturgy with the daily tkhines

The *Seyder Tkhines* provided, in effect, a new and parallel daily liturgy in Yiddish for women. It was based on the ancient, fixed Hebrew prayers that are recited three times a day in synagogue. The three prayer sessions are known as: *Shakhris* (morning service), *Minkhe* (afternoon service), and *Mayrev* (evening service). Women have no obligation to attend these time-bound services,[15] but the daily *tkhines* gave them the opportunity to fulfill their obligation to pray once a day.[16]

The daily *tkhines* appear at the beginning of the *Seyder Tkhines*. It can be seen from their rubrics that two *tkhines* are said each day. The first and longer *tkhine* of the two, entitled "This *tkhine* is said every day," is the fixed part of daily worship. In addition, one of seven *tkhines*, one for each day of the week, is recited, for example: "This *tkhine* is to be said on Monday with *kavone*." The daily prayers in the *Seyder Tkhines* provided women with a prescribed liturgy, printed within the synagogue prayer book, which could be said at a prescribed time.

A comparison between the Hebrew daily synagogue prayers and the daily *tkhines* offers evidence as to whether or not the *Seyder Tkhines* did, in fact, present an alternative daily liturgy to that in the *Sider*. As the daily *tkhine* liturgy is intended for recitation in the morning, it is compared here with the *Shakhris* service. The content and structure of the daily *tkhines* are based on a reordering and reformulation of various prayers from Hebrew morning prayer, supplemented with new material.

The order of the *Shakhris* service is set out below in Table 1. Table 2 shows the order of the *tkhine* liturgy in the *Seyder Tkhines* and suggests how the Hebrew liturgy is apparently rearranged and adapted so that parts of it are represented, to some extent, throughout most of the *tkhine* liturgy.

Prayers from the Sider directly transferred to the Seyder Tkhines

Certain prayers from the *Sider*, namely *Moyde Ani* and *Ma Toyvu*, from which women would normally be exempt, are found in some editions of the *Seyder Tkhines*. These usually appear in their original Hebrew (e.g., Amsterdam 1649), and occasionally in Yiddish translation (e.g., Frankfurt am Main 1696). *Moyde Ani* is said immediately on waking, before carrying out the first required daily commandment of hand washing, and is alluded to on the title page of the *Seyder Tkhines*. *Ma Toyvu* is the first prayer said upon entering the synagogue. The direct

TABLE 1
DAILY SYNAGOGUE LITURGY (*SHAKHRIS* SERVICE)

1. *MOYDE ANI*	(I give thanks). Recited immediately after waking.
2. *MA TOYVU*	(How good [are your tents]). First synagogue prayer, to be said on entering the synagogue.
3. MORNING BLESSINGS	Predominantly male blessings for phylacteries (boxes containing scriptures strapped to man's head and arm during morning synagogue prayer), tallis (fringed prayer shawl), and *tsitsis* (fringed garment worn by men beneath clothing). Includes thanks to God "who has not made me a woman" (*sheloy osani isho*).
4. *AKEYDE YITSKHOK*	(Binding of Isaac: Gen. 119). Abraham's binding of Isaac.
5. *KORBONES*	(Sacrifices). Includes *ketoyres* (incense), *avayey havo mesader* (order of daily Temple service), Temple ritual, worship, and sacrifice.
6. *PESUKEY DE-ZIMRO*	Praises of God as Creator. Psalms and sections from Bible (1 Chronicles, 6:8–36) introduced by a benediction and concluded by a benediction.
7. *SHEMA* (Hear)	Women are exempt from saying this prayer.
9. *AMIDE* (Standing prayer)	Main prayer of *Shakhris* service. Opening and closing correspond to opening of daily *tkhines*.
8. *TAKHNUN* (Supplication)	Same etymological root as *tkhines* but not directly part of them.
9. TORAH READING	Mondays, Thursdays, Sabbath, and Festivals, read by men only, with no parallel in the *tkhines*.
10. *ASHREY*	Praise of God. Includes a request for the Messianic age.
11. *OLEYNU*	Praise to the eternalness and oneness of God.
12. *SHIR SHEL YOYM*	(Psalm of the day). Final part of the morning service.

transference of these prayers into the *tkhine* prayer book suggests that the daily *tkhines* were intended to fit within the familiar framework of the established Hebrew prayers. They were to provide a recognizable parallel to them, and were not a rejection of the structural arrangement of established liturgical tradition. This is achieved, in part, by beginning with the first Hebrew prayers of the day and ending with an equivalent to the Psalm of the Day (see Table 2). However, while the basis of the Yiddish liturgy is found within the Hebrew liturgy, the *Seyder Tkhines* is a new form of prayer book with features of its own.

TABLE 2
DAILY PRAYER FROM THE SEYDER TKHINES

Order of prayer in the Seyder Tkhines	Suggested source from daily Hebrew liturgy
Moyde Ani In its original Hebrew in some editions of the *Seyder Tkhines*	*Moyde Ani*
Ma Toyvu In its original Hebrew in some editions of the *Seyder Tkhines*	*Ma Toyvu*
Opening of daily *tkhines* (translation of opening of *Amide*)	*Amide*
Praising of God	*Pesukey De-zimro* (Praising of God), *Ashrey*, *Oleynu*
Female Prostration	No parallel in Hebrew prayers
Supplications	Some from Hebrew liturgy, some original
Statement of number of commandments plus women's commandments	Blessings for phylacteries, *tallis*, and *tsitsis* in which number of commandments are stated, excluding women's commandments
Supplications	Some from Hebrew liturgy, some original
Temple ritual	*Korbones* (Temple ritual)
Reference to Abraham's binding of Isaac	*Akeyde Yitskhok* (Binding of Isaac)
Supplications	Some from Hebrew liturgy, some original
Tkhine of the day	*Tkhine* of the day
Standard opening: praise of God	Standard opening: praise of God
Daily reference to parallel day of creation	Daily reference to parallel day of creation
Female prostration	Female prostration
Supplications	Supplications
Shir Shel Yoym (Psalm of the day) Like third paragraph of the *Shema* and *Pesukey De-zimro* and first half of *Adoyn Oylom* hymn that ends the service	*Shir Shel Yoym* (Psalm of the day) No parallel in Hebrew prayers Some from Hebrew liturgy, some original
Leave-taking (corresponds to close of *Amide*)	*Amide* (final lines)

77

A shared framework

The shared framework is further reinforced in the opening and closing lines of the entire daily *tkhine* liturgy. These are virtually the same as the opening and closing lines of the Hebrew prayer from which it has most likely been derived, known as the *Amide* (Standing prayer), which is the name I use here. It is also known as the *Shmoyne esrey*, meaning "eighteen," denoting the eighteen blessings of which it originally consisted, or simply as *Tfile* (prayer). The similarity between the opening lines of the Hebrew *Amide* and the daily *tkhines* is evident:

Opening lines of tkhines:	Opening lines of Amide:
Lord of all the world,	*Blessed are You*
God, my God,	*Lord our God*
And God of my forefathers,	*And God of our forefathers*
Abraham, Isaac, and Jacob,	*God of Abraham*
Great and strong and	*God of Issac and God of Jacob*
awesome God . . .	*Great and Strong and*
	awesome God . . .

The *Amide* as a model for the opening of the daily *tkhines* is one indication that a new standard liturgy was based on the existing Hebrew liturgy. This is even more apparent when examining the final lines of the daily *tkhines* that corresponds to the final lines of the *Amide*:

tkhines	Amide
May the speech of my mouth	*May the speech of my mouth*
And the thoughts of my heart	*And the thoughts of my heart*
Find favor before You,	*Find favor before You,*
God, my Creator and my	*God, my Rock and my*
Redeemer.	*Redeemer*

The daily *tkhine* liturgy is not only derived from the *Amide*, but also borrows from prayers that precede and follow it in the morning service. It also features additional elements of its own.

Internal structure

A distinguishing feature of daily *tkhines* that is wholly absent from the Hebrew prayers is the method of linking sections of prayer with bridging passages. The daily Hebrew liturgy is constructed from a succession of complete abstractions from various sources such as

the Bible (e.g., Numbers 28: 1–8 during *Korbones*), the Talmud (e.g.,
Yoma 33a, also during *Korbones*), together with whole Psalms (e.g.,
Psalm 24 for Sunday's psalm of the day), and blessings (Heb.
brokhes) that have either fixed formulaic beginnings, endings, or
both. Some prayers are in the form of a self-contained acrostic of
the whole Hebrew alphabet (e.g., Psalm 145). In contrast to these
clearly defined beginnings and endings found in the Hebrew blessings and prayers, there is no clear-cut separation between sections
in the *tkhines*. Instead, there are linking or bridging passages that
are not part of the previous or ensuing sections, which prepare the
worshipper for a change of subject matter. Three separate sections
of supplications are found in the *tkhine* that is said every day. Preceding each of these sections, is a preparatory declaration of self-ef-
facement and prostration by the worshipper. Such a bridging
passage introduces the first supplicatory section:

> *So I come before Your Holy Name*
> *With my body bowed in great submission*
> *To revere Your Holy Name,*
> *And to beg before You*
> *Like a pauper at the door of a rich man.*
> *God, my God . . .*

Such declarations are also found preceding sections of supplication
in the *tkhines* for each day of the week, and are a recognizable indi-
cator of the opening of a new section of supplications. They are immediately followed by a series of requests, all beginning with the
words: *gib mir* (give me). In the bridging passage preceding the third
supplicatory section, references are made to God as "Father and King,"
echoing the Hebrew liturgical prayer *Ovinu Malkeynu* (Our Father,
our King), a prayer of repentance and a plea for God's forgiveness of
sins. This link indicates subsequent supplications for forgiveness in
the *tkhines* because of the association with the Hebrew liturgy. It
also indicates another parallel between the two liturgies, as the *Ovinu
Malkeynu* prayer is said during *Shakhris* after the *Amide* on certain
days.[17]

Each section of supplications in the *tkhines* ends with requests for
the prayers to be received by God. The following lines complete the
preceding section of supplications and lead into a section citing practices of Temple ritual:

And as you accept the prayers
Of all those who repent,
Those who serve you,
And bow down before you,
May you accept my prayer
Today, and every day of my life.

These bridging passages demonstrate a structural technique absent from the Hebrew liturgy that provides continuity and unity for the various sections of the *tkhines*. While the framework and content are appropriated from the Hebrew liturgy, the difference in internal structure reflects the two different methods of collation. The Hebrew liturgy is a composite of different prayers, psalms, and biblical excerpts in various styles and from different sources and periods of history. The daily *tkhines*, on the other hand, is composed as one contemporaneous, cohesive work.

Adaptation of Exclusively Male Prayers

There are 248 positive commandments in Judaism (those that should be performed) and 365 negative commandments, or prohibitions. In both the Hebrew and Yiddish daily liturgies, these commandments are seen as the obligation of all Jews. The daily prayers in the *Sider* that refer to those commandments are intended to be said exclusively by men when donning *tsitsis*,[18] *tallis*,[19] and *tfilin* (phylacteries),[20] which are ritual items traditionally worn by men only:

> I am ready to wrap my body in tsitsis, so may my soul, my two hundred and forty-eight organs and my three hundred and sixty-five sinews be wrapped in the illumination of tsitsis which has the numerical value of six hundred and thirteen. Just as I cover myself with a tallis. . . .[21]

There is a parallel to the above prayer in the *Seyder Tkhines*:

You gave 252 Commandments
To Your children, Israel, to carry out,
And 248, as many as men have parts of their body
That must be observed and kept . . .
And You have given a further 365 Commandments
To Your children Israel
Which they are forbidden to perform.

The contents of the *tkhines* are extended to encompass commandments that do not appear in the Hebrew liturgy and are relevant only
to women:

> *And You have given to women*
> *To correspond with our four limbs,*
> *Four Commandments of our own:*
> *To kindle lights for the holy Sabbath,*
> *To purify ourselves from impurity,*
> *To divide the* khale *dough,*
> *And fourth, to serve our husbands.*[22]

Unexpectedly, there is mention not only of the usual three women's
commandments, but of four. An additional new women's commandment is added that entails an obligation on the part of all Jewish
women to serve their husbands. The appearance of this extra commandment, and its absence from earlier precedents of rules for women
and from any subsequent sources, imposes on seventeenth-century
Ashkenazic women a religious obligation of servitude and obedience
to their husbands. Even in a liturgy exclusively for women, which
would have elevated women's religious and cultural status, male prece-
dence is stressed.

The fourth commandment, however, could be viewed as a possible
literary device rather than a sign of oppression. It may well have been
thought up by the author as a convenient way of imitating the Hebrew
prayer by equating the number of extra commandments with parts of
the human body. The four limbs were an available and obvious
choice, but as there are only three women's commandments, an extra
commandment had to be devised. It could not appear as if the author
was introducing a new religious law, so the obligation to serve one's
husband was added to round up the figures.

Another unusual aspect found in these lines from the *tkhine* is the
author's addition of the four women's commandments to the usual
248 positive commandments. This total of 252 is not found elsewhere
and seems to be a phenomenon only of the *Seyder Tkhines*. It could
be viewed as an outrageous flouting of the principles of Judaism, since
the addition of four new commandments to the number of positive
commandments alters the total from the significant, universally acknowledged number of 613 that stem from the Torah. It also implies

that the women's commandments had not, until the existence of the *Seyder Tkhines*, been regarded on a par with the rest; but in this book, they were elevated to equal status.

The daily prayer for men in the Hebrew liturgy has its parallel in the female liturgy with the addition of the women's commandments, but omits exclusively male references. This suggests that this part of the Hebrew liturgy, intended only for men, was adapted to allow women to recite important tenets of Judaism from which they would normally be excluded. The *tkhine* offers women an alternative to the male-orientated Hebrew prayer, not a supplement to it.

Sacrifice and Temple ritual: a Yiddish parallel to the daily Hebrew korbones *prayers*

Daily synagogue liturgy is derived from, and acts as a substitute for, the original daily Temple sacrifice ritual, which was the earliest form of daily Jewish public worship.[23] Both liturgies keep Temple ritual alive by recalling it daily. The *Shakhris* service includes a section called *Korbones* (Sacrifices), which describes, in detail, the practical elements of Temple ritual. The daily *tkhine* liturgy also has a section devoted to this subject, though its references are more general. The positioning of these sections in the structure of the two liturgies does not coincide,[24] but the *tkhine* parallels this section in its own way:

> *And one part of the offering was burnt each time,*
> *And one part was eaten,*
> *The steam gave off a delicious scent,*
> *And beatified You.*
> *In that Holy House*
> *Dwelt Your Holiness,*
> *Your Divine Presence.*
>
> *But now we have no Priest,*
> *And no sacrifice.*
> *We have no Levites*
> *Who sang at the sacrifice,*
> *Accompanying their holy songs*
> *On harps and lutes.*
> *They played on all sides*
> *To honor Your Holy Name.*

> *And now we have no Temple,*
> *And no Altar,*
> *And no Menoyre,*[25]
> *And no Ark,*
> *And no atonements.*[26]

Evidence that the daily *tkhines* were an alternative to the daily Hebrew prayers is provided in the following lines from the *tkhine* to be said every day:

> *May You accept my prayer*
> *Today, and every day of my life.*
>
> *And accept my prayer*
> *As You accepted the sacrificial offerings*
> *That the Priest brought*
> *To the offering stool,*
> *At the time when Your House stood*
> *In great purity and holiness.*

Just as the synagogue liturgy stands as a substitute for Temple ritual, the daily *tkhines* also serve that function.

"Tkhine of the day": The Yiddish parallel to the Hebrew "Psalm of the day"

Although there are parallels to the prayers in both liturgies, it is clear that their positions in the order of prayer do not always coincide. A further example of this appears in the section in *Shakris* concerning Abraham's intended sacrifice of Isaac,[27] the *Akeydas Yitskhok* (Binding of Isaac), which is most likely the source of the lines on the same subject in the daily *tkhines*.

However, the corresponding outer framework is kept intact with the "Psalm of the day" (*Shir Shel Yoym*), which concludes the *Shakhris* service and its equivalent at the end of the *tkhine* liturgy, the "*Tkhine* of the day." The "Psalm of the day," one for each day of the week, was sung in the Temple by the Levites.[28] These psalms have been continued in the *Sider* and consist entirely of one psalm, whereas the *tkhines* consist of a section that refers to the Creation, followed by a section of supplications. The content of the Hebrew and Yiddish forms resemble one another in that they both refer to the

83

particular day of Creation that corresponds to the day on which they
are recited.

The female perspective

A vital feature distinguishing the *Seyder Tkhines* from the established
daily Hebrew prayers is its exclusively female nature, expressed
through a woman's voice. This Yiddish prayer book was not intended
for men, however uneducated they might be. Men and women had
alternative prayer paths. Because of their obligation to pray three
times a day, men would not have been able to fulfill their obligation
with a once-daily liturgy. Even in a prayer book containing both the
Seyder Tfile and *Seyder Tkhines*, men would have been obliged to pray
in Hebrew from the former, whether or not they understood the
prayers. Women, however, were offered the choice, and though some
might have chosen to pray in Hebrew, the *Seyder Tkhines* provided
women with an alternative that catered to their needs, while allowing
them to fulfill their religious obligation.

CONCLUSIONS

The comparison between the two daily liturgies suggests that they cor-
responded to one another to an extent that cannot be considered co-
incidental. While the works differed in style, it is evident that the
tkhine liturgy was based on the Hebrew liturgy and was set within its
framework. The *tkhines* functioned as a substitute for Temple ritual
in the same way as did the synagogue service. The *Seyder Tkhines*
had additional, new elements relevant to women that made the parallels specific to them. The *Seyder Tkhines* provided a new, daily, vernacular liturgy, exclusively for women, based on the *Shakhris* service,
which served as an alternative to the traditional Hebrew liturgy. The
tkhine liturgy can also be viewed as a substitute for the three synagogue services, since women fulfilled their entire daily prayer obligation by praying only once.

As a newly composed liturgy for women, the *Seyder Tkhines* represented a product of the coalescence of existing influences with a
revolutionary development in Jewish religious literature. Its accept-
ability stemmed from the fact that it was a new liturgy based on an
old, established one, and was related, in a highly specific way, to some

of the most sacred Hebrew prayers. At the same time, it offered additional prayers to fill the gaps left by the Hebrew liturgy. At any other period of history, a separate liturgy for women, in a language other than Hebrew, might have seemed either an outrageous break with custom or, in more recent times, a degrading segregation. However, by the middle of the seventeenth century, it was a natural progression from the Yiddish moral and religious books and prayer book translations that women had become accustomed to reading for over a century. For the Messiah to come, every man and woman, educated or uneducated, would have to pray every day, and for that prayer to be effective, it would have to be understood and heartfelt. Women were able to utter appropriate, formulated sentiments from a female point of view, through a female persona. Nothing was left to chance. This is the only period in Ashkenazic history when such an alternative women's liturgy existed.

The Introduction to the *Seyder Tkhines* stated that it was intended for women who could not understand Hebrew prayer; so it never presented a challenge to the status of the Hebrew liturgy. Because it never was, or claimed to be, anything other than a prayer book for women, perhaps that is why the religious authorities permitted it to be printed side by side, in the same book, with the Hebrew liturgy.

Notes

1. Lev. 15:19-24; 18:19.
2. One such example is the synagogue in Worms, France, built in 1175 to which a separate women's synagogue was added in 1213.
3. Lowenthal 1977: 271-73. Glikl of Hameln (1646-1724) recorded her memoirs in Yiddish between 1690-91 and 1719. Lowenthal provides an English translation.
4. Ibid., 49.
5. Exod. 25:8.
6. For the purpose of this book, I am giving a simplistic explanation of a very complex concept, and I recommend texts such as those by Gershom Scholem, mentioned in previous notes and in the bibliography, for a fuller explanation.
7. I am again giving a simplistic explanation of a very complex concept. Further reading is again recommended.
8. See Kay 1993: 49-96.
9. Mendele Moykher Sforim (c. 1834-1917), known as "the grandfather of modern Yiddish literature."
10. 1869.
11. Tsinberg 1943: VI: 279. First edition, Vilna 1935.
12. See Chapter 1 and the translation of Toybe's song in Part 2, "Single Prayers and Songs in *Tkhine* Language."
13. Weinreich 1973:1:258.
14. Ibid.
15. Mishnah: Kidushin 33b.
16. Chapter 1. See also, *Berakhot* 3:3 (from the Mishnah, the code of Jewish law that dates mainly from middle of the first century to the second decade of the third century C.E.).
17. Between the New Year and the Day of Atonement, with certain exceptions, and on fast days.
18. Fringes attached to the corners of garments as a reminder of the commandments. See Num. 15:37-40 and Deut. 22:11.
19. Prayer shawl to which fringes are attached.
20. Boxes containing scriptures strapped to a man's head and arm during morning synagogue prayers.
21. Translation from *The Complete Artscroll Siddur*.
22. From the *tkhine* to be said every day.
23. See Megila 31a, Ta'anis 27b.
24. See Table 2.
25. Seven-branched candelabrum that stood in the Temple in Jerusalem.
26. *Tkhine* to be said every day.
27. Gen. 22: 1-19.
28. Mishnah, *Tamid* VII, 4.

6

A Rare Manuscript Lost and Found: Book of Tkhines for a Pregnant Woman

The absence of extant manuscripts of the *Seyder Tkhines* suggests they were a phenomenon of the age of print and did not, like many early printed works of literature, originate from earlier handwritten versions. There is, however, a manuscript of a single, anonymous collection of *tkhines* stored away in the Bodleian Library in Oxford.[1] It has never appeared in print and has been virtually unknown until now. A translation of this rare manuscript appears in Part 2 of this book. It is listed in Neubauer's catalogue of Hebrew manuscripts in the Bodleian Library as "Occasional prayers *(tkhines)* in Hebrew-German cursive characters [incomplete]."[2] In the unpublished revision to Neubauer, the manuscript is referred to as "Ashkenaz, early 17th century."

The content is unique, and because it is mainly concerned with pregnancy and childbirth, it appears to have been intended for a pregnant woman who was presumably rich enough to have had the book written especially for her. The manuscript is an exciting addition to the corpus of women's prayers from the seventeenth century.

CONTENTS

The manuscript, like the *Seyder Tkhines*, is a sequence of prayers for a female reader composed in the voice of a female persona, yet its content is quite different. It consists of a number of daily *tkhines*, a *tkhine* asking for financial security, a *tkhine* in eight parts for a pregnant woman, and a *tkhine* to be said on fast days. At certain points in the text, there are rubrics instructing the reader to recite particular psalms, although only the numbers of the psalms are provided and not the psalms themselves. None of the *tkhines* in the manuscript can be found in the *Seyder Tkhines*, or anywhere else in *tkhine* literature, although they contain unmistakable similarities in style that reflect a shared literary form. The manuscript also prescribes far fewer occasions on which the *tkhines* should be recited.

Most of the manuscript is in Yiddish and written in cursive Hebrew characters. At certain points in the text, short passages in Hebrew are interspersed with the Yiddish. These Hebrew lines, written in square characters, consist of short phrases cobbled together from various sources proclaiming the oneness and truth of God, with much repetition of God's name. They derive mainly from the psalms, but also include the second line of the *Shema,* which women are usually exempt from saying. This line is significant to kabbalists because of its association with the eternal name of God. In the Hebrew text, the names of God are adorned with scribal flourishes. The repetition of God's name and the decorated form in which it is written conveys a preoccupation with the name of God that belongs to the kabbalistic tradition. There are no similar Hebrew passages in the *Seyder Tkhines*, which apart from one brief Hebrew blessing, is entirely in Yiddish. The level of knowledge that would have been required in order to read the Hebrew text and understand the significance of its derivation, seems to indicate that the manuscript was intended for a highly educated woman with an interest in mysticism.

ORDERING THE MANUSCRIPT

At first glance, the manuscript appears to be incomplete, as Neubauer indicates. It is bound inside a modern hard cover and the last page ends abruptly in mid-sentence. On closer inspection, however, it is evident that all the pages are there and can be rearranged to form a complete book.

My rearrangement of the pages in my translation of the manuscript is guided by the order of the *Seyder Tkhines*. As the text was presented to me, the first *tkhine* had no rubric or introduction. The second *tkhine* was for fast days, unlike the *Seyder Tkhines*, where the *tkhines* for fast days appear toward the end of the book. Daily *tkhines* followed those for fast days, but these were not consecutive. They were, instead, interspersed with *tkhines* concerning pregnancy. The final *tkhine* was another for daily recitation, which had a long introductory title. Though the variety of occasions on which *tkhines* are to be recited is considerably smaller in the manuscript than in the *Seyder Tkhines*, I have rearranged the text so that it now corresponds to the sequence of the *Seyder Tkhines*, beginning with daily *tkhines*, continuing with those for pregnancy, and ending with those for fast days.

The other aid to reordering the text was provided by the catchwords at the bottom of each page that correspond with those at the top of the following page. On some pages there are no catchwords, but the text follows continuously. Where the same catchword appears on a number of pages, both the catchword and the structure of the *Seyder Tkhines* is taken into account to determine the page order. In its newly arranged form, the manuscript has a beginning, middle, and end.

DATING THE MANUSCRIPT

The exact date of the manuscript is unknown. By examining the style of handwriting and the paper, all investigations so far are unable to estimate the date more specifically than early seventeenth century. With some margin for error, this might signify a period beginning fifty years earlier than the extant printed *Seyder Tkhines*, and extending to a period contemporary with the *Seyder Tkhines*. If it were an ancestor of the *Seyder Tkhines*, it would testify to the existence of the *Seyder Tkhines* in an early stage of development before the middle of the seventeenth century and would also suggest that other similar manuscripts might have been produced. But in the absence of other known manuscripts, it seems unlikely that one manuscript in Germany, for one woman's personal use, would have influenced a whole prayer book form. It is more likely that it is a unique example of the many known by-products of the *Seyder Tkhines*.

PURPOSE OF THE MANUSCRIPT

The manuscript appears to be a private commission for a pregnant woman because, unlike the *Seyder Tkhines*, it does not contain *tkhines* requesting a successful conception. A large proportion of the manuscript does, however, consist of *tkhines* for a healthy pregnancy and the safe delivery of a baby.

The manuscript follows the convention in Jewish prayer of making collective pleas, and the female persona prays both on her own behalf and for "all Israel." But unlike the *Seyder Tkhines*, there are no collective female phrases such as "we women," which further supports the supposition that the manuscript was intended for the personal use of one particular woman.

LANGUAGE

The language of this rare manuscript is a mixture of formulaic stock phrases found in the *Seyder Tkhines* and a more skilled literary style that conveys a spontaneous outpouring of devotion, using vivid imagery through metaphor and simile. The kinds of stock phrases from the *Seyder Tkhines* include "God, my God, and God of my forefathers," "with all my heart," and the likening of human life to "a shadow on a wall." In its general tone and style, the language resembles the familiar *tkhine loshn*. The fact that the manuscript conforms to certain linguistic features of the *Seyder Tkhines* suggests that there was some knowledge of it and some connection with it. But unlike the *Seyder Tkhines*, the *tkhines* in the manuscript are not composed solely in the voice of the female persona. There is more than one voice and more than one audience addressed by the prayers. The literary device used in the opening passage of the manuscript is not a common feature of *tkhine* literature. Instead of addressing God, the worshipper addresses herself in the following emotional outpouring:

> *My heart, my heart,*
> *Do you not know*

> *That you were created to die,*
> *And return again to the earth?*

Self-address is a comparatively rare phenomenon in Jewish prayer, including the Hebrew *tkhinot* and other liturgical poems intended for personal devotion. However, such a device can be found in certain psalms where the worshipper addresses his or her soul. For example, Pss. 103 and 104 begin with the same line: "Bless the Lord, O my soul." This opening of the manuscript is replete with the emphatic urging to consider the transience of human life. The worshipper forcefully takes herself to task for ignoring the inevitable time when her sins will have to be accounted for. These lines convey a personal, tortuous, inner struggle that contrasts with the conviction expressed by the declaration of faith at the opening of the *Seyder Tkhines*: "Lord of all the world, God, my God, and God of my forefathers," and continues with lengthy, repetitive praise of God. The manuscript's opening conveys a sense of immediacy and demonstrates a seventeenth century pregnant woman's fear of sudden death and of dying before she has repented.

The theme of anticipated death is continued in more prosaic language when the woman of the manuscript makes practical requests that seem to depict her as a business woman in her own right:

> *And may my livelihood and my earnings*
> *And my luck in my business dealings*
> *Be blessed so I live and do not die.*

She is asking for her life to be spared in order to materially support her child.

The woman of the *Seyder Tkhines* believes that it is her lot to suffer in childbirth, as all women must, to atone for the sin of Eve, and she thanks God for it. In contrast, the woman of the manuscript seems confident in her expectations and demanding in her requests:

> *And may I live in Your great mercy and grace,*
> *So I may bear my child into the world*
> *Without pain, like the saintly women*
> *Who were not inscribed as Eve*
> *So they did not need to suffer in pain.*

She regards herself as being superior to other women and worthy of painless childbirth, which is granted only to the matriarchs and other saintly women.

Although these *tkhines* appear to be tailor-made for one particular woman, they also incorporate with more general material. The author skillfully creates a strong individual voice, yet supplies rubrics that seem to apply to a wider audience. In one example, she writes: "Whoever recites this new *tkhine* every day with *kavone* while weeping and wailing, and who takes their sins to heart, may be sure of having a share in the world to come." Another is entitled, "A delightful *tkhine* for a pregnant woman to say." It is as if a prayer book has been created that must possess the authority of a general prayer book, while pandering to the specific interests of its patroness.

The use of powerful imagery of a kind that is absent from the *Seyder Tkhines* and other women's prayers of the period is found in the *tkhine* to be recited on fast days, which recalls the ritual of Temple sacrifice. Sacrifice can be carried out only in the Temple and only by the *Kohanim* (Priests). This has not been possible since the destruction of the Temple in the first century C.E. Therefore, daily synagogue prayer is regarded as a substitute for the daily Temple sacrifices until the time when Jews are redeemed and the Temple restored. In this *tkhine*, the female worshipper's kitchen becomes a substitute for the Temple. She recreates the Temple ritual through familiar objects in the home and human sensations experienced during fasting. The cooking pot, uncharacteristically redundant during the fasting period, evokes the utensils of the Temple ritual. Hunger heightens the worshipper's perception, so that routine kitchen objects take on heightened significance and symbolism. She does not complain of the bitterness of hunger; instead, she welcomes it as an opportunity to re-create the experience of the Temple sacrifice. The suffering sounds of the worshipper's weeping and wailing are transformed into the voices of the Levites singing psalms. The transformation of kitchen into Temple imbues the home with a potential for great sanctity, implying that holiness can be perceived even in what is most familiar and mundane. The images in the *tkhine* create contemporary parallels that evoke the taste, smell, and sound of the Temple and link them to associations with which an Ashkenazic woman could strongly identify.

This *tkhine* manuscript offers evidence that individual collections of *tkhines* existed in the seventeenth century in addition to the *Seyder Tkhines*. It is the most highly crafted literary contribution to the *tkhine* form that has yet been discovered.

Notes

1. Bodleian Library Shelfmark: Opp 666.
2. Neubauer 1886.

CHAPTER

Other Yiddish Prayers and Religious Songs and Their Authors

At the same time that the *Seyder Tkhines* was being printed through-out Europe, other Yiddish prayers and religious songs entitled *tkhine*, *tfile*, or *lid* appeared in print. These were usually single works, either newly composed or adapted into the *tkhine* style and language from Hebrew models. While the *Seyder Tkhines* was exclusively for women, these single prayers were mainly, but not exclusively, so. A significant feature that distinguishes them from the *Seyder Tkhines* is the self-proclaimed identity of many of their authors, some of whom are women. Prayers and songs of this type by six Jewish women can be found in Part 2 of this book. I have included among them a song written by a man because of its depiction of women.

VARIETIES OF TKHINES

Yiddish tkhines as inserts between Hebrew prayers in the Sider

The source of Yiddish *tkhines* can be traced back to the earliest known works entitled *Tkhine*. These were Hebrew and Aramaic liturgical poems known as *piyutim*, which were composed from about the eighth century[1] until the sixteenth century.[2] These *tkhines* (modern Hebrew, *tekhinot*) were generally recited as meditations during regular worship services in synagogue. Unlike Yiddish *tkhines*, some of these Hebrew and Aramaic works have made their way into the Hebrew liturgy, particularly as part of the penitential services that precede the festivals of the New Year and the Day of Atonement.[3] They did not originate as a manifestation of the Ashkenazic community, but stemmed from the great individual literary minds of the Middle East, Spain, and Italy. Also, unlike the plainly expressed Yiddish *tkhines*, their Hebrew and Aramaic counterparts are highly crafted, poetic works that reflect the unique talents of their composers. They were never intended as prayers for women. In fact, they were geared toward men and synagogue prayer as part of the Hebrew service. In spite of the differences, the composers of Yiddish *tkhines* adopted the name of the earlier Hebrew and Aramaic supplications while developing a form and style appropriate to the seventeenth-century Ashkenazic community.

Like their Hebrew ancestors, single Yiddish *tkhines* were often intercalated as "extra prayers" between the established Hebrew prayers in certain editions of the *Sider* (e.g., Frankfurt am Main 1697, Amsterdam 1715). There was often a *Seyder Tkhines* at the end of the same *Sider*. These *tkhines* are for recitation by women who make requests on behalf of themselves, their husbands, and their children. They ask for forgiveness "through the merit" of biblical figures, including the three patriarchs and the Jewish exemplars—Pinkhes, Elijah, Solomon, Daniel, and Mordecai. No female examples are given, as they are in the *Seyder Tkhines*. The presence of these *tkhines* confirms an acceptance of Yiddish *tkhines* as an integral part of the synagogue service during this period, as their Hebrew forerunners had been. However, Yiddish *tkhines* did not become a permanent part of the synagogue liturgy.

Tkhines attributed to great mystics

There are various features found in Yiddish prayer literature that testify to the influence of the messianic movement. There are claims in some *tkhines* that they are written by Isaac Luria or by one of his adherents, Yeshaye Hurvits (c.1555–c.1630), author of the mystical work *Shney lukhes habris* (Two tablets of the Ten Commandments).[4] The following attribution to Yeshaye Hurvits is made on the title page of *Eyn sheyne naye tkhine* (A beautiful new *tkhine* printed in Zolkiev in around 1692-94): "Several new *tkhines* from Reb Yeshaye's book collected and translated into Yiddish." It is difficult to substantiate the claim of Yeshaye Hurvits's authorship, as his book, *Shney lukhes habris*, was an ethical work and not a prayer book. A more likely source would have been Hurvits's prayer book, *Sha'ar ha-Shomayim* (Gate of heaven), edited by his great-grandson, but that was first printed more than twenty years later, in 1717.

The claim of Luria's authorship is also suspect because of the absence of any direct writings by him. An incomplete book of daily *tkhines* entitled *Tkhines khadoshoys* (Holy *tkhines*) was printed under Luria's name in Prague in 1708. The prayers are intended for both men and women. The editor, Yitskhok ben Leyb Yudls Kats, identifies himself on the title page and hints enticingly that he might be offering hitherto unknown writings by Luria. He explains that the *tkhines*, never before printed, came into his possession and have been translated by a Moyshe Tshuve (Moyshe the penitent) in Prague.

More crucial than the actual source of the content is the fact that these works, entitled *tkhine*, were attributed at this time to great mystical figures, especially Luria. He was being popularized through Yiddish prayer as the introduction to *Holy Tkhines* reveals: "Soon the whole Diaspora of Israel will become acquainted with his [Luria's] good name, because a certain Moyshe Tshuve in Prague translated it into Yiddish." Around thirty years after the death of Shabbetai Tsvi, producers of Yiddish prayer literature were still according great importance to such men as Luria and Hurvits and their kabbalistic teachings.

Tkhines claiming to originate in the Holy Land

The messianic turmoil of the mid–seventeenth century also exuded a strong strain of mystical Zionism. Another of the kabbalistic writers of the time, Nathan Shapira, who published his *Tov ha-arets* (Goodness of the land) in Venice in 1655, stressed the pivotal role of the Holy Land in bringing about the redemption of the Jews, and therefore of mankind. He insisted that it was in the Promised Land that the true preparations for redemption were taking place. The Jews in Diaspora prayed daily for a return to Jerusalem so that they could fulfill their religious obligations.[5] To add to their attraction, some seventeenth-century *tkhines* proffered claims that they had been discovered in the Holy Land and imported to Europe.[6] One such *tkhine*[7] expressed the fears of accounting for one's sins on the "day of judgment." The link with these *tkhines* and the Holy Land, whether contrived or real, raised their spiritual status.

Menoyre

A prayer entitled *Menoyre*, consisting solely of Psalm 67, that was printed in the shape of a seven-branched candelabra, was a powerful visual example of the influence of kabbalism. The psalm is associated with the *menoyre* because of its seven verses (plus an introductory verse). The prayer appeared as the central motif in a small collection of *tkhines* published in Prague around 1650 and 1700 under the title *Menoyre*. It also cropped up on a full page in some editions of the *Seyder Tkhines* (e.g., Prague 1700, Sulzbach 1794) as well as in various *Sidorim* that contained a *Seyder Tkhines* (e.g., Frankfurt am Main 1707, Sulzbach 1712). The psalm is printed either in the original Hebrew (e.g., Prague c. 1650) or is translated into Yiddish (e.g., Prague 1700).

The second line of the Hebrew *Shema* prayer is always printed at the base of the candelabrum. It proclaims God's "oneness" and is recited at both the morning and evening synagogue services: "Blessed is the Name of His glorious kingdom for all eternity." This line is of special interest to kabbalists, as is the Hebrew phrase, "I long for your salvation, Lord," which always precedes the psalm. This is because of its emphasis on the names of God. The phrase is usually chanted three times, changing the order of the words each time, and forms various names of God.

Like the *Seyder Tkhines*, the *Menoyre* prayer book contains *tkhines* composed for women, in the voice of a female worshipper who refers to herself as *dayner meyd* (your maid) and addresses God as *Got, mayn, Got* (God, my God). The psalm and accompanying prayers are for daily recitation: "Whoever says these psalms every day and seeks the image of the seven-branched candelabra finds favor and wisdom in the eyes of God, blessed be He." The female worshipper asks for God's acceptance of her prayers and her song, meaning Psalm 67, which she claims appeared with the *Menoyre* on the shield of King David when he went into battle.[8] It was foretold that the Messiah would be a descendant of King David,[9] who is mentioned on many title pages of Yiddish books in connection with the hoped-for redemption. The shield was invested in legend with magical qualities of protection. Another tradition suggests that Isa. 11:2, enumerating the six aspects of the divine spirit, was inscribed on the shield in the outer six triangles of the hexagram of the *mogen dovid* (star of David; literally: shield of David). It is certainly true today that the *mogen dovid*, generally associated with King David's shield, is the most popular and universally recognized symbol of the Jewish People, both within and outside of the Jewish community. However, it was the menoyre that served as the primary Jewish symbol from antiquity until the post-Renaissance period. In the seventeenth century, both symbols were associated with messianism, as the *mogen dovid* was a popular motif among the followers of Shabbatai Tsvi. In time, the *mogen dovid* replaced the menoyre in legends about David's shield.

While in some editions of the *Menoyre* the words of the Psalm 67 are printed within the outline of the branches of the candelabrum (e.g., Frankfurt am Main 1707), in others, the words of the psalm themselves are arranged in the candelabrum shape (e.g., Prague c. 1650). This intertwining of graphic depiction with the actual recitation of the psalm is an interesting feature. In fact, it can be said that the psalm is recited in the shape of the menoyre, because the words are printed up and down across its branches and base in one uninterrupted line, so the menoyre itself is drawn with the words of the psalm. Each recited word of the psalm contributes to the completion of the shape of the menoyre. Therefore, the psalm has a subtle extra dimension of sacred meaning by reconstituting the symbol of the original menoyre that stood in the Temple in Jerusalem.

Circumstantial tkhines and songs

Additional songs and prayers in Hebrew or Aramaic, composed for particularly tragic events, have always been part of Jewish prayer tradition. For example, the *piyutim* of eleventh-century liturgists Menakhem ben Makhir and Yitskhok ben Meyer, were inspired by the horrors of the massacres of the First Crusade in 1096, which Menakhem witnessed.[10] Toybe Pan's "A beautiful, newly written song in *tkhine* language" (Prague [1680]) and Matesyohu ben Meyer

Sobotki's,[11] "A new tkhine for the people who died here in the plague" (Prague 1719), are both Yiddish works in this genre. They are both inspired by the outbreaks of plague in Prague. Sobotki's prayer conveys the distress caused by the hasty and chaotic burial of victims in unmarked or mass graves: "This *tkhine* is to be said in synagogue for the people who died in the plague because, alas, we do not know which grave we should visit." Toybe's appears to have been written during the epidemic as heartfelt appeals are made for God's help to end the suffering: "Beloved lord God, help us out of this pain." Toybe's *lid* is translated in Part 2.

The Yiddish Lider

A number of Yiddish works of the period that are entitled *lid* are not prayers but religious songs, and several were written by women. Some of these are moral tales, for example, "A beautiful new song of three women" (Prague [1650]); some are stories, such as "A new song about the *Megile*" (Amsterdam 1650-55) telling the story of Queen Esther;[12] and others are songs of praise, usually to God, like the song composed by Rivke Tiktiner for the festival of *Simkhes Toyre*,[13] or "A beautiful new Torah song" (Prague [1605-23]) in praise of the Torah. The songs are always in rhyme and are directed in their rubrics to be "sung," unlike *tkhines*, which are directed to be "said." The rubrics of the *lider* sometimes gave the name of a particular tune in which the *lid* was to be sung, for example, "A new, beautiful song on the Ten Commandments in the tune of Joyous Month," which is written by a woman called Sheyndele.[14] Most of these tunes have either not survived the centuries or are no longer known by the same titles. Three songs of this type, all by women, are translated in Part 2.

The unacceptable face of Yiddish prayer

Not all new Yiddish prayers were acceptable to the communal authorities, as the rejection of one particular book clearly demonstrates. Arn ben Shmuel of Hergeshausen contributed to Yiddish prayer with his prayer book entitled *Liblikhe tfile oder kfreftige artsnay far gur un neshome* (Beloved prayer or great remedy for the body and soul), believed to be printed in Hergeshausen in 1709. Several prayers, entitled *Tkhine*, are included in the contents, including "A beautiful *tkhine* that should be said every day" and "A beautiful *tkhine* for an unlearned countryman." This book was for both men and women. Arn ben Shmuel was not a learned man, as he admits in his preface. He claims to write for the uneducated because his poor knowledge of Hebrew prevented him from reading the "sacred books." His insistence on the importance of religious study for children in Yiddish, rather than the traditional Hebrew, so that they could more easily understand the texts, is an idea that would not have appealed to the rabbis. Unlike the *Seyder Tkhines* and other *tkhines* and prayer literature cited in this chapter, Arn ben Shmuel's prayer book was not rooted in established Hebrew prayer. His book included psalm translations, but the rest was entirely new and poorly composed in poor Yiddish. Outrageous for its time, the Yiddish book was printed not in *mashket*, but in square Hebrew characters with diacritic vowel points, both of which were used only for Hebrew texts. The notion of a prayer book for the uneducated would itself not be inherently objectionable. All Yiddish prayer claimed to serve this purpose.[15] But because it was a new prayer book by an avowedly unlearned man, its circulation was never permitted. All but a few copies were seized as soon as it was printed. They were hidden away for more than a century in an attic in the synagogue in Hergeshausen, where hundreds of copies were discovered in 1830.[16] This suggests that even though there was a drive to establish Yiddish prayer, this new prayer had to conform to certain acceptable standards. There is no recorded opposition in the seventeenth century to the *Seyder Tkhines*. To the contrary, the work can be seen as part of the seventeenth-century rabbinic movement to intensify religious education and moral awareness through vernacular literature.

AUTHORSHIP
The earliest known printed work in Yiddish by a woman

Royzl Fishl's rhyming preface to a Yiddish translation of the Book of Psalms published in Krakow in 1586 is the earliest known printed work in Yiddish by a woman. It appears as twenty-eight lines of rhyming couplets on one page, yet the preface has received attention through the centuries, being catalogued and mentioned by scholars as a work in its own right.[17] It combines prayer and supplication with Royzl's religious curriculum vitae, how she brought the book into print, and her motivations for doing so. Royzl tells how in Hanover, Germany, she discovered a Book of Psalms that Rabbi Moyshe Shtendl had rendered into Yiddish in "the rhyme and tune of the *Shmuel-bukh*." As a duty on behalf of her deceased father, Royzl brought the book back to Krakow, copied it out ready for printing and brought it into print for "men, women, and pious girls" so that they might praise God. The printer, whose name appears as Yitskhok ben Hakhor Aren, confirms her story.

Like other Yiddish authoresses that came after, she establishes her religious authority through the status of the men in her family:

> I, Royzl Fishls as people call me, have done this because my father, of blessed memory, is unable to do so. Yoysef Leyvi is his name, of the Levites, those who are all God's servants. And his father, Yude Leyvi, the elder, may his soul rest in peace, who spent fifty years at the *yeshiva*[18] in the holy community of Lodmir: they praised beloved God. . . . Here I thank and praise God for making me a Levite, and hope He will continue to be merciful to me. He does not forget the struggle of the poor. I pray that He will stand by me.

Every morning in synagogue men say a prayer thanking God for not making them a woman. There is a parallel prayer for women thanking God for making them "according to His will." The Levites inherited priestly duties that they performed in the Temple. This included the singing of psalms, which is particularly relevant to Royzl's psalm book. But only males performed these duties, and her assertions that not only is she a Levite, but that she is substituting for her father in her religious duty to produce the Book of Psalms, are bold claims for a woman to have made.

Royzl was author of the preface, copyist of the whole book, and is also believed to have been the owner of the printing house.[19] She was certainly involved in promoting the sales of the book as well as performing a religious duty. In spite of her tone of piety and prayer, Royzl explicitly connects the Book of Psalms that she is introducing, with the popular Yiddish epic romance, the *Shmuel-bukh*, which would have enhanced its commercial value. Her multifaceted role in both the practical and creative production of this book is typical of the time. Though her work is only a preface, it unmistakably contains elements representative of the classic *tkhine loshn*. It is a personal, devout praising of God and supplication in a woman's voice. The rhyme does not resemble the short rhyming lines of title pages, but is reminiscent of the long lines of devotional rhyme found in Yiddish liturgical works by women such as Toybe Pan and Rivke Tiktiner. Royzl's preface stands out as a key transitional work for both female authorship and the expression of spirituality.

Authorial evolution

Today, a literary work will unambiguously display the name of its title and its author. But as Royzl's preface demonstrates, in sixteenth- and seventeenth-century Yiddish printing, things were not so clear-cut and the roles of author, adaptor, editor, printer, copyist, and typesetter often overlapped considerably.

Acrostics

An acrostic was usually a clear indication of authorship. Rivke Tiktiner, the daughter of Meyer of Tiktin, is the acknowledged authoress of a song that is translated in Part 2. Her work imitates the commonly used device known as an acrostic, found in Hebrew and Aramaic liturgical songs, where the first letter of each line or verse represents a letter of the Hebrew alphabet, and the remaining lines or verses begin with the letters of the author's name. The acrostic RIVKE BAS MEYER ZATSAL (Rivke daughter of Meyer of blessed memory), which appears in Rivke's song, conveys that she is its author.

We also know that Rivke was the author of a book entitled *Meynekes Rivke* (Foster mother or wet nurse Rebecca), published in Prague in 1609, which is an ethical work on women's religious obligations. She was hailed in seventeenth-century Christian-German scholarship by Johann Christof Wagenseil (1674) as the first female Yiddish writer. Four hundred years after the first appearance of "*Meynekes Rivke*," Rivke's song is printed here in English.

New writers

The new popular vernacular literature, with its new, mass readership full of messianic hope, changed the nature of authorship. Changes had already begun with the production of Yiddish manuscripts. Entertainment literature, often secular-based, had different authorial requirements than the learned Hebrew texts. The term *"shrayber,"* which literally means "writer," was a term attributed to the scribe or copyist of Hebrew manuscripts, the man who physically wrote it out. But it is now believed that authors of the Yiddish epic romances such as the *Shmuel-bukh* could be "sought in the contemporary Jewish middle-level 'intelligentsia' which included copyists, *nakdanim*,[20] *melamdim*,[21] and the like . . . a stratum in which proficiency in Hebrew and the midrashic literature might be expected."[22] In an excellent article on the subject, Professor Chone Shmeruk gives the example of Oldendorf,[23] who was the copyist of some texts, but was also the author of two poems, one in Yiddish and one in Hebrew. Thus, in the production of manuscripts, a *shrayber* could also be an author.

The revised meaning of this term was carried forward into printed books where not only the *shrayber*, but also, on occasion, the printer took a hand in authorship. The term *shrayber* or "writer" lost its literal meaning and came to mean "author," as it does today. Another term, *soyfer*, retains the fundamental meaning of "scribe" or "copyist." The father of Rokhl, another authoress whose work is translated in Part 2, was known as Mordkhe Soyfer (Mordecai the scribe), a term that refers to the practical writing of text. This skill is still practised in the writing of Jewish texts such as Torah scrolls and mezuzes.[24]

The new order

When Yiddish *tkhines* and songs first came into print, "new" was the order of the day. Authorship of new works by the educated rather than the learned was established and women were brought into the authorial arena. Their education might not generally have been as extensive as that of learned men, and their religious authority not as highly regarded, but the literature they produced was of a new type and for a new readership. The term *shrayber* was feminized to *shrayberin* in order to accommodate them, and in her *tkhine*, Beyle Hurvits (daughter of Hazakay Hurvits, wife of Yosi Khozn) introduces herself as *Ikh, shrayberin Beyle* (I, Beyle, authoress).[25]

Women were not confined to writing only for women. The idea that they were writing new prayers and religious works was certainly remarkable; but the fact that they often wrote for both genders widened the scope of their involvement and influence in the mainstream religious arena to a degree not equaled before or since. These women often state specifically in the introductions to their works that they are writing for men and women. In a sermon entitled "*Eyn hipshe droshe*" (A delightful sermon) printed under the name of Khane Kats, which is discussed below, the title page begins: "For men and women, young and old," and the sermon begins: "Listen, you beloved men and women. . . ."[26]

The newness of a work was proudly proclaimed on the title pages, and as long as the "new" understood its place in the scheme of things and did not go beyond what was considered acceptable, as did Arn ben Shmuel, all was well. The word "new" was incorporated in the title of many Yiddish prayers and songs, usually accompanied by the words "beautiful" or "delightful." One such example is "A beautiful new *tkhine*," attributed to Yeshaye Hurvits, cited above. Another, "A new, beautiful song about the Ten Commandments,"[27] by Sheyndele (wife of Gershon ben Shmuel zatsal from Tarnigrad [Galicia]),[28] combines originality with established religious tenets. In "A beautiful newly written song in *tkhine* language," Toybe Pan, the wife of Yankev Pan and daughter of Leyb Pitzker, claimed originality for her work, which was newly composed and concerned a current event. However, her use of the phrase "Father, King" to begin or end each verse, depending on the edition, links her song to the Hebrew "Our Father, Our King," recited in synagogue during the Ten Days of Penitence, and at the end of the morning service on the Jewish New Year. Authors wrote original works within certain accepted boundaries, producing works that reflected the new religious fervor by looking forward as well as back.

The printing trade reflected the prevailing messianic movement in its transcendence of social class and all levels of learning. In addition to the new breed of printers, learned men like Menasseh ben Israel[29] could be both printers and authors of scholarly works. Menasseh printed sacred texts, Hebrew prayer books, and philosophical works as well as his own new, messianic writings in Spanish. He was also the printer of the new Yiddish *Seyder Tkhines*.

Definition of authorship

There are various terms found on title pages and in colophons of early Yiddish books that became synonymous with authorship. The popular *Bovo-bukh*, published in Isny in 1541, is a valuable source of such evidence. On the title page, Elijah Levita, also known as Elye Bokher (Elijah the bachelor), is referred to unequivocally by the Hebrew term *Elye ha-makhaber* (Elijah the author). The book itself begins: "*Ikh Elye Leyvi der shrayber . . .*" (I, Elijah Leyvi the writer . . .). He is not the scribe, and in any case, the book is printed, not handwritten. In verse 649, toward the end of the work, he writes "I will let you know *ver dos bukh hot gemakht un geshribn*" (who made/created and wrote this book). So all these terms: *makhaber, shrayber, gemakht*, and *geshribn* (the past participle of the verb related to the noun *shrayber*) are used synonymously and denote authorship from the earliest days of Yiddish printing. Both Toybe Pan and Sheyndele claim to have "*gemakht*" their songs. They make these statements not on a title page or in a colophon, but in the actual lines of verse, so that their names and claims become an integral part of the work itself. Toybe also states that she has "*oysgetrakht*" the song, which means "thought up" or "invented," a further sign that she has created the work. It is evident that Toybe and Sheyndele are the actual authors of their works.

It is not the fact of authorship that is necessarily in question, but the extent and nature of that authorship. This covers a range from simple translation, to adaptation, where old material is reworked and new material added, up to a high proportion of originality. Though the *Bovo-bukh* was an adaptation from the Italian *Buovo d'Antono*, which itself was based on the English *Bevis of Hampton*, the work of Levita goes far beyond adaptation. Just as Chaucer's *The Knight's Tale* or Shakespeare's *Romeo and Juliet* would not be regarded as mere adaptations of Boccaccio, even though their source is clear, Levita's *Bovo-bukh*, composed in ottava rima, is a work of creative brilliance in its own right, and he can rightly be viewed as its author. When Shmeruk refers to Levita as "the greatest poetic personality of Old Yiddish literature," it is with the *Bovo-bukh* in mind.[30]

Khane Kats's booklet

A booklet printed toward the end of the seventeenth or beginning of the eighteenth century in Amsterdam, under the name of Khane Kats (Khane, daughter of Yehude Leyb Kats, widow of Yitskhok Ashkenaz), is more complicated to assess in terms of authorship. The booklet contains four works: "A delightful sermon," "Sabbath prayer," "*Ma Toyvu*" (How good), and a penitential *tkhine* entitled "This *tkhine* is said from the first day of the month of *Elul* until the Day of Atonement when the shofar[31] is blown." Two of these works are translated in Part 2. Although Khane makes no claim of authorship, the entire contents have been attributed to her.[32] It is still unclear, however, whether or not she did, in fact, write any of it. The title page conveys the information that the book has been produced "*Al yad ha-al-mone Khane* . . ." (lit. "by the hand" of the widow, Hannah). The use of this term usually denotes a printer rather than an author, though the roles were no longer clear-cut.

It is unlikely that Khane wrote the penitential *tkhine*, as it was printed frequently elsewhere under the claimed authorship of Beyle Hurvits. A further possible confirmation of Beyle's authorship may be seen from the title page of some editions of the *tkhine*, which bear an interesting and unusual feature regarding her identity. There are two words on the title page that are larger and bolder than the rest. One is her name, "Beyle," which is spelled with the Hebrew letters *beys, yud, lamed, hey*, and appears in the sentence in which she claims authorship: "*Ikh, shrayberin Beyle, bas hagooyn hagadoyl hakoydesh* . . ." (I, **Beyle**, the authoress, daughter of the great and holy man of learning . . .). The other larger and bolder word is *libe*, which appears in the phrase "**libe vayber**" (beloved women), with which the title page begins. But instead of using the usual contemporary spelling of *libe*, an anagram of her own name is used, reordering the same four letters that are used for "Beyle" (*lamed, yud, beys, hey*). The two words "Beyle" and "libe" stand out from the rest because they are highlighted.

In later printings of these *tkhines*, including the one that appears in Khane Kats's collection, Beyle's name does not appear, but the anagram of her name in *"libe"* remains in its highlighted form as the largest and boldest word in the text. The anagram reinforces the belief that Beyle is the *shrayberin*, or authoress, of this *tkhine* and not Khane, who merely included it in her prayer book.

The *Ma Toyvu* prayer is an adaptation into *tkhine loshn* of the Hebrew synagogue prayer, but like Elijah Levita, the adaptor of this prayer goes beyond translation and creates an entirely new work. But was Khane responsible for its creation? As far as the sermon is concerned, it is made clear from the outset that it is written by a female persona:

> *Listen beloved men and women,*
> *I apologize to you all*
> *For stepping in with this sermon*
> *For you will say:*
> *"How is it that this woman comes to admonish us?"*
> *But you know, my beloved folk,*
> *I could neither rest nor sleep over this sermon.*

Therefore, this could either have been the work of Khane, or that of another, unknown woman.

If Khane composed the rhyming title page, which was a prevailing custom of the printer (for example Corneleo Adelkind's title page to Elijah Levita's psalm book translation), she may well have composed the "Sabbath prayer," which is in a similar style of rhyming couplets as the sermon. Khane's booklet is an eclectic selection, consisting of some adaptation into Yiddish, some redeployment of appropriate contemporary material by another author, together with a substantial proportion of newly created material that may have been written by the printer, Khane herself. Neither the *Ma Toyvu*, the "Sabbath prayer," nor the sermon appear elsewhere, nor is there any other candidate for their authorship. The booklet is indicative of how Yiddish prayer literature was pieced together. In this case, the printer, editor, and the likely author turn out to be the same woman. Whatever Khane's exact role might have been, the booklet and its contents are forever associated with her.

Multi-attribution

Another problem encountered is the accurate attribution of author-ship when a work is printed in different editions, under different names. This is highlighted in the *lid* entitled "A new, beautiful song of the Ten Commandments," by Sheyndele, wife of Gershon ben Shmuel zatsal from Tarnigrad (Galicia).[33] Modern scholars have made various proposals regarding authorship.[34] In his catalogue of Hebrew printed books in the Bodleian Library in Oxford, Cowley attributes one edi-tion of this *lid* to a man, Meyer ben Shimen Verter,[35] but attributes all other editions of the identical *lid* to Sheyndele. The same work reap-peared in the nineteenth century, and Noakh Prilutski, in his article "The unknown old Yiddish poetess Yente bas Yitskhok,"[36] claimed that it was the work of Yente bas Yitskhok. The most likely author of this *lid* is Sheyndele, who predated Yente by two centuries. Sheyndele states in the final stanza of the *lid*: "Madam Sheyndele, wife of our teacher Rabbi Gershon son of our teacher Rabbi Shmuel of blessed memory made this song." She uses the word *gemakht*, as does Elijah Levita and Toybe Pan, who are both authors. The only claim made by Meyer ben Shimen, not in the lines of the text like Sheyndele's, but in the colophon of the c. 1685 version, is as follows: "I, Meyer, son of Shi-men Verter, have prepared and stitched this cover, dressed fit for a king." Meyer is not referred to in any way as author. Therefore, the *lid* seems to be mistakenly attributed to him by Cowley. The third possibility is that it is the work of the "unknown" Yente bas Yitskhok, whose name appears in her preface (verse 10 in Prilutski's reproduc-tion of the text), where she addresses the readership as "*khosheve frume vayber*" (respected pious women), a phrase not commonly found in seventeenth-century texts. The work presented by Prilutski contains different features from the earlier work. For example, it is in stanzaic form, and each stanza in Yente's version ends in the word "Hal-lelujah." Neither of these features appears in the seventeenth-century version under Sheyndele's name, which suggests that the "Hallelujah" response was added at a later date. The language of Yente's version is generally more modern, and material has been added or changed from Sheyndele's earlier work. Prilutski was apparently unaware of the ex-istence of the seventeenth-century version, and Sheyndele survives as the main contender.

These examples demonstrate some of the difficulties encountered in attempting to define and attribute authorship to seventeenth-century Yiddish prayers and songs. The evidence points to the conclusion that an acrostic, and the terms "*shrayber*" and "*gemakht*," signify the creation of a work. It was common practice for those involved with the practical side of printing to also turn their hands to authorship. But the accurate identification of the author or creator of the "new" religious, ethical, and prayer literature was not the vital issue. Neither was the authenticity of claims like those in the *tkhines* attributed to Isaac Luria and Yeshaye Hurvits. The main concern was that a work was part of the new order that enabled the readership to pray, repent, and praise God with understanding and hope.

Notes

1. E.g., Amittai 780–50 C.E.
2. E.g., Yehude Moscato of Mantua.
3. *Slikhes.*
4. Hurvits was born in Prague, became an influential rabbi in Poland, and finally settled in the Holy Land in 1621. He died in Safed in 1630. He is known by the acronym deriving from the name of this work, *SheLoH hakoydesh*, "the holy *Shelo*" or simply the *Shelo*. His book was edited by his son and published posthumously in Amsterdam in 1649, a year after the first *Seyder Tkhines* appeared in print.
5. See *Avoyde* blessing in the Hebrew *Amide* prayers.
6. E.g., Meyer ben Shimshen, Prague 1688 and c. 1691.
7. Amsterdam eighteenth century.
8. 1 Chronicles 17: 11–14.
9. *Kehoyshato odom* (As you saved Adam) by Menakhem ben Makhir (eleventh century); *Yisroeyl amkho* (the people of Israel) by Yitskhok ben Meyer (eleventh century).
10. The fifteenth-century Spanish philosopher and kabbalist Isaac Arama claimed that Psalm 67 was engraved on King David's shield in the form of a *menoyre*.
11. Meyer Sobatki also wrote a book of *tkhines* printed in Prague in 1728.
12. By Efrayim bar Yehude Haleyvi, Amsterdam 1650–55.
13. See later in this chapter and in Part 2, "Single Prayers and Songs on *Tkhine* Language," where Rivke's *lid* appears in translation with an introduction.
14. Translated in Part 2.
15. See, for example, Epshteyn 1697: page between title page and preface.
16. Erik 1928: 212–14; Tsinberg 1935:VI:258.
17. See Wagenseil 1705; Steinshneider 1852–60: no 1280; Erik 1928: 446; Tsinberg 1935:VI:274, 434, Shulman 1913: 25, Korman 1927:xxxvi, Shmeruk 1981:81, Niger 1913:131–35. See also Kay 1990:165–67.
18. Seminary.
19. Tsinberg 1935:VI:271.
20. Those who add the diacrytic vowels or points above and below the Hebrew letters on a manuscript.
21. Teacher at primary level.
22. Shmeruk 1986:22.
23. Ibid., 33.
24. Lit. "doorpost." A receptacle attached to the doorposts of houses containing a scroll with passages of scripture written on it.
25. Translated in Part 2, "Single Prayers and Songs in *Tkhine* Language."
26. Amsterdam seventeenth to eighteenth century.
27. Translated in Part 2, "Single Prayers and Songs in *Tkhine* Language."
28. [Prague] c. 1685 and 1686, and also Fürth 1700.

29. See Chapter 3.
30. Shmeruk 1986:16.
31. Ram's horn.
32. Cowley 1929:229; Niger 1913: 131; Korman 1928: xliii.
33. [Prague] c.1685 and 1686 and also Fürth 1700.
34. Cowley 1929:422; Prilutski 1938: 13:2-4, 36-54.
35. Opp 8° 1050 (10) in Cowley 1929:422.
36. Yivo-Bleter 1938:13:3-4; 36-54.

Seyder Tkhines in the Twenty-first Century: The Messianic Inheritance

Scarcely a trace of the *tkhines* that were an integral part of Ashkenazic prayer life three hundred and fifty years ago survives today in mainstream Judaism. By the middle of the eighteenth century, when the messianic movement had played itself out on center stage, all the things that the *tkhines* had come to represent were no longer relevant, and the *Seyder Tkhines* were no longer a part of common prayer life. While orthodoxy resumed its status quo, conserving what had gone before, manifestations of the *Seyder Tkhines* lingered on and remain today in the twenty-first century prayers of two Jewish movements that are at opposite ends of the spectrum of orthodoxy: Reform Judaism and Hasidism.

Both these movements had their roots in the second half of the eighteenth century. Reform Judaism sprang from the seeds of the Berlin Enlightenment (*Haskole*) in Western Europe, which expressed a fervent distaste for mysticism in an age of reason. The movement rejected a separate Jewish language and culture in its drive to foster the assimilation and acceptance of Jews into the wider community. This was the beginning of modern, secular Judaism.

Hasidism, in contrast, is a deeply mystical movement that has intensified traditional orthodoxy, while preserving the traditions of Eastern European Jewish culture. It originated in eighteenth-century Podolia, in the Ukraine, and thrives today in many parts of the world. A large proportion of its followers speak Yiddish as their everyday language, and since the foundation of their movement, Hasidim[1] have composed a continual line of Yiddish prayer.

Though appearing to have little in common, these two movements, Reform Judaism and Hasidism, share the legacy of the *Seyder Tkhines* and have common aspirations that were relevant to *tkhines*. Both sought a spiritual vitality and regeneration they could not find in mainstream Judaism, and both advocated vernacular prayers, comprehensible to everyone, which would be imbued with a deeper, inner meaning.

VERNACULAR PRAYER

Vernacular prayer is an important part of Reform liturgy and the Reform Movement has claimed that the *tkhines* were the forerunners of their vernacular of prayer. In one of the most comprehensive works ever written on *tkhines*,[2] the Reform rabbi, Solomon B. Freehof, adopted *tkhines* as the nucleus of his research in order to justify Jewish vernacular prayer.[3] Freehof quotes various authoritative sources that sanction certain prayers being said in the vernacular.[4] According to Freehof, an important justification for the existence of vernacular prayer such as *tkhines* is the need for the individual to freely and spontaneously express his or her own particular concerns in prayer.[5] But it is clear that the *Seyder Tkhines*, and other contemporary Yiddish prayers, were standard, formulated prayers that were neither individual nor spontaneous.

Freehof's assertion that *tkhines* serve as a prototype for Reform movement prayer, because they are composed in the vernacular, depends on how the term "vernacular" is defined. Vernacular prayer within Reform Judaism usually consists of newly composed works or those translated from Hebrew prayer, recited in the national spoken language. Until modern times, Polish Jews did not pray in Polish, nor Dutch Jews in Dutch. This would, however, be the case today in Reform Judaism. Meditative literary works appear in Reform prayer books, for example, poems by the twentieth-century American poet Allen

Ginsberg and excerpts from the works of Franz Kafka, which were never intended as prayers or targeted at any particular religion. All of these literary works and quotations are either composed in, or translated into, the national vernacular. *Tkhines* however, are composed in Yiddish, which is quite different in nature. Yiddish is a specifically Jewish language, written in the Hebrew alphabet, which was never confined to national boundaries. In fact, Reform Judaism is known for its fervent rejection of Yiddish in favor of the national language.

Hasidism, on the other hand, has produced a continuous stream of mystically inspired Yiddish prayer that is specifically Jewish, some of which closely resembles *tkhines*. Of the various types of Hasidic prayer, *tkhines* seem to have most in common with those described as "intimate presence" prayers[6] of the variety composed by Rabbi Levi Yitskhok of Berditchev. These Yiddish devotions, expressed simply and directly to God, may be recited by man, woman, or child, the educated or the uneducated. The worshipper praises and makes supplication to God in a personal voice, without need for any specialized knowledge of mystical theology or meditative techniques that are a feature of other Hasidic prayers. It is in these Hasidic prayers that the line of vernacular prayer, as it was understood in the *tkhines*, has survived. However, the acknowledgment by Reform Judaism of the *tkhines* as a precedent for their own prayers, establishes *tkhines* as a source of inspiration and influence.

CHALLENGING THE RELEVANCE OF THE HEBREW LITURGY

In 1913, a Reform rabbi, H. G. Enelow, pointed out that the early leaders of Reform Judaism sought to eliminate all prayers not in accord with the convictions and ideals of the people.[7] He continued: "It has been the common fate of religious ideas, no matter how vital and genuine at first, to lose their inner meaning and force in the course of time" and that religious practices "continue in sheer mechanical fashion." Freehof brings *tkhines* into the discussion: "It may frequently be that an old traditional book will contain ideas that are no longer vital to the worshipper, and are retained merely through the preserving force of tradition. . . . Their [the *tkhines*] very existence seems to imply an inadequacy in the regular prayer ritual."[8] Eighty years earlier, the introduction to the first edition of the prayer book of the English Reform movement claimed the following:"History bears us out in the assumption, that it becomes a congregation of Israelites to adapt the ritual to the wants of its members; and it must be universally admitted that the present mode of worship fails to call forth the devotion so essential to the religious improvement of the people."[9]

These excerpts clearly present the Reform view and practice that once prayer is deemed irrelevant, it should be removed and replaced with new prayers that will revitalize the liturgy. Freehof views *tkhines* as an early example of new prayers, relevant to their time, which replaced the existing liturgy. Freehof's suggestion that *tkhines* were a more relevant and vital form of prayer cannot be reconciled with the fact that in the seventeenth and early eighteenth centuries writers and printers of *tkhines* and other Yiddish religious literature made no claims that the Hebrew liturgy was irrelevant, or less relevant. In fact, the opposite was true. *Tkhines* may have provided new prayers for occasions and concerns missing from the Hebrew prayer book and even an alternative service for women, but there were no claims that the traditional Hebrew liturgy was redundant. Relevance of the Hebrew liturgy to a specific historical period was not an issue. The traditional prayer book was accepted as perennially relevant because of its sanctity, its historical significance, and its direct link with the ancient Temple in Jerusalem, which represented the pinnacle of Jewish spiritual life. The Orthodox Jewish community prayed, and still prays, daily for the resurrection of the Temple and its ritual. Prayers intended for recitation during the sacrifice rituals in the Temple, which were no longer part of their daily life, were kept alive and are still included as a major part of Orthodox prayers. Therefore, Freehof's suggestion that *tkhines* were composed because the established prayer book had become irrelevant is unjustified. The Hebrew prayer book had certainly become increasingly less accessible because of its language, but no attempt was made to depose Hebrew prayer or replace it with vernacular prayer in the synagogue service. The much quoted example of an attempt to do this, by Arn ben Shmuel and his new Yiddish prayerbook, suffered the consequences.

In the tradition of *tkhines*, Hasidim continued to compose prayers in Yiddish in order to enhance their prayer life. However, like *tkhines*, Hasidic prayers may be additional to the liturgy, integrated with it and sometimes parallel to it, but not as a replacement. Since the foundation of their movement, Hasidim have elevated the status of Yiddish prayer to a central position, but they have never considered the Hebrew prayer liturgy irrelevant, and have never tried to replace it with Yiddish prayer. While the *tkhines* may have more in common with Hasidic prayer, it is Reform Judaism that has adopted them as a source of influence.

KAVONE

Kavone is an integral component of *tkhines* and both the Reform and Hasidic movements have stressed its importance as an essential aspect of their own prayer. Influenced by the emphasis on *kavone* by Lurianic kabbalism, the *Seyder Tkhines* and other seventeenth-century Yiddish prayers have rubrics that stipulate recitation either "with *kavone*" or "with great *kavone*." Some go even further and insist on weeping and beating the breast, adding an outwardly expressive dimension. The author of the contemporary ethical manual *Lev tov*[10] quotes an earlier Hebrew source: "Prayer without *kavone* is like a body without a soul."[11]

The word *kavone* is difficult to translate, but may approximately be defined as "intention," "deep concentration," or "spiritual intensity." *Kavone* has been identified as a basic ingredient of prayer through the centuries, and Rabbi Akiva (first to second centuries B.C.E.) viewed it as a state of sustained devotion throughout an entire prayer. Maimonides (1135–1204) insisted that the absence of what he termed "*kavone* of the heart" prevented the efficacy of prayer. He defined *kavone* as follows: "What is the definition of *kavone*? It means that one should empty one's mind of all thought and see oneself as if one were standing in the presence of the *Shkhine* (Divine Presence of God)."[12] A German contemporary of Maimonides, the mystic Yehude ha-Khosid (d. 1217), author of the ethical treatise *Seyfer Hasidism* (Book of the pious),[13] declared that praying without *kavone* was like erecting a building on unsound foundations.

Hasidism attempts to convert prayer from an act of routine or semi-consciousness "into an experience in which one is more fully present."[14] This coincides, to a point, with Reform Judaism's concept of *kavone* as sustained concentration. The insistence by the Reform movement on vital new prayer was bound up with *kavone*, and it was claimed that if prayer "ceased to express the ideas, beliefs and hopes of the people . . . the inner correspondence [i.e., *kavone*] was gone."

However, Hasidism extended the concept of *kavone* even further. It has been described as "the art of spiritual consciousness-raising,"[15] and can even take the extreme form of frenzied prayer.

Exponents of Reform Judaism have strongly criticized Hasidic interpretations of *kavone*. Enelow concedes that the two movements coincide in their objective "to reintroduce the true idea of *kawwana* [Enlow's spelling of *kavone*] as a means of increasing genuine devotion and awareness."[16] But his disapproval is evident when he writes, "Kabbalistic aberration usurped the place of true devotion" and was an "exploitation of the idea of *kavone*." He expresses his disgust with the mystical varieties of *kavone* at the time of the *Seyder Tkhines* and regards the striving for higher levels of spiritual awareness and experience as deplorable "hocus-pocus." He goes on to accuse the seventeenth-century mystic Yeshaye Hurvits[17] of being a perpetrator of it: ". . . *kawwana* was turned into a grotesque play with letters, words and ideas. It assumed magic significance. Even the best of the kabbalists were not free from this fault, Isaiah Horwitz, for example. . . . Similarly, all religious performances, and especially prayers, came to comprise supernal objects and metaphysical mysteries, occult *kawwanoth*, and one was supposed to refer to *kawwana*, or recite it, whether or not one understood it, or whether or not, indeed, it had any meaning at all." But in Enelow's view, the ensuing Haskole, from which the Reform Movement grew, did bring "some improvement."

Both Reform Judaism and Hasidism employ *kavone* to enhance the spiritual intensity of their prayers, so that prayer is focused and not automatic. But it is in the Hasidic prayers, inspired by mystical sources, where the fundamental character of *kavone*, as expressed in the *tkhines*, can be found. Again, the liturgical line appears to lead from *tkhines* to Hasidism.

LOCATING TKHINES IN THE TWENTY-FIRST CENTURY

An echo in the Sider

Today, Yiddish prayers are not found in the mainstream Hebrew *Sider*. There is, however, one exception. In the widely used *Artscroll Sider*,[18] there is a Yiddish prayer that has been included in recent years. It is exclusively for women to recite each week at the end of Sabbath, although it was originally intended, by its author, Levi Yitskhok, the Hasidic rabbi cited above, to be read by men, women, and children. The opening words of the prayer echo the opening words of the *Seyder Tkhines*: "*Got fun Avrom un fun Yitskhok un fun Yankev, bahit dayn folk yisroel ...*" (God of Abraham and of Isaac and of Jacob, protect Your people Israel). Thus the *tkhines*, through its descendants in Hasidic prayer, have found a modest place in a widely circulated modern edition of the Hebrew *Sider*.

The direct descendant of the Seyder Tkhines

Unlike the Reform movement, the Hasidic movement has never claimed the *tkhines* as a forerunner of its prayers, yet it is within this community that an enlarged, revised version for women of the Yiddish *Seyder Tkhines* is still being printed and used. This direct descendant of the *Seyder Tkhines* contains 121 *tkhines* for different occasions, and is entitled *Tkhine:A shas tkhine af a gants yor* (Tkhine for the whole year).[19] It continues to be published in Israel today and is intended for women in the Hasidic community. From the rubrics, it is clear that the modern *tkhine* book is no longer considered as an alternative liturgy, but as a book of prayers to be used in addition to the Hebrew liturgy, such as the "*tkhine* for after prayers on Sunday." The days of the week in the rubrics of these prayers are in Hebrew—for example, Sunday appears as *Yoym rishoyn* (lit. first day)—rather than in Yiddish as in the seventeenth-century edition in which Sunday would be *Zuntik*. The publication of these *tkhines* in Israel, coupled with an intensification of ties to traditional orthodoxy by Hasidim, may explain why, in spite of their preservation of the traditions of Eastern European Jewish culture, the shift in emphasis found in the rubrics indicates a reorientation of the Yiddish *tkhines* away from their original European cultural and geographic base.

Tkhines in stereo

A cassette of songs, specifically intended for Hasidic women and girls, is an example of another modern-day manifestation of *tkhines*. While

Reform and other denomination synagogue services integrate the seating of men and women in the main body of the synagogue, the custom of segregation of the genders in their social and religious roles, as advocated in the ethical manuals of early Yiddish literature,[20] is still adhered to today in the Hasidic community. It is strictly retained both at prayer and during other communal activities, such as schooling, dancing, and all forms of public entertainment. The cassette entitled *Devorah* (the name of the female singer and composer of some of the songs on the cassette) is an example of many recordings available to the Hasidic community. The subtitle "An Album for Women and Girls," is reminiscent of the title pages of the *tkhines* that were addressed to *vayber un meydlekh* (women and girls). The directions and claims that appear on the cover of the cassette reassure the listener that it is suitable for the most orthodox of women: "Please give this tape a rest on *Shabbos* (Sabbath) and Jewish Festivals," and "This album was produced according to strict halachic (legal religious) standards." Modern life presents modern dilemmas. Books of *tkhines* can be read on Sabbath and Jewish Festivals, but these songs cannot be played on electrically operated machines on these sacred days and must therefore be restricted to elevating the spirit on weekdays. The songs are in Yiddish and English with a psalm in Hebrew, which suggests that in some parts of the Hasidic community, Yiddish is gradually being replaced by the national language of the local community. The subject matter reflects concerns expressed in the *tkhines* for observance of commandments, the kindling of Sabbath candles, the wish for an end to *goles* (exile from the Holy Land), and the coming of the Messiah accompanied by restoration of the Temple in Jerusalem. The cassette is a form of entertainment, rather than a book of prayers. In their time, the *tkhines* were also a popular medium. The lyrics on the cassette display the same pious devotion attached to a yearning for the Messiah that was found in the *Seyder Tkhines*, and could have been composed by Rivke Tiktiner over three hundred years ago:

> *Oh, we'll stand against this goles*
> *There's no cause for despair*
> *Through Torah and mitsves this goles*
> *Will vanish into thin air*
> *And together we will sing*
> *And dance so full of joy*

Meshiekh[21] *will arrive*
The third Beys Hamikdosh[22] *will float down*
From the skies.

THE WORLD TO COME

Today, women are writing new prayers in the vernacular, for a growing number of women of various Jewish denominations. The Reform rabbi Tracy Guren Kliers recommends a revival of *tkhines* to release women from the "spiritual desert" in which they find themselves today."[23] She also urges women to write new, relevant prayers for women.[24] The modern-day collection of *tkhines*, the *Shas Tkhine*, has become a much-altered anachronism, relevant only to a specific group of women, and does not serve as a general model. Looking back, however, to the earliest type of Yiddish *tkhines* that are presented in this book, it is clear that they represent a time of unprecedented religious and cultural prestige for women. They broke new ground in the realms of women's prayer and of Jewish prayer in general. Women were authors of a new religious literature that was mainly for women. Their prayer book, the *Seyder Tkhines*, was at the heart of the messianic movement, and they played an essential role in the spiritual life of their communities. At the very least, these *tkhines* can be seen as a beacon of inspiration in the history of Jewish women's prayer.

From the middle of the eighteenth century, when *tkhines* ceased to be relevant to the mainstream of pan-European communal Jewish prayer, they took root in the beginnings of the Hasidic movement. They continued to exist both in the form of a revised version of the *Seyder Tkhines* and as a recognizable model for popular types of Hasidic prayer. The *tkhine* sprang up, grew, and flourished in the cultural and religious life of Ashkenazic Europe. In the Hasidic community, which perpetuates the traditional lifestyle of its Ashkenazic ancestors, the Yiddish *tkhines* remain to this day. They will continue to exist where messianic hope prevails and where Yiddish manages to survive on the brink of extinction.

Ñotes

1. Exponents of Hasidism.
2. Freehof 1923.
3. Ibid., Freehof uses, for his examples, the *Seyder Tkhines u-Vakoshes* first printed 150 years after the *Seyder Tkhines*, a collection that was no longer part of mainstream Jewish prayer.
4. Ibid., 382. Freehof includes the following examples: Mishna (Sota VII, 1); Babylonian Talmud (b. Sota 327, B. Sota 33a), Palestinian Talmud (J. Sota 216); Maimonides *Hilkhoys Kerias Shma; Yankev ben Oshers* Tur Oyrakh Khayim, No. 62; and Joseph Karo's *Shulkhan Oruckh: Ora Khayim* No. 5:2.
5. Ibid.
6. Blumenthal 1982:148ff.
7. Enelow 1913:107.
8. Ibid., 379, 384.
9. London 1841.
10. See Chapter 2.
11. Bahya ibn Paquda, Jewish philosopher who lived in Saragassa, Spain, in the first half of the eleventh century.
12. Hilkhot tefile 4:16.
13. Published in Bologna 1538.
14. Blumenthall 1962: 112.
15. Ibid., 112.
16. Enelow 1913:106.
17. See Chapter 7.
18. New York 1984: 620.
19. The title *Shas* imbues the highest sanctity to the book. *Shas* is the term used traditionally for the *Gemore*, an interpretation of the Mishna, which is the collection of traditional Jewish law and ethics. Together with the Torah, the *Gemora* and Mishna form the Talmud, the body of Jewish civil and ceremonial law and legend.
20. See Chapter 2.
21. The Messiah.
22. Temple.
23. Kliers 1984: 27.
24. New York 1984.

PART TWO
PRAYERS IN
TRANSLATION

The Seyder Tkhines

The Yiddish *Seyder Tkhines* was printed for all Ashkenazic women across Europe. I have been asked if it was intended for "religious women," but such a concept would not have existed. Some women may have been more naturally pious than others, and a few better educated. In fact it was the better educated who might have chosen to pray in Hebrew rather than Yiddish, so the *Seyder Tkhines* would have particularly appealed to those who were not able fully to understand the Hebrew prayers, which would have been most women. However, there is strong evidence presented in this book that whether or not women could read Hebrew, many had a preference for reading prayers in Yiddish. Three hundred and fifty years ago, Jewish women across eastern and western Europe read these prayers and continued to do so for three generations. It is left for today's reader to decide to what extent they remain relevant and if they serve any liturgical purpose. They offer the opportunity to resurrect daily and other occasional prayers written from a woman's perspective, and are brought into print here to stand as a memorial to the enhanced spiritual lives of Jewish women at an extraordinary time in history.

DAILY TKHINES

The daily *tkhines* fulfilled two functions. They allowed women to perform their religious obligation to pray once a day. They also offered women an alternative to the Hebrew synagogue service on which they were based, but they were composed especially for women in a language that was more accessible than Hebrew.

Every day, two *tkhines* were to be recited. The first was for every day of the week and is the longer of the two. There followed a second for each day of the week. Together, the two *tkhines* were the recognized daily liturgy for women.

 This tkhine is to be said every day

Lord of all the world,
God, my God,
And God of my forefathers,
Abraham, Isaac, and Jacob.
Great and strong and awesome God,
And Lord over the whole world,
Above and below,
One Lord over everything on earth,
Every creature, flesh and blood,
And all that grows under the sun,
And Lord of the angels in Heaven above,
And of the sun, the moon, and the stars,
Everything is of His making,
And He governs alone.

He counts and He calculates,
And each and every thing is created
According to its needs,
According to its nature,
And according to its purpose.

And You, Blessed God,
You need no creature in Heaven
Or on earth,
Or under the water,
For You are one God, alone.

You are eternal,
And were alone before the Creation

Of the heavens and the earth,
And You will remain
After all Creation goes down to eternity.

Your Name is praised.
Your kingdom is higher than all others.
Your Name is praised for all eternity.

They seek Your Name in fire
But they do not find it,
And they fear Your Name.

They seek Your Name in the earth,
But they do not find it,
And they tremble at Your power.
And they speak with fear
Of being far from home.

And in all dwellings,
Above the earth
And in the graves below it,
They tremble in fear
Before You.

And the blessed ones
Who enter Paradise
Will praise and respect Your Name
With a loving heart,
And the mountain will spring up high, once again
Like a young sheep
To honor Your Holy Name.

So I, Your devoted maid and daughter,[1]
Was created from the earth,
And must return to the earth.
I am part ashes and part earth,
Part blood and part flesh,
And I will fade like a shadow on a wall
That is soon gone,
And like a blade of grass that bends
And trembles in the wind,
And soon withers.

So I come before Your Holy Name
With my body bowed in great submission
To revere Your Holy Name,
To beg before You
Like a pauper at the door of a rich man.

God, my God,
Listen to me with great mercy.
Answer me.
Favor me,
Be gracious to me,
And be merciful to me.
Bless me,
And inscribe me in the book
In which are inscribed for eternal life
All saintly men and women,
All those who speak before You with love.

And give me my share in this world
And in the next,
And give me Your blessing
And Your mercy.
God Almighty,
Grant me good luck
In all my endeavors.

I spread out the palms of my hands
And raise them to you
And ask for mercy and eternal life.
Open the gate to Your garden
Forgive all sins and wrongdoings,
And open to me
The gate of wisdom and justice,
And the gate of nourishment.

Grant me power and strength
And a good heart,
And good thoughts,
So I may be at peace with my sins,
And repent entirely before You.

May evil thoughts never provoke me
Into evil actions.
Reach out Your right hand to me
And fill me with goodness.
Let me be among those
Who turn toward You
With all their hearts,
And direct me in all my ways.

Strengthen my bones,
So I may stand before You
In awe of Your Name,
To worship You
With all my heart
And with all the limbs of my body,
That You alone created.

You gave 252 Commandments
To Your children Israel to carry out,
And 248, that must be observed and kept,
As many as men have parts of their body.

And You have given to women,
To correspond with our four limbs,
Four Commandments of our own:
To kindle lights for the holy Sabbath,
To purify ourselves from impurity,
To divide the *khale* dough,
And fourth, to serve our husbands.

And You have given a further 365 Commandments
To Your children Israel
Which they are forbidden to perform.

God, my God,
Allow no evil to enter me
At any time,
So I may do only good for You,
So no evil may leave my lips
And weaken the holiness of my speech.

I ask You, God, my God,
Send me a good angel
To intercede at all times
On my behalf,
Who will speak to You
On my behalf
At the Court of Your judgment
Over the living and the dead,
And may all who speak ill of me without cause
Be condemned and never again be brought
Before Your holiness.
And may You view all my deeds in this world
In a good light.
And may You recognize my few good deeds
And may You turn Your eyes
Away from my sins
And overlook them.

Let my prayers reach You
Free from the interference of devils,
Or evil spirits who hinder prayers,
All those who are excluded from Your holiness.

And make a space for me beneath Your throne,
As you made a space for King Menassah
When You accepted his prayer,
And reviewed and forgave his great sin,
When he bowed down before You,
And repented.

And as You accept the prayers
Of all those who repent,
Those who serve You,
And bow down before You,
May You accept my prayer
Today, and every day of my life.

And accept my prayer
As You accepted the sacrificial offerings
That the Priest brought
To the offering stool,

At the time when Your House stood
In great purity and holiness.

These are good memories,
The holiest,
The most joyful.
For then all the children of Israel
Worshipped You
And confessed their sins,
As they lined up to acknowledge their wrongdoings.

And one part of the offering was burnt each time,
And one part was eaten,
The steam gave off a delicious scent,
And beatified You.
And in that Holy House
Dwelt Your Holiness,
Your Divine Presence.

But now we have no Priest,
And no sacrifices.
We have no Levites
Who sang at the sacrifice,
Accompanying their holy songs
On harps and lutes.
They played on all sides
To honor Your Holy Name.

And now we have no Temple,
And no Altar,
And no *Menoyre*,[2]
And no Ark,
And no atonements.

And the city of Your holiness, Jerusalem,
Is deserted and dead and wiped out.
And where once people carried out Your will,
Now Your beloved people Israel
Are driven beneath the rule of other peoples,
And suffer bitter, hard exile.
So my eyes pour with water

131

Like a spring,
Day and night,
Endlessly.

For I am without my remembered mountain, Zion,
Without Your city, where Your Name was proclaimed,
And where Your Divine Presence was among them
As they called out to You
From the depths of their hearts,
Assured of Your mercy and grace,
As You assured Your servant, Moses
That man of truth,
May his soul rest in peace.

Lord of all the world,
At this time we do not have
All the words to praise Your Name,
But accept from my lips
What I say here and now
In all humility,
As you assured Abraham, our forefather,
When he brought his son Isaac to be sacrificed.
Then You made a covenant with him,
And swore to give the Holy Land to his seed,
So that Your Name could rest among us.
You swore to forgive their sins
And their wrongdoings
If they acknowledged them
And showed remorse,
And brought offerings.

And through the prophet,
You let it be said
That when Your children remember their sins,
And repent,
You will grant them forgiveness,
And Jerusalem will be rebuilt,
And the Temple,
So that Your Holy Name
May rest there.

Here I stand, a poor woman,
Before You and Your Holy Name,
And acknowledge my sins
With great remorse,
And will never repeat them.

I ask you as a Father and one and only King
Forgive my sins,
And grant eternal pardon.
Do not leave me penniless
For my wrongdoings.
Help me to speak modestly,
And be merciful to me,
And to my husband,
And my children,
And all my household,
And over all Your children Israel,
And bring us good luck,
And help us in all we do.

And protect us from those who are evil,
Those who break the law,
And those who incite people to do wrong to others
By ruthless persuasion,
And from those who are malicious,
And gossip and lie,
And curse and swear,
Sitting in the streets, criticizing others,
And who never have a good word to say,
And have no shame.

Lord of all the world
May I, and mine,
And those who do not belong to me,
Have their share of this world
And the world to come.

Protect us from all the evil in the world,
And protect us from an untimely death,
And from captivity,

And hunger and thirst,
And corruption and evil decrees.

Let us not be shamed before You,
Nor before others,
And do not allow the evil inclination
To manifest itself in the world,
But unite us in goodness
As it should be.

Shelter us in Your shadow,
Beneath Your wing,
And enable us to worship You
And to keep Your Commandments,
Which You commanded us to keep
In Your holy Torah.

And let us know how to take instruction
From those who instruct us to do good,
So we may serve Your Name in holiness
And never again shame ourselves
When we speak.
And accept the words
Only of those who speak the truth.

Do not allow the evil inclination
To hinder us from rising early
To praise Your Holy Name
And to thank You
For all the good You have done
For Your maid
At all times.

And may we be worthy always to be
Among good, pious people,
Those in Your service
Who fear God.
Make good all my bad thoughts,
And let bad thoughts
Have no place in the world.
And may my feet walk toward goodness,
And may my hands do only good,

And may my ears hear the Torah
And the praising of Your Name,
And may those who read the Torah
And keep Your Commandments,
Never be shamed by their speech.

And may my eyes see only good.
And see the wonders of Your creation.
And may my body and limbs
Praise Your Holy Name
And know no evil.

Give me a pure, fresh heart
That is not despondent,
So I may worship You
With all my heart,
And without falsehood,
Not grudgingly or sadly,
But gladly and joyfully,
So I may carry out Your Commandments
With great happiness.

And may I become pregnant
In purity,
So I may raise my children
To fear Your Name,
And keep Your Commandments,
And praise and sanctify and honor You
At all times.

And may my health be good
So I may do You justice through truth
And through *Kashres*[3]
And with no deceit or *Treyf,*[4]
No blasphemy,
Or desecration of the Sabbath or Festivals
So all the work of my children may be
For the glorification of God.

And when I lie in my bed,
Protect me from bad thoughts,
So my body and my heart

May lie safely at rest.
And do not allow me to be
Smothered by my covers,
So that I may live to honor Your Holy Name,
Which is honored by the entire world,
Which is entirely Yours.

And let no shame come to me,
Or my husband or children,
Or my household,
Either between ourselves
Or among others.

And may I never condone
Those who wrong Your Name,
Or act in spite against You,
But only let me see
Those who always do good,
And worship You with their whole heart,
And love Your Name,
And fear You.

Let us not crave great houses,
And beautiful clothes,
But let us desire from Your mild hand
Only that which we need,
And let us not set ourselves apart
From those who have nothing,
But unite all good people,
So our children show great respect
To all pious people,
Those who fear You
And love You greatly,
And keep Your Commandments,
And earn their keep through their own efforts.

And let us benefit from the merit
Of Abraham, Isaac, and Jacob,
Moses, Aaron, David, Solomon,
Sarah, Rebecca, Rachel, Leah,
Hannah, Abigail,

And other saintly men and women.
And pious men and women.

And may we live to see
The Temple rebuilt,
So we may bring sacrifices,
And again go three times a year
To Jerusalem, that Holy City
Which you chose to house
Your Divine Presence,
And celebrate to see
The great friendship and love
That You have for all Your people Israel.

Almighty God, hear my prayer,
And answer me always.
Purify my heart,
And fill it with love and fear of You.
Send us the prophet to beg from us
So You may send us Your holy Messiah.
And heal my heart and my soul
So they are mended,
And favor me and all others,
And give us the vision and wisdom
To know and fear Your Holy Name.

Master of all the world,
Accept this prayer
From Your devoted maid and daughter
Who has called to You in her need,
With all her heart,
As You accept the prayers
Of all those who pray and call out to You,
With all their hearts,
As You accept all the prayers
Of Your children Israel
Who praise and thank You
For accepting their prayers today,
And always,
And for all eternity.

Amen.

This tkhine is to be said on Sunday with kavone[5]

May it be granted, God, our God,
And God of our forefathers,
Creator of us all,
And Creator of all the world,
You were one God, alone
When the world began
And will be one God throughout eternity.
Only You can rule this world,
And the world to come.

On this day,
From the purity of
Your Divine Presence,
You created for the world
Great and good and pure light,
So the world,
And everything in the world,
All those in Heaven,
And on earth,
Would benefit from that light.

Then You saw
With great clarity and insight,
That creation was not worthy
To benefit from this holy and dignified light,
So you divided it, and lifted
The greater light
Into the concealment of the next world,
For the benefit of those who worship You,
And fear and love Your Name
With all their heart.

Lord of the whole world,
May I, and all mine,
Live to be worthy to enter
The great pure light

138

In the Garden of Eden
With other saintly men and women
And to receive great blessedness
From the radiance of the light
Of Your Divine Presence

And let us know the magnificence
Of the holiness of Your Name.
For in Your light shall we see light.
As the holy verse says:
When we enter eternal life with You
We shall see light in Your light.

May the speech of my mouth
Find favor before You,
God, my Creator and my Redeemer.

 This tkhine is to be said on Monday with kavone

May it be granted, God, our God,
And God of our forefathers,
Creator of us all,
And Creator of all the world,
You were one God, alone
When the world began
And will be one God throughout eternity.
Only You can rule this world,
And the world to come.

On this day You proclaimed Your holiness
By extending the skies,
And You separated the water from above,
And the water from below,
And You took a stool to sit upon
To judge with justice
On the day when You judge
The just and the unjust.

And You have today
Created Hell to punish the sinful,
Those who do not fear You
And Your grim fury.

Therefore Lord of all the world,
I spread open the palms of my hands
And bow down before You
With all my heart
So You may protect me and all mine
From Your severe judgment
And from Hell.

Protect us from water and from fire,
And from evil winds and thunder and lightning
That may strike us
Awake or sleeping,
In our homes or on the streets.
Protect us from the terror,
Of great floods and storms,
When sudden waters come rushing
From below or above.
And protect us from all evil encounters
Wherever we stand or walk
So we may worship Your Name with joy.

May the speech of my mouth
Find favor before You,
God, my Creator and my Redeemer.

 This tkhine is to be said on Tuesday
with great kavone

May it be granted, God, our God,
And God of our forefathers,
Creator of us all,
And Creator of all the world,
You were one God, alone
When the world began
And will be one God throughout eternity.

Only You can rule this world,
And the world to come.

On this day of Your creation
You created food:
Grass, green vegetables,
And all the needs of Your creation.
And You divided the earth from the waters
So that all Your creation
Could live on the land,
And grow on it all their needs
With great mercy and grace,
Each one with its mate apart,
According to its nature.

How great is Your wonder.
You have no equal.
There is no such master in Heaven or on earth.
We believe in Your Name for ever and ever.

I, Your devoted maid and daughter,
Come to honor You
With my body bowed
In great submission
And with broken spirit.
I beg like a pauper
At the door of a rich man,
That You may grant good health
To me, and my husband and children,
And to all my household,
And may Your mild hand
Provide us with food at all times,
In correct measure,
Not from the hand of others
But honestly, and without shame.

And give us a secure dwelling
Within the city boundaries
Without struggle,
So none can claim it from us,
And none will claim it from us.

And give us houses that are near to the synagogue,
And not far from the study house,
So that I, and my husband and children,
May come quickly
To worship Your Holy Name,
And never be prevented
From worshipping You
With all our hearts.

May the speech of my mouth
Find favor before You,
God, my Creator and my Redeemer.

This tkhine is to be said on Wednesday with kavone

May it be granted, God, our God,
And God of our forefathers,
Creator of us all,
And Creator of all the world,
You were one God, alone
When the world began
And will be one God throughout eternity.
Only You can rule this world,
And the world to come.

On this day,
The day that is blessed
And praised by Your creation,
You set the sun and moon and stars
Each in their own firmament,
So that Your people Israel
Could calculate the days and years,
And reckon the Festivals
And the start of the months,
And epochs of history
From heaven's design,
And to give light by day,
To divide night from day,

And the darkness from light,
And the greater light from the lesser light.

Because of these changes,
On this day
The state of all pregnant women
Is threatened by harm,
And some of their children
Could be possessed by evil spirits
Or even suffer death.

I, Your devoted maid and daughter,
Come before You with my body bowed
    down to the earth
To confirm Your holiness
And to ask You
For great mercy and grace.
May You be merciful over me,
And over my children,
And over all the women and children
Of Your people Israel,
Those who fear the justice
Of Your Court.

Almighty God,
Let no harm come to me,
Or my children,
Or any of the children of Israel,
And protect us from
The evil in the air
That goes around today,
On this day in the world
That might do us harm.
Cover us with Your wing
And protect and guard us,
For You are protector to all those
Who would be unprotected without You.

As the verse says:
"Those who are the servants of God,
God will protect."

May the speech of my mouth
Find favor before You,
God, my Creator and my Redeemer.

 This tkhine is to be said on Thursday
with kavone

May it be granted, God, our God,
And God of our forefathers,
Creator of us all,
And Creator of all the world,
You were one God, alone
When the world began
And will be one God throughout eternity.
Only You can rule this world,
And the world to come.

On this day,
Lord of all the world,
You created all the life
Under the heavens:
Cattle and sheep,
Worms and birds and fish,
And blessed them
So they should multiply
In the world
And procreate
So they should be of help
And benefit to all Your creation,
Who worship You with all their heart
And read Your Torah
And keep Your Commandments,
While You sit with Your Holy Court
To judge with justice
The righteous and the unrighteous.

So I come to You again
I, Your devoted maid and daughter
In great recognition of Your holiness,

144

So that You may give me honest nourishment,
With great blessedness,
To benefit Your creation,
And to benefit and protect me,
And my husband and children,
And all those who rely on You.
And give me,
And all those women under Israel
Who suckle their children,
Good breasts at all times,
So my milk shall be free of suffering
When I nourish my young.

And help me to teach them
To worship Your Holy Name,
And to fear You and love You,
So that I, and my husband and my children
Are righteous in all our ways
When You bring us before Your Court.

And stop up the mouths
Of all those who speak ill of us.
Ignore their advice,
And wipe out their memories.
But listen to those who speak well of us
Before Your justice.

May the speech of my mouth
Find favor before You,
God, my Creator and my Redeemer.

This tkhine is said on Friday with great kavone

May it be granted, God, our God,
And God of our forefathers,
Creator of us all,
And Creator of all the world,
You were one God, alone
When the world began

And will be one God throughout eternity.
Only You can rule this world,
And the world to come.

On this day,
All Your holiness went out
To humankind,
For them to govern all creatures
Under the heavens, on earth
And beneath the water.
And You created people on earth,
To be your servants at all times,
To praise and honor
Your Holy Name,
And to tell of Your wonder,
And of the wonderful creation
As it was created with perfection
By Your hand,
So that everything is in exact measure,
And nothing is too small or too large,
And everything is created
According to its need.

You created the people out of earth,
And blew a loving breath
Into their nostrils
With great grace and mercy.
And You gave them speech
So that they might speak out
In praise of Your Holy Name.
And You shaped the people
From the shape of Your holiness,
And commanded them to multiply the world
And then flee the earth.
You created the Garden of Eden
So they should benefit from their good work
For all eternity.

And You created Hell
To punish evil deeds,

And You created repentance
For everyone in the world
So that when remorse sweeps over them
And they keep Your Commandments and repent
You will with Your right hand
Waive their sins in forgiveness.

So I, Your devoted maid and daughter,
Come before Your holiness, God, our God.
I beg You to give me
A heart of flesh,
And a prudent mind,
And the good sense to understand
All Your Commandments.
So that I may benefit
From the world,
Give help to it
And not damage it,
And urge everyone
To praise Your Holy Name,
And not to oppose it.
And help me to be helpful
In Your world,
And to multiply in great light
And piety.

And help me to teach
Others to do Your service,
And to praise, honor, and sanctify
Your Holy Name
All the days of their lives.

And if we have erred,
May our sins be forgiven,
And may we never sin again,
But keep the Commandments
Of Your holy Torah,
So that when our lives come to an end
We may benefit
From the great light and beauty

In the Garden of Eden,
With other saintly men and women,
Those who kept Your Commandments
And acknowledged Your holiness,
With their flesh and blood.

May the speech of my mouth
Find favor before You,
God, my Creator and my Redeemer.

SABBATH TKHINES

 This tkhine is to be said on Sabbath with great kavone

May it be granted, God, our God,
And God of our forefathers,
Creator of us all,
And Creator of all the world,
You were one God, alone
When the world began
And will be one God throughout eternity.
Only You can rule this world,
And the world to come.

On this day You completed
The six days of Your work
With great skill and judgment,
And then You created rest,
And You rested and made this day
Holier than all other days,
And You blessed it for Your people, Israel,
So that they would rest
After spending the whole week
Attending to their needs.

But on this day,
They should read the Torah

And think of the *mitsves* they should do
All the days of their lives.
And on this day You gave Your people
The opportunity to rest in this world
In preparation for the great rest
And the blessedness
Of the next world,
Where they will enter
Eternal Life,
In the Garden of Eden,
With their Creator,
In the radiant light
Of Your Divine Presence.

Lord of all the world,
I, Your devoted maid and daughter
Beg before Your holiness
And ask You to give us blessed rest
Today, on this day,
So we may praise and thank
Your Holy Name for all the gifts
And the food that You have given us
For the past six days.

And may the food we have today,
And the sweet spices and beautiful clothes,
Enhance and honor
Your holy Sabbath,
In peace and tranquillity.

Give me the ability and strength
To rest, and to keep Your Commandments,
On this day when Your Divine Presence
Rested and sanctified it above all other days.

May I, and my husband and children,
Be worthy to be brought at our time
With great honor
Into Your service
In the next world,
To sit in the Garden of Eden

With those who have honored,
And made holy, and observed,
The Sabbath.
May they intercede for us
When we are judged by Your holiness,
As Adam was redeemed in death.

Lord of all the world,
I feel safe in Your assurance
To Your children,
Your people Israel,
That all those who rest and praise and observe
Your holy Sabbath,
Will, like Jacob our father,
Receive their reward
In this world
And in the next world,
And I know that You will remain constant
And keep Your word.

May the speech of my mouth
Find favor before You,
God, my Creator and my Redeemer.

 Tḥis is said witḥ great ḥavone wḥen sḥe divides tḥe ḥale douǥḥ[6]

You are beloved, God our God,
And God of our forefathers.
You have sanctified your people Israel
Above all people,
And have commanded
That when we bake our Sabbath bread,
We should separate one part of the dough
For You, God Almighty,
As it was done for the Priest,
Who was free of all impurity,
Just as You separated a part of the earth
From which You created humankind,
And gave each one a pure soul.

Where the High Priest stood
There was no corruption.
Now we are punished for our sins
And the sins of our forefathers.
And His city, Jerusalem, is destroyed,
As is the Holy House
In which Your Name was made holy
Through the Priests
Who brought offerings
To the offering stool,
According to the law.

Through the worthiness of the Priest,
The holy bread was eaten
For You, God, my God.
But now we have no Priest
To keep the Commandment
Of Your holy Torah.

I wish to keep Your Commandment,
And wish to divide off
Part of the dough
To praise and honor
Your Holy Name.

And I wish to burn it,
So none of Israel
Shall be tempted to eat it.
And I beg You,
God, my God,
To allow me and my children
To live to see Your Holy House
Built again in Jerusalem as before,
And all Your people living again
In the Holy Land
That You made holy with Your Name,
So that we may again
Give the separated portion of dough
To the Priest,
Who is free from all impurities,
In great happiness

With Israel gathered together
In God's name
Amen.

And make this blessing:[7]

Blessed are You, Lord our God, King of the Universe,
Who has sanctified us by Your Commandments
And commanded us to set aside a part of the dough.

And she says this when she places the Sabbath loaves into the oven

Lord of all the world,
The blessing of all things
Is in Your hands.
So I come to honor Your holiness
And ask You to bestow Your blessing
On this dough.

Send an angel to protect it,
So that it may bake well,
And rise well,
And not burn,
In order to honor
The holy Sabbath,
That You have chosen
As a day of rest.

So, I make this holy blessing
As You blessed the dough of
Our mothers, Sarah and Rebecca.

God, my God,
Hear my voice.
You are God
Who hears the voices
Of those who call out to You
With all their hearts.

You are beloved for ever.

152

This is said with kavone when she kindles the Sabbath candles

God, You are our Lord,
And Lord over all lords.
You have sanctified
Your people Israel
Above all peoples.

With Your Commandments,
And with Your holy Sabbath,
You have given
Your people Israel
Rest in this world.

You have hidden away
The most glorious rest
In the Other World
Which is like the holy Sabbath,
And it is our duty
To honor the great gift
That You have given us
Above all other peoples
On earth.
So we must light candles
On this holy day,
To give light
And rejoice in it.

May we be worthy
Of the lights,
And of the joy
Of eternal life.

Lord of all the world,
I have done all my work
Over six days,
And wish now to rest
As You have commanded,

And to light two candles
As it is written
In the Torah,
And taught by your sages,
In order to honor You,
And to honor
The holy Sabbath.

I, Your devoted maid and daughter,
Ask for Your mercy
And for Your great compassion,
So that You may grant my wishes
As You have granted the wishes
Of all those who deny their will
To do Your will.

Let these candles be accepted
In Your eyes
As the lights that were kindled
By the Priest in the Temple,
And do not allow our candles
To be extinguished,
But let them light the way,
And lead our souls
To the lights of Paradise,
With other saintly men
And saintly women.

In God's name,
Amen.

 This is said after she has kindled the Sabbath candles

God of Your people Israel,
You are holy,
And have sanctified
Your people Israel,
And have sanctified
The Sabbath,

And You are one.
You have chosen
Your people Israel
From all peoples
To serve You.

You have singled out
The Sabbath for rest,
So we may honor it
And rejoice in it,
And illuminate it
With candle light,
To serve You joyfully today
On Your holy Sabbath,
Which we are bound to honor
And keep in all things,
Like a king his queen
Or a bridegroom his bride,
Because in the words of our sages:
The Sabbath is queen and bride.

So I,
Your devoted maid and daughter,
Have kindled two candles
At the bidding of Your sages
Who know Your Torah,
To honor and sanctify
Your Name,
Your Torah,
And the Sabbath.

God Almighty,
On this holy Sabbath
Give to me and my husband,
And to my children and my household,
Health, peace, blessedness,
And light.

Protect us from all evil occurrences,
Encounters and events,
Which are wont to come

155

On this day,
And from the rule of evil stars.

And from those who cry out,
From those who desire
Respite from their pain,
But whose souls
Are bound for Hell,
And from those who come
To claim their dues
From the living.

May my candles
Shine with purity,
To drive away the evil spirits,
Devils and Igres daughter of Makhales[8]
Who come from Lilith,
So they may all flee
Before the candles
That I light
To honor You
According to the Torah,
In honor of the Sabbath,
So they may be able to hurt
Neither man, nor woman, nor child
Among Your people.

Lord of all the world,
Give me children
Who are enlightened
By Your Torah
And understand Your Commandments
And who teach them to others,
And do at all times
That which gains favor
In Your eyes,
And in the eyes of others,
So we may be worthy
To rest on this Sabbath
And exult in peace
And tranquillity,

Without encumbrance
Or distraction.

Send us Your blessing
With the good angel,
The one who is at Your right hand,
And may the evil angel
Say "Amen,"
And let us be worthy
To inherit this day,
That is a mere foretaste
Of the Sabbath on which
Rest those who live for ever.

May the speech of my mouth
And the thoughts of my heart
Find favor before You,
God, my Creator and my Redeemer.

NIDE TKHINES

 This tkhine is to be said when women dress themselves in white[9]

God and King of Mercy,
Who can know or tell
Of the Justice of Your judgment,
Which is as profound
As spring water
At its deepest source.

You punished Eve, our Mother,
Because she persuaded her man
To flaunt Your Commandment.
And he ate from the tree
Which You forbade.

This troubled You so greatly
That You decreed that all her descendants,

All women,
Must suffer every month
When their time comes.
Your word is true.

I have once again had my time
With a sorrowful heart,
And I thank Your Holy Name
And Your great justice,
And I have taken my punishment
From my great Friend, with love.

I observe Your Commandment,
As every woman under Israel
Should observe the Commandments
Of our sages,
And of the Torah,
And now comes the time
When I must immerse myself.

God, my God,
Let my act be acknowledged,
And let me remain pure
Until I reach the *mikve*
Where with Your help,
Those who desire to be pure
Shall be cleansed.

May the speech of my mouth
Find favor before You,
God, my Creator and my Redeemer.

 She says this when it is her time to go to the mikve

Lord of all the world,
You have sanctified
Your people Israel
Above all peoples,
And have commanded
That a woman must

158

Cleanse herself of impurity
By immersing her body in water,
So that she may be cleansed.

God, my God,
The time has come today
For me to cleanse myself
Of my impurity.

God, my God,
May it be Your will
That my cleansing
In the water of the *mikve*
Be counted with the purification
Of all pious women under Israel,
Who go to the *mikve* at their time
To cleanse themselves.

God Almighty,
Accept my prayer,
As You accept the prayers
Of all Your children Israel.

May the speech of my mouth
Find favor before You,
God, my Creator and my Redeemer.

When she leaves the mikve she says this with kavone

Creator of all the world,
Lord of all souls,
Who sits on high
And dwells among
His chosen people Israel,
And who with great love
Commanded us to be pure,
And to cleanse ourselves
From all impurities.
You are pure,
And all Your servants

159

Are pure,
And among them
Is no impurity.

God, my God,
I, Your devoted maid and daughter,
Have lovingly kept
Your Commandment today,
And cleansed myself
Of my impurity,
So that I may come purified
To my husband to unite
With him in radiance
And with pure thoughts,
And may I bring him
To the blissful observance and fulfilment
Of Your Commandment,
So we may honor and sustain
The world.

Merciful God,
Send Your angel
To meet me
When I come to my husband,
So we may encounter
No impurity.

Cleanse my heart and my thoughts
So I may think no evil.
Give my husband a pure mind
So he may have good, pure thoughts,
Not unseemly thoughts,
When he unites with me.

And may all his actions
Be suffused in great light,
And may he be neither timid nor bold.
Send me a good angel
To intercede respectfully before You
So my womb is made worthy
To accept the seed.

Almighty God,
May it be Your will
That a righteous, pious son
Results from this act,
One who will fear Your Name,
And keep Your Commandments,
And find grace in Your eyes,
And in the eyes of all the people.

May he study Torah
Day and night,
So he need never be shamed
In the *yeshive,*
And may he never stumble
Over Halakhah.[10]

For then it is better
To have a daughter,
So grant me a daughter
To be a guiding light
And not immodest,
So she may learn to accept the guidance
Of all those who teach her.

Merciful God,
Be merciful to me.
Do not allow my womb
To be obstructed,
And let me not desire
That which is unclean,
Or inappropriate
Or that which is unhealthy
For me or for my child.

Let me worship You anew,
Restored, refreshed, and strong,
And in good health
At all times,
In great happiness
And in God's name.
Amen.

Before giving birth, she should say this

God Almighty,
Judge and Justice,
You have punished us women
With truth and righteousness
Since the creation of humankind,
So that we give birth to our children
In pain.

It is in Your making
That when You punish,
Then we are punished,
And when You are merciful,
We are graced by Your mercy.

God be merciful to me
Through the merit of all saintly men and women
As You have shown mercy
To those whose prayers
You have accepted
When they prayed to You,
And called out Your Name,
Asking You to open their wombs.

You opened their wombs
With grace and mercy
And allowed them to give birth
At their time.

God, our Father,
You existed before the Creation
Of the world,
And You will support
The whole world
Until its end,
With great mercy.

Silence and subdue
The bad angels
And banish them from Your Court.

Let them not stand before You
And do not accept their words
If they speak of my sins and evil deeds.
Stop up all the holes
In Your holy gates
So that their voices cannot be heard.

But allow the good angels,
Those who speak well
Of Your children Israel
To intercede for me,
And may they do so
With only good words.

And take the key to my womb
In Your right hand,
And unlock me without pain,
And without suffering,
And allow this birth
To be free of all harm,
Without sickness,
And without the *yeytser hore*,[11]
So my child may from the start
Be good-natured.

Protect me and the child
From all evil spirits
And evil people,
And may the evil eye
Not harm us.

God Almighty,
Accept my prayer,
And take my tears in Your vessel
Like the tears of Hannah,
Whose prayer You granted
When You allowed her to speak to You
Through the prophet,
And brought her happiness.

God of Israel,
May it be Your desire

To accept our tears
As You have accepted
The tears of other pious women,
For You are the one
Who accepts the prayers
Of those who call out to You
With all their heart.

May the speech of my mouth
Find favor before You,
God, my Creator and my Redeemer.

 She says this when she leaves the childbed
before going to the mikve to cleanse herself

Lord of all the world,
You accept all the prayers
Of those who call out to You
With all their heart
And are in awe of You.

Lord God,
I thank You as a Lord
For making my bitter suffering
Disappear after childbirth,
And for giving me milk
To nourish my child,
And for the ability to rise today
From my bed to serve again
Your Holy Name,
Just as when the Temple stood
And I was required
According to Your Torah
To bring an offering
After my purification
To honor Your Name.

Now, because of the sins
Of our forefathers,
The Temple is destroyed

And we have no Priest
And bring no sacrifices.

Lord of all the world,
Accept my words and my prayer,
And my calling out
To Your Holy Name
From the greatest depths
Of my heart,
As an offering,
And continue to protect me
From all evil,
With all Your people Israel
Who depend on You.

Continue to guide me and my husband
So we may raise this child and our others
Without difficulty,
And with delight in our hearts.

God, our God,
Give me Your help,
So my child may worship
Your Name at all times,
With honesty and sincerity and love.

Amen.

FAST-DAY TKHINES

The next tkhine is a good example of a Hebrew prayer being adapted into the *tkhine* formula. The Fast of the Ninth of Av is a day of mourning for the destruction of the first and second Temples in Jerusalem, which occurred, according to tradition, on the same date, the Ninth of Av, in 586 B.C.E. and 69 C.E., respectively. Hebrew liturgy has traditionally incorporated additional prayers and liturgical poems into liturgy for fast days to allow worshippers to express their mourning. *Kines* (*Kinot*), meaning "Elegies," from the Book of Lamentations (*Eykho*) are a major source. Both the Hebrew and Yiddish prayers relate the story of the destruction of the two Temples. The *Eykho* was also reproduced in Yiddish with Yiddish explanations in the *Tsene-rene*, which gives a close rendering of the Hebrew original. The author of the *Seyder Tkhines* creates a separate prayer dimension that co-exists with and complements the material in the *Tsene-rene*, but does not overlap with it. An interesting and salient parallel between the *tkhine* and the *Eykho* is that in both, the outward expressions of grief are voiced by a female narrator (the *tkhine* worshipper and the voice of the city of Jerusalem, which is initially described as "her," but then becomes "I").

 ## To be said on the Ninth of Av

Judge of all the world,
Your judgment is right and true,
And without injustice.
You are our true judge forever.

On this day our forefathers,
Those whom You led out of Egypt
Through Your servants Moses and Aaron,
Committed many misdeeds.

Again they did not trust in the promise
That You made to our forefathers,
Abraham, Isaac, and Jacob,
So they were not permitted to enter the Holy Land,
Where Your Divine Presence rested
At all times, and where Your Name
Was murmured by Your true servants.

And on that night they all cried,
And their eyes ran like spring water,
And they did not trust in Your assurances.

And when they discovered
Through Your servants Moses and Aaron
That the gift was also to be withheld from their children,
As it happened through Your truth,
They cried many tears on this day.

On this day of Your great splendor,
Both Temples were destroyed and wiped out.

The crown fell to earth,
And we can no longer bring sacrifices
To the offering stool
In honor of Your holiness,
And can no longer go three times a year
To see the beauty of Your Divine Presence.

With our faith and conviction
In the great happiness
With which the Holy Divine Presence
Rested among the cherubim,
And spoke with Your children
On the High Holy Days
In the face of great bravery,
Against great wealth,
And against great hope
Everything was burnt in a fire from Heaven,
And they chose crooked ways, not good ones.

And women and children who were gentle and educated
Were taken into captivity,
And the maidens were shamed.
And the young men had to drag
Millstones around their shoulders and necks.
And the chains around their feet made them stumble.

And they craved bread in their hunger,
And had no water to quench their thirst.
There was great and bitter frustration
For all the people,
And for this city,
The crown of all cities
And all lands,
One city that was above all others
Suffered great and bitter frustration.

And they called out for mercy
To overturn this hatred.
They called out to their Friend for help,
But no one answered them

Except with evil,
Mocking their Sabbaths and Festivals,
Extinguishing their candles,
And creating darkness.

Lord of all the world,
I stand before You
With a sad heart,
Wailing and weeping,
My eyes run like spring water,
And my heart sighs and cannot be free
Of the memory of the disruption
Of Your children Israel
In the broken city of Yehuda,
And Israel
And their Kingdom.

So they went into captivity,
And the Priests who worshipped in Your House,
And the Levites who sang and beat on all sides
Playing the holy songs,
Are now dispersed,
And all the holy vessels
Have come into unclean hands.

May Your Name be merciful.
My eyes are swollen with great weeping,
And my heart is weak with sighing before You,
And my strength deserts my body,
And the marrow forsakes my bones,
And my limbs are feeble with great lament
For Your children Israel.

Who can heal them like You?
You are the One who heals all sickness under Israel,
And you are one Lord over all lords,
Who forgives transgressions
In Your great mercy and compassion.

Turn Your ears toward the cries of Your people Israel,
And open Your eyes and see the plight of Your holy city
Where Your voice called out to them,

And hear how Your children are mocked and shamed
   among the peoples,
Where their goodness is lost with all their hope.

Give your strength to them,
And let the strength of others come to nothing,
And may they be shamed,
And tremble in awe before the grim severity of Your
   holiness.
And help us, and gather us together
From all four corners of the world,
From among the peoples,
So we are happy again.

And free us from the pain You gave us,
And remember the covenant with our forefathers.
Let it not be lost to us among the peoples,
And rebuild the holy city again with Your continuity.

As the prophet said:
In honor of You
I wish to receive Your mercy and compassion.
For You forgive the misdeeds of Your people Israel
Out of love
When our eyes and our hearts are faithful to You,
And when we serve You,
You are our consolation.

Therefore console us in our unhappiness
And protect us from further sadness,
And send us Your beloved
Who will beg only for the good of Your children Israel.

And on this day, may we celebrate,
And praise Your Name,
And tell of Your great wonder.
And may You save us now
As You saved us from Egypt,
So we may soon rejoice
In our day.

Amen.

This tkhine is to be said on the Fast of the tenth of Teyveys[12]

Creator of all the world,
You are absolute in all Your work.
You punish us with righteousness,
And the mercy that You showed to our forefathers
You sent through Your prophets
To help lead them on the right path,
To serve You, and to keep Your Commandments,
And Your Torah.

But they did not listen.
They mocked You,
And did not believe Your word.
Nor did they learn Your Holy Name,
And Your Holy Name is long to learn.

And on this bitter day,
You stretched out Your mighty hand
And sent an unmerciful king,
One with many people.
And the city of Jerusalem,
Which was the crown of the whole world,
Where Your Holy Name rested,
And from where came all the prayers
Of Your children Israel
And where You accepted the sacrifices and the incense
Which gave off a holy scent,
This city was overwhelmed with hatred,
And Your children were locked in great need.

So they cried out to You,
But You did not listen to them.
You stopped up all the holes under Your throne,
Where the prayers of saintly men and women come
Before Your holiness,
And their cries could not enter the city
And were hindered by those

Who lie in wait to hinder prayers.

Lord God, my God,
We fast today,
And torment our bodies,
And remember the great downfall
That happened to our forefathers,
Which we still suffer on this day.

We cannot regain what we have lost.
So acknowledge our pain and our pleas,
And accept my prayer,
And hear my cry,
And help Your people Israel once more,
And remember the covenant
You made with our forefathers,
Abraham, Isaac, and Jacob,
That their children would be helped
For all eternity.

And be merciful to us,
Like a father to his children.
Unload this burden from us,
And bring us out of this long exile
And into happiness.

And on this day,
Let us say through Your prophet
That on tenth of *Teyveys*
Your people will live happily
In God's name

Amen.

 ## Say this tkhine on the Fast of Esther

One and only God, You sit on high
And await the prayers of Your children Israel,
And hear them pray from the depths of their hearts.

And You protect them from all tyrants
Who offend Your children Israel,

And just such a tyrant was held high
By an evil king
Where Your children lived under his rule.

The same evil king sold Your children
To rob them of their money.
And to bring about their downfall.
And the king vowed to destroy
The whole Jewish race.

And then they wept,
And their hearts sighed to Your Holy Name,
And they remembered their sins,
And they dressed themselves in sackcloth and ashes,
And fasted, and tormented their bodies
With hunger and thirst.

All the angels were merciful at Your throne,
And called out
And the holy Torah was heard.
And Your children dressed in mourning clothes,
And the holy man, Elijah the prophet,
Heard them, and hurried to our forefathers,
Abraham, Isaac, and Jacob, Moses and Aaron,
To let them know of the great and bitter evil decree
That was commanded to be done to all Jews
Throughout the kingdom of Ahasuerus.[13]

And Mordecai[14] commanded all men,
Women, and children to fast
For three days and three nights,
And ordered that they should
All call out to Your Holy Name,
All at the same time.

And You were merciful and protected them
From the hands of their enemies.
And the evil man, Haman, and his children,
Were hanged on the tree
That was intended for Mordecai,
That saintly man.

And You endowed Esther
With great renown throughout the world,
So all the world should torment their bodies
And always fast on this day,
So that our sins might be forgiven.
And all Israel be full of joy,
As they were in the days of Mordecai and Esther,
And we should be happy
On Purim every year,
In the truth of God's name.

Amen.

This tkhine is said on the Fast of the Seventeenth of Tammuz[15]

Living God,
You are the source of life,
And You lit the world
From Your light,
And You have given us
The holy Torah
Which is light,
And its *mitsves* are light,
And they light up Your children's eyes.

And our forefathers in the desert,
Those whom You led out of Egypt,
Their eyes darkened,
And they made the golden calf
That caused Moses to break the holy tablets
That were written by the fingers of God.
And they infuriated You.
So You sent Your enemy,
Who divided and broke up
The city of Jerusalem
As it is today.

And Your Holy House,
Where the purity of Your Divine Presence rested,

Was desecrated and destroyed,
And the jewel was stolen from Your children.

They were without a city.
And where every evening and morning
Sacrifices were brought,
Suckling babies were brought instead
And slaughtered there.

God, and King over all kings,
Be merciful to Your people Israel,
Those who are in exile
For so very long
Because of the sins of their forefathers,
And the sins that we commit every day,
And the sins we commit among the people,
That shame us among them.

God, my God,
Protect us and help us
And forget the sins of our forefathers
And forget our sins,
And take before You the saintly men and women
Who kept the faith at all times
And whose merit and good name You do not forget.

Gather us from all four corners
Of the earth,
And bring us again to the holy place,
Where Your Divine Presence
Shall rest among us.

Merciful God,
As I have today
Inflicted my body with pain,
And poured out my heart
Before Your Holy Name,
You have let us know
Through your prophet
That in the fourth month,
All our fears will turn to joy

In our time.
In God's name,

Amen, seloh.

FOUR GRAVESIDE TKHINES

I have translated only a selection of the graveyard prayers because of repetition in the content from one to the other. Women are traditionally excluded from saying *Kaddish*, the traditional prayer of mourning and these *tkhines* offer the comfort of a ready-made prayer, while requests for intercession evoke spiritual communication with the deceased.

 ### When the cemetery has not been visited for thirty days or more, she recites this blessing[16]

Beloved is God,
Our God, King of all the world,
Who created us with justice
And nourishes and sustains us
With justice.

And with justice He will restore us to life again.
Beloved is God, who restores the dead to life.

 ### She says this at the graveside

All you saintly men and women
Who lie buried here,
May it be granted,
Before God our Lord,
That your souls
And the souls of your friends
And the souls of your pupils
Shall rest in the great eternal rest,
At rest with the Holy Divine Presence,

And may they be beatified
In eternal beatitude.
In Your resting place.

For you walked in God's ways
And always united the people,
And showed His truth to them,
And the true path they should take.
And you put things to right
Between them
And led them to learn Torah.
Your reward is immense.
Your reward is immense.

God ,our God,
Creator of all creatures on earth,
Light of the heavens,
Your name is praised.
You are visible to Your saintly men.
You are beloved by Your saintly men,
And by Your holy angels.

Lord God, Almighty God.
May it happen soon in our times
That they are awakened from their internment
To see Your serene face,
Like the light from heaven.

And may the merit of good deeds
And the truth of the Torah
Protect me, and my husband,
And my children, and my household
In everything we do.

Give us good luck
In all our deeds,
And may our feet not stumble
In this world,
And may we sit at rest
In the next world
With saintly men and women,
Those who have been buried,

And now dwell
With the Holy Divine Presence.

God, our God,
Accept my prayer,
And turn with great mercy
To my prayer and my *tkhine*,
And reward me
As You reward the mild,
And bestow mercy and grace
On those who love You
For all eternity:
The saintly and pious men,
And the saintly and pious women.

Bring them out of their graves
And let them live forever,
And lead us into the great meadow
Where those who fear and love You
Are protected in safety,
And in eternal truth.

When she prostrates herself upon a grave she says this

God Almighty,
You created humankind on earth,
And gave them their souls from above,
And gave their bodies back to the earth,
Deep in this place
Where they are taken,
According to their dues.

Here lies buried
A saintly man / a saintly woman.[17]
Their souls are under the throne of Your holiness
Near to the Divine Presence,
And every day when the living are judged,
And nourishment is apportioned each to his own need,
I, poor woman, remember that I am earth,

And must again return to the earth,
As everyone must.

And all the days that I live,
I cannot know what is shouted out in Heaven.
Our sages say that which is shouted out in Heaven
Is unknown on earth.

Therefore, as you were my beloved friend in life,
Be my friend, and love me
And hear what we call out,
So that you may convey my prayer
Accurately to God, the Holy One,
So He will be merciful to me,
And to mine,
And to all the children of Israel,
And we may all be fed with honor,
And nourished with piety,
And not with levity.

And may we be protected from all evil occurrences,
And let us go along the righteous path.
And may we benefit from the merit
Of all saintly men and women,
All those who lie buried here,
Beloved friends, both male and female.
Ask our forefathers, Adam, Abraham, Isaac,
And Jacob, to be good mediators for us
As they were for Caleb
When he spread himself out on the grave in Hebron.

So you rest an eternal rest,
Among your friends, the saintly men and women,
Till the time when God, blessed be He,
Will let the dead fall from Heaven,
And make them live again,
And lead them, with great honor,
In their piety, to become worthy
To see the radiance of the Holy Divine Presence,
With all saintly men and women.

Amen.

This tkhine is said when she wishes to leave the graves

I ask You Almighty God
To allow me to benefit
From all Your merit
In the divine reckoning.
Greet me and bless me
And protect me
And light up my eyes
With Your Commandments
Favor me throughout my life
Grant me wealth and respect
And longevity,
Protection and blessings,
And help and trust,
And food and nourishment.

Wipe out our sins
With Your mercy and forgiveness,
And protect me and all my gender,
And all the people of Israel
From a bad name,
And from shame.

And let us look forward to redemption
When all Israel
All those who are worthy
Will gather together
Free of pain and suffering
In the time of the Messiah.

Protect us from harassment,
And from all bad luck
And from the court of Hell
And the suffering of this grave,
From illness and evil tales
And everything that undermines our goodness
And hardens our hearts.

And when the time comes
For me to die
Send a good angel
To initiate my soul
So that I may turn again with beatitude
To the Holy Place
Where I will be placed
Among the pious men and women
All those who have entered there
Since the world began:
Angels, prophets, and sages.

Quicken the time when they will rise up again
To live as You assured us they would
Through that joyful man, Daniel,
In God's name,

Amen.

 ## This is said at the grave of a husband or wife[18]

Beloved Lord of all the world,
Hear my prayer
And welcome it
With Your great mercy and grace.
And allow me to benefit
From the merit
Of all those saintly men
Who are known by their own holy names,
And through the merit of the Torah,
And for their good deeds.

So I have come to this grave
To praise Your holy name,
And prostrate myself upon the grave,
And beg You, Lord of all the world,
To give us long life
In happiness and wealth,
Honor and good fortune,
And good health.

And may we never lack
Food and nourishment,
And may we live long lives
In the Jewish way
Of Torah and good deeds.
And may I fulfill
The desire of my heart,
So when my soul
Is separated from my body,
It may come here to You,
And to the soul of this saintly man / saintly woman[19]
Who lies buried here,
And may it be worthy to rise again
With the souls of other saintly men
And saintly women of Israel.

Amen.

NEW YEAR AND DAY OF ATONEMENT TKHINES

 She says this when she kindles candles on the eve of New Year and eve of the Day of Atonement

May it be granted, God, our God,
God of Abraham, Isaac, and Jacob,
Sarah, Rebecca, Rachel, and Leah,
That for these two candles I have lit,
You will give me children
Who will learn the two Torahs,
The written Torah, and the oral Torah,
And may they love You and fear You,
And keep and learn the whole Torah,
All of Your Commandments,
To the very smallest.
Even a Commandment for how a man
Should walk his horse,

So he may practice what Moses
Put in the Torah,
And what our sages commanded,
May it be so.

Amen, Seloh.

 ## This is said after kindling the candles on the eves of New Year and Day of Atonement

Angel of Joy,
Peace and happiness to you.
There is a joy of joys
In your coming.

Bless us with joy
As He has commanded
And hear our joy.

The venerable King who commanded His people
And will be gracious to them
When they obey Him,
Hears this happiness,
And will bless us with joy.
And You shall make us worthy
To find grace and wisdom
In Your eyes
And in the eyes of everyone.

May we be forgiven
All our sins and misdeeds,
And may You make me worthy
To welcome the Sabbath
And the High Holy Days
With the slightest of sins
Of which You shall absolve me,
And my household,
And my offspring,
Now and forever.
And give us prosperity,

And cure us of all sickness,
And soothe our sighs
In our day.

And let me think of You with love and awe
For You are the King.

Notes

1. This is how I have translated the problematic phrase "*ikh, meyd, tokhter, dayner maid.*" See Chapter 4 for discussion.
2. Seven-branch candelabrum that stood in the Temple in Jerusalem.
3. Fulfilling requirements of Jewish law.
4. Not fulfilling requirements of Jewish law.
5. Spiritual intensity; deep concentration.
6. When the *khales* (Sabbath loaves) are prepared on the eve of Sabbath, a portion is set aside as a symbol of the offering given to the Priest in the ancient Temple in Jerusalem.
7. This blessing appears in Hebrew before the Yiddish *tkhine* begins.
8. Igres (Igrat daughter of Mahalath), with Lilith, Naamah, and Mahalath, is one of the four queens of the Demons. She is sent out to do harm on the nights preceding Sabbaths and Wednesdays (see, for example, Zech. 5:5-11).
9. The time of purification when all signs of menstruation have ended for the month, prior to the required visit to the ritual bath (*mikve*) for a woman to cleanse herself before resuming sexual relations with her husband.
10. Jewish Law.
11. The evil inclination.
12. The fast that commemorates the siege of Jerusalem.
13. King of Persia from 485 B.C., known also as Xerxes I.
14. The uncle of Esther.
15. The fast that commemorates the breaching of the walls of Jerusalem in the first Temple period.
16. This prayer is extracted from a longer Hebrew prayer that appears in the *Sider.*
17. Insert whichever is appropriate, either "saintly man," "saintly woman" or if buried together, "saintly man and woman."
18. This is the only tkhine in the *Seyder Tkhines* that may be said by either a woman or a man. A man would say this in order to ask his dead wife to intercede with God on his behalf.
19. Whichever is appropriate.

Book of Tkhines for a Pregnant Woman

A prayer book for an unknown, pregnant woman. From a manuscript written in Germany in the seventeenth century.

There is no evidence to suggest that this book has ever before been printed or had more than one reader.

TKHINES

Whoever recites this new tkhine *every day with* kavone *and with crying and wailing, and who takes her sins to heart will be sure of a share in the world to come.*

It is a harsh lesson for all who fear God that in their minds and hearts they must accept that they will die. So, mercifully, they must remember that they should sin no more and should address themselves like this:

 Tkhine One

Part I

My heart, my heart,
Do you not know

185

That you were created to die,
And return again to the earth?

Since the first moment you entered the world
Why have you not thought about
The end of your life?
You must know full well
That in this world
You are as a shadow on a wall,
Like rain on the wind,
Like a puff of smoke
That quickly disperses.

Your days have a measure,
And your life has a reckoning,
And each and every day
Drops away, leaving you
Closer to death and to your grave,
Into which you will fly
Not on wings, but carried by others.

So why do you not consider
Yourself to be a sinner?
Why do you not remember
That you are ash and earth?
Why do you not think about
Your bitter death,
When you and your senses
Will be lost?

On that day your tongue
Will cleave to your palate.
It is a day when you will be carried
By your elbows and thrown underground,
And all your deeds will be recalled,
And like the dew
You will evaporate,
But your fire will not be extinguished.

It is the day on which the book is opened
And you will see your sins measured.
A toll of good and bad deeds

Will be calculated,
And there will be a goblet
In God's hands,
From which you must drink,
And you will eat the fruits of your works
And answer for what you have done.

And if you should die like an animal
And make no reckoning,
You will go from here
Not as you should,
But to a place in the darkness
Of the shadow of death
Where death is bitter.

And fear and anxiety
Will engulf you,
And you will be covered with shame,
And your body will be earth and worms,
And sulphur and pitch will be spread on you
And set on fire,
So nothing of you
Will remain.

God Almighty, answer me here.
My body and soul are in Your hands.
You are praised,
And Your Holy Name is praised.

Lord of all the world,
I am a humble being
Who comes before You.
May my prayer fly to You,
And may You grant mercy
From Your holy seat of judgment,
And when the time comes
For You to claim me from this world,
Take my soul
So that Satan shall not have it,
And let no evil spirits be of hindrance
From today until the day I die,

May I observe the Commandments
That are commanded to be done,
And those which are forbidden to be done.

The sins of which I am guilty
May, God forbid, condemn me to die within the year
Such a death as the Court of Law decrees,
For the sages declared that man
Should not transgress from the Commandments.

May my soul be virtuous and pure
When it leaves me,
So I may go to Paradise
Among the holy souls of other saintly men and women,
And with the souls of our forefathers,
Abraham, Isaac, and Jacob,
In the place that I desire.

And, God forbid, if Satan comes to tell
That I have, God forbid, not observed
Even one of Your Commandments
That You commanded in Your beloved Torah,
Heaven forbid, and God forbid, that I should deny
Your Torah, and Your Holy Name,
For from the very moment when a person dies,
Great fear and anxiety descend upon him.
He is lost and does not know what he says.
But such is death.

I make confession with all my senses,
With my will and my reason,
And implore that whatever I, God forbid,
May say, that is not correct,
Let it become null and void,
Like a broken skull.

And I declare that the Holy One, Blessed be He,
Is true and one over the whole world,
And the Torah of Moses our teacher,
May his soul rest in peace,
Is true, and You are one alone,
And there is no one above You.

You always were, and will remain forever,
God, the one King who rules,
And will rule eternally,

Amen. Seloh.[1]

The following lines appear in Hebrew.

God, He is the God[2]
God, He is the true God
And His Torah is true
And Moses the prophet is true
The blessed name of His glorious kingdom is true.

After that, say Psalm 21, Psalm 87, Psalm 4, and Psalm 120 with great kavone.

Part II

I confess to You, God my God,
And God of my forefathers,
For I have sinned and transgressed before you.
I acknowledge my sins
And that the healing is in Your hands.

I beg that You, God,
Will choose to heal me
Body and soul
Completely
For You are God
The merciful healer.

You are praised by everyone
You are right in everything
And if it is judged to be the time for me to die
I beg You that in death
I shall atone for all the sins
And misdeeds and errors
Of which I am guilty before You:
Those that were committed in my youth,
In middle age, or in my old age.

Whether they were committed unknowingly

Or with good intention,
Let them be known and answered before You.
My deeds cannot be concealed from You,
God my God,
They are the sins I have committed
From the day I entered the world
Until today.

It is as if my soul,
The one within this body,
Had entered another body.
So my God, it is for You to help,
For in Your Holy Name
Is our hope, dear God,
That you will forgive.

So I beg you to forgive us
We poor human sinners,
For You are my God,
My King and Merciful Redeemer.

Part III

I beg You God,
Creator of the whole world,
You created me and You raised me
And fed me from the day
That I entered the world
Until today.

And I confess to You that I have sinned
And am guilty of transgressions,
Many thousands of sins.
Woe is me that I have sinned so greatly.

And You are full of mercy,
As it says in our Holy Torah,
One God, a merciful Lord, slow to anger,
Full of grace,
Do not bring me low into the depths of Hell,
Because of my great sins, Beloved God.

Only You are able to forgive,
And lead the world with mercy.
And with Your compassion.
You created repentance
When You created the world,
So You know how Your people thank You
Who are sinners from their youth.

You have created repentance
To provide a cure for fear.
Therefore I come as a sinner
Who is full of sin
Which I send in flight to You.
Forgive my sins and erase my guilt
From this day forth.

Since You created the world,
You have forgiven all those
Who turn to You in repentance.
Therefore, beloved God
Enfold my poor body and soul
In mercy and compassion
And do not calculate my evil deeds in haste
But only with mercy.
And may You cast all my sins
Into the depths
So they disappear forever.

How should I prepare myself for Your Holy *Shkhine*?
How should I approach Your Holy Name
To ask You to pardon the sins
That I have committed for so long
And have repeated so often?
May You grant Your forgiveness of these sins,
For I am a poor weak human
Who acknowledges before You, God my God,
And God of my forefathers,
That I have sinned and erred and strayed.

Do not rush to judge me for my quick words
For now, my God, and for everything,

I turn to You in a rush of remorse,
Terrified, and ashamed of my deeds,
Not knowing how I can lift my face to You.

And if only You will answer my prayer
And absolve me of my sins
I ask You God
Just as a slave would ask a Lord
Or a serving maid their mistress or master,
That I, poor sinner,
Turn my eyes to You, my Lord,
Full of weeping
And cry out to You
So You may forgive me.

So I cry hidden away in my concealment
And sigh inconsolably where I lie
Full of sin
And I approach You
With a broken heart
And in despair.

God my God
Who opens His hand to all penitents
And helps them to cleanse themselves
Of their sins,
I ask You to open
Your beloved, holy hand to me
And pardon me
Through my repentance
And my prayer.

And may a righteous mediator
Come before Your Holy Name
To plead on my behalf .
And if there is, heaven forbid, no mediator for me,
Make a space for me under Your Holy Throne of Mercy
As You did for King Menassah[3]
When he called out to You in his pain and prayed
And You helped him out of his pain.

Your help for a true penitent

Has reassured us that You would also help us.
And it is written in Your beloved Torah
That you should make supplication to your God
And apply yourself with all your heart.

Praised is He, the Holy Name,
Who said to the prophet:
Say to Israel, that I, God, say
That I do not desire the death of the evil
For if they repent of their sins
And forsake their evil ways
Then they shall live.

His standing in heaven and His words are true
And His beloved words exist in heaven
And His words are true
And His beloved words exist forever
And shall remain true for me.

Through Your beloved words
May You pardon those sins
Of which I am guilty,
The sins of my youth,
And of my old age,
With the deeds or thoughts
In another incarnation.[4]

May we, beloved, one and only God,
Be forgiven,
And when the time is right
For my departure from this world,
When I must turn toward You,
Then I will be prepared for my death
With the love of the Merciful Lord
For You are loved at all times.

To You, God my God,
God of my forefathers,
God of my body, and my soul,
May You grant, God my God,
And God of my forefathers,
That my death shall atone for all my sins,

Be they small or large.

And may my soul
Be received in happiness
When You take it from me,
And on the day on which I pass on,
May You grant my going,
And send me merciful angels
Who will not oppose me,
But who will take me in happiness
So that I go directly to Paradise
Where I shall sit among
All the saintly men and women,
And pious men and women.

And may I be beatified
In the purity of the Holy Divine Presence,
And may I rest in peace and contentment,
And may this be my concealment
And dwelling place
Under the shadow of Your wing.

Sustain me
And hear my prayer,
And beloved, one and only God,
Help me, and do not turn a deaf ear
To my cry, for You are the Lord of Justice
Who reassures me.

May You accept
The speech of my mouth
And the thoughts of my heart,
For You are my Creator
And my Redeemer
For all eternity,

Amen, Seloh.

These lines follow in Hebrew:

I long for Your salvation, God.[5] In Your hand I shall entrust my spirit. You redeemed me God, God of Truth.[6] I lie down, I won't be scared. My sleep is pleasant. I will in righteousness see Your face.

*I will be satisfied when awakening from Your slumber.[7] God, He is
God. Hear O Israel, the Lord our God, the Lord is One. Blessed is
the Name of his glorious kingdom for all eternity.[8]*

Then follows in Hebrew, the blessing of the Priests (*Cohanim*).

 Tkhine Two

This tkhine should be said by a woman every morning with kavone, so
the Blessed Name [God] will surely accept her prayer and give good
luck and blessings to her husband in all he does, and protect them both.

> I make a plea to You, Lord of all the world,
> God, the one and only God in the whole world,
> No one can be helped without Your help.
> You are God over all lords.
> There is no other God.
> You alone are King over all kings,
> A merciful King who created heaven and earth,
> And all creatures,
> And You have given all of them
> Food from Your gentle hand,
> With Your mercy.
> Even the worms in the earth are fed
> By Your trusted hand.
>
> And You created mankind with Your wisdom,
> And You commanded man
> Not to eat from the Tree of Knowledge,
> And when he did,
> The King of the whole world
> Punished him severely and painfully
> And we must bear this punishment always.
>
> So merciful Father,
> We accept Your punishment
> Whenever you send it to us,
> And bear it with great love,
> For You punish no one without reason,
> For we are sinful

And we deserve Your punishment.
You are full of mercy when You punish mankind
And they must earn their bread with pain and sweat.

So I come before You, a poor sinner
To beg God Almighty, King of the whole world,
Helper over all helpers,
I beg You, merciful God,
To protect my husband
From all evil,
And guide him in his ways,
And ensure that he earns his living with honor
So we may never need the help of another,
Or suffer the shame of being fed by others.
May we be fed only from Your gentle hand
At all times,
And may You show us mercy
As You did our forefathers,
Through the hand of Moses our teacher.

May my husband journey on safe paths,
And may You send angels to accompany him
Along the route on which he travels,
As You protected Jacob our forefather,
May his soul rest in peace.
And may his every step
Be shielded from all evil
Wherever he goes.

And may he return in good health
To his beloved wife and children,
To a peaceful and joyous home.
And may the merit of the children
Support them all,
And cleanse them from their transgressions.

Lord of all the World,
If my husband has sinned,
And You have, God forbid, decided
That he should perish on his journey,
I beg You, Almighty God, Merciful God,

Do not judge him from a legal standpoint,
But in a merciful manner.

You are a merciful Father over Your children, Israel,
So let him not be placed in danger
When he travels on his journey.
And let us profit from the merit of our fathers,
And the merit of our children,
Who are quickly cleansed from sin.

May we, God forbid, not be separated and scattered,
And let us grow old in honor,
And live out our time in happiness and strength,
With our hearts worshipping You,
So that we may know Your beloved face.

Strengthen the hearts of my children
So they, God forbid,
Do not stray from Your Commandments
Like our enemies, from whom we may seek revenge.
Banish all thoughts of evil and hatred,
So that the evil inclination may be confronted
And turned away
And their hearts may turn to goodness.

I beg You, God, our God,
Who is merciful Father over Your children, Israel,
I beg You, merciful Father, be merciful to me,
And to my beloved husband,
Like a merciful father over his child,
And accept this prayer from me, a sinner,
As I have prayed to You.

Set aside my accusers
Who were created from my sins
And let my good defenders
Who were created from my good deeds
Speak to You.

And send us the Angel of the Messiah
In our days,
So we may be redeemed

And released from the heavy yoke of exile.

We praise You, God
Who hears the prayers of Your people, Israel.

Amen, Seloh.

 ## Tkhine Three

A beautiful tkhine to say every day

In the name of the God of Israel,
Who sits with the cherubim,
In the name of God,
Be merciful and hear
With grace and compassion
This prayer
That I say before You.

God, my God, I appeal to You in earnest,
With all my heart,
Hear me, and forgive the sins
That I have committed.

Have mercy, King who sits
Among the cherubim,
King who sits on the Seat of Mercy,
Forgive my sins,
Banish my sorrow,
And hear the prayer that I make to You,
And deliver me in joy and gladness.

Almighty God,
Hear me and forgive my sins,
So I may praise Your Holy Name.
Merciful Saint who sits on the Seat of Mercy,
Hear me and forgive my sins,
Redeem me,
Save me from my sinfulness
As only You can.

Loving God, redeem and hear me,
As You redeemed and heard our forefathers.
God, let my enemies not shame me while I live.
Banish my sorrows in Your Name.
You are all grace and mercy.

And let my prayer be answered,
As Hannah's prayer was answered.
And do not let my prayer go astray.
Be merciful to me.
I call out to You faithfully every day.
You are all mercy and grace.
You are a merciful God every day,
Every hour and every morning
To the prayers of Israel.

Therefore, I beg You, Almighty God,
Do not let my enemies take revenge,
Or bring disgrace upon me while I live.
And may You accept my prayer
In the Name of the Holy Words,
And may my enemies not stand before You
When I call out to You.

King of Kings, be my defender.
You know my sorrow and my grief.
You are the adjudicator of the Judgment,
And it is not fitting to speak
Of the benevolence shown by You.
You are the Lord and Father
Who is merciful over Your children.
Over widows and orphans,
You are God,
And there is none higher.

You provide my needs,
You give me life,
You send a cure for my illness,
And heal my wounds.
How could I not pray to You?

Give me strength and might,
So I may present my petitions
Before the greatest of all lords.
And I beg Your Holy Name to answer my prayer,
As You answered the prayers of Sarah, Rebecca, Rachel, and
    Leah,
And the prayers of our forefathers.

And may I live out my years with all Israel,
Free of the help of others,
Without sin and shame,
Without suffering and without imprisonment.
And may I die in my bed when my time comes,
And may I be worthy to dwell
With my forefathers
In Paradise.

Amen.

 Tkhine Four

How to pray for an easy livelihood

God, my God, and God of my forefathers,
May You grant food, blessed and sure,
For the nourishment of my household,
And for the nourishment of Your people, Israel
As a sweet gift from Your hands.
So I may never deprive any man,
Of their gift from Your full and holy hands,
Those blessed hands.

And may my livelihood
And my luck in business
Be blessed so I live and do not die.
And may I live to help others do good.
And may many people be nourished through my efforts,
Just as You provided for our forefathers
When they came out of Egypt.
You gave them their food without labor or toil,

And You protected them from all evil,
And sustained them,
And blessed them.
Your blessing is a righteous blessing.
You helped with Your gifts and Your mercy
As the verse says:
All eyes look to You in hope,
And You give them their food in their time.
You open Your hand and bless all Creation.

May their holy souls and their pure souls
Pray to God for me
And may He bestow good fortune upon me.
So I find favor in His eyes
And in the eyes of His people,
So I may serve God with all my heart,
All of my days,
And do much good for many people.

And may I be taken from the world
With a good name and in a good hour,
And at a great age.
And may I have my share with the saints
In the Garden of Eden.

Amen and amen.

 The prayer that a pregnant woman should say when she wishes for an easy labor

May it be Your will, God, my God,
And God of my forefathers,
To ease the suffering of my pregnancy,
And increase my strength
Every day of my pregnancy,
So I do not weaken.

And strengthen my baby
Against all worldly troubles,
And protect me from the curse of Eve:

"You shall bear children with sorrow."

And may my pregnancy
Run its full course,
And may my labor not begin
Before its time,
And may my baby enter
The air of this world
Quickly and easily,
Without injury to myself or to my baby.

And may it be born at a good hour,
And a lucky hour, to live in joy.
And may it have good health and grace,
And honor and riches,
And not be an exile from Your land.
And may You reckon his days in full complement.

And may my husband and I always
Lead a good life in Your service,
According to the teachings of Your holy Torah.
And may neither I, nor my baby be harmed,
And may my baby not be without limbs,
Without flesh or without organs,
And may my body receive no injury.

Increase my strength,
And strengthen my mood
And my bones,
For as the verse says:
God will heal your body
And refresh your bones.

I wish to be strengthened by God's healing,
So I pray that You will answer me, God, my God.
And I wish to be happy with God's help.
Protect me, God, my God,
Hurry to my aid, hurry to help me,
God, my Helper.
Hear my voice, be merciful, and answer me
Through the righteousness and the learning
Of our holy forefathers

And their good deeds.
And may all the world invoke their love.

And bless me, and let my seed live,
And protect me from death and miscarriage,
And from all illness and pain,
And bless me as You promised us
In Your holy Torah,
Through the hand of Moses Your servant.
As the verse says:
And He will love you and bless you
And will bless the fruit in your belly.

May You bless me and answer me,
And lengthen my days
With sweetness, as the verse says:
Long days will I give you,
And I will show you my help.

Amen and amen.

 A delightful tkhine for a pregnant woman
to say

Part I

Lord of the world, my God,
I humbly beg You, with a broken heart,
And with my weak body,
To confirm my baby in Torah,
As a person of honor and riches.

I beg You, Lord of the whole world
Do not diminish my honor
When You give me a child,
So it may have honor and riches,
And be honored by You,
For it is written in Your holy Torah
That we should multiply and people Your holy Torah
To learn and carry out Your Commandments.

So may the blessing of Abraham,
Isaac, and Jacob be confirmed
As You promised.
Oh, Lord of the Universe
Accept my tears,
So they may not be locked away forever.
Hear my weeping, so I may be worthy,
Like Hannah, the saintly woman,
To have a son, as she had her son,
The prophet Samuel.

I beg You to bestow me with honor
So I may be worthy to have a son,
A talmudic scholar.
And I beg You, merciful God, to make kosher
The seed of all the daughters of Israel,
That come into the world.

And may I give birth to a strong and tall man,
Fine of figure,
To honor Your Divine Presence.
And may he be a rich man, a talmudic scholar,
A strong and handsome man, and tall.

I beg You, merciful God
Give me a son, a talmudic scholar,
Or a daughter who may marry a talmudic scholar,
For to be the wife of a talmudic scholar is
As good as being a talmudic scholar.

I beg You, loving God of truth,
Whose Name lives for ever,
Answer me, forgive my sins,
And accept my prayer.
Hear those who call out to You,
Hear them and answer them.

Holy God, loving God,
Your true Name is eternal.
I beg You to answer this plea
That comes from the bottom of my heart,
And may my prayer be answered.

Be merciful to me,
So I may be worthy to bear a kosher child,
Who will have no blemish,
And no deformity.
And may You put good words into his mouth,
The words of Your beloved Torah,
So that he will know how to carry out
Your Commandments,
And to keep all 613 that You commanded
On Mount Sinai.

And endow him with a fine face and good hearing,
And straight limbs, both arms and legs.
And may he soar like an eagle,
And be strong as a lion,
And run like a deer,
To fulfill Your beloved Commandments,
The Torah, and all good deeds.

Beloved one and only God of all creatures,
I beg You to honor me and be merciful to me,
And to heal me like a doctor.
But doctors are only mortals.
When they heal,
They combine healing with payment,
But they are not sure
Whether or not their cure will work.
And those they have helped
May need to return to them, uncured.
But Your healing is eternal,
And the sick do not need a second visit.

Therefore, beloved Lord God,
Heal me with Your healing.
You know the people that You created.
Be merciful over me,
And open my womb in virtue,
So I may give birth to a talmudic scholar.

And may my seed smell sweetly,
And not be spoiled,

And not go unblessed,
But blossom into fulfillment
Just as good, rich earth
Yields its grain from a fine crop.

May my seed also grow to praise the Blessed Name,
And to make Your Name holy,
And to worship You alone,
Always and forever,

Amen.

Part II

And in supplication,
Archangels Michael, Gabriel, and Raphael,
I beg you as your servant to put my case
To the Holy One, Blessed be He,
So my prayer may be answered
And I may be worthy to bear beautiful children,
Of fine figure and full of grace in God's eyes,
And in the eyes of the people.

And may my prayer be accepted by You
As once the priests made sacrifice in the Temple.
May our lives now be reckoned like the sacrifice
So we might receive Your forgiveness,
And may my words be accepted like the blessed spices.
And may You accept our prayers,
And may You give me beautiful, fair children,
Tall and strong,
To be your servants.

Amen.

Part III

Raise your eyes to the heavens and say this:

I stand before You, God, my God
God on high, You are the Lord of the whole world,

And Your kingdom is great and strong,
And You know the thoughts that Your people
Have in their hearts.

I stand before You
And ask from the bottom of my heart,
To be forgiven and pardoned by everyone
For everything that I have done
Either by word or by deed.
For I forgive,
I forgive everyone their sins,
Be they man or woman,
Young or old.

So I beg You, mighty God on high,
You are forgiveness and pardon,
And before You the whole world trembles,
And may all whom You have created forgive me.
At this time
As I call out to You.

May my prayer come before You
And may You answer it
As You answer the prayers
Of all saintly men and saintly women.
And may You lock up the mouths of my accusers
Who would speak ill of me before You.

Amen. Seloh.

Part IV

God, God of Israel, who sits with the cherubim,
King, King of kings,
And Ark of arks,
Blessed is the Name of His glorious kingdom for all
   eternity[9]

I beg You, God,
You, who created the whole world,
And all Creation.

You are God, and there is no other,
You reassure me day and night.

And all the highest angels in heaven, on earth,
And on the mountains, tremble at Your beloved Name.
And all are frightened and tremble at Your mighty Name.
You are mighty and Your great wonder is mighty.
Who can tell of it?

And even when our mouths are full,
We still cannot find the words to tell one part of Your
    wonder.
And we are silenced by all Your wonder,
And You have performed great wonders for our forefathers,
And every day You do more
Than we can ever express.

Part V

Lord of the World, Master of Mercy,
I beg You, highest of Lords,
Who is merciful to all
Those You have created,
From the smallest to the greatest,
And who nourishes them with Your great mercy,
And with Your immense grace,
So I beg You, my God, and God of my forefathers
Be merciful to me,
And to the fruit I carry in my body,.

And may You overlook the sins and misdeeds
Of my youth and of my adulthood,
And forgive all the sins
That I confess to You
With all my heart.

Say with great kavone

Master of Forgiveness,
I come to You to call out for Your help,
And I call out to You from the depths

Of my burdened heart that weighs heavily in me.
May You help me and the fruit in my body,
As only You can help
A child in its mother's body.
As King David, may he rest in peace, said,

The next two lines appear in Hebrew

I thank you for I am awesomely, wondrously fashioned.
Wondrous are Your works and my soul knows it well.[10]

I beg You, God, my God,
To let me benefit from the merit of
Abraham, Isaac, and Jacob,
And Sarah, Rebecca, Rachel, and Leah,
And the merit of all saintly men and women
Since the beginning of the creation of the world.

May their merit benefit me,
And may You send the holy angels
To protect me and the child in my body.
Beloved Lord God, I beg for mercy.
May You be merciful to me,
And may You give strength and energy
To me and to my child.

Part VI

God of Hosts
I call out to You
To protect me and my child,
And when it comes to the time
When my child shall be brought into the world,
May You protect me, mighty God
And powerful God,
And awesome God.

I place myself and my child into Your hands,
As You hold the key to these things.
No one can override the highest angel in Heaven,
And in Your hands is great mercy and grace,

Which You bestow on a child
As it is born into this world

Therefore I beg You, God on high, God of mercy,
In Your great mercy is my assurance of a safe birth.
For help is Yours
As You are named God Full of Mercy
And may I live in Your great mercy and grace,
So I may bear my child into the world
Without pain, like the saintly women
Who were not inscribed as Eve
So they did not need to suffer in pain.

Lord of the whole world, God on high.
Great and awesome God,
Who can praise You enough?
Who can know how to speak
Of the great strength that You give to me?
I beg You, God on high,
Let my prayer be accepted by You,
As You accepted the holy sacrifices
That were brought every day
To the Altar.

And may my prayer be accepted
As You accepted the prayer of Hannah the prophetess,
When she was blessed with her fruit.
You heard her prayer
And she gave birth to the prophet Samuel.
So may my prayer
Which I send to You
From the bottom of my heart,
Come before You,
And may You answer my call
With great mercy and compassion.

And I beg You, God on High,
And God of my forefathers,
Accept my prayer.

Amen. Seloh.

Part VII

Lord of the world, I begin to speak,
I beg without forgiveness,
My tongue is silenced by the enormity
Of the sins I have committed
That remain unconfessed,
And lie heavily upon me,
Like the harshest sins that are no longer remembered.

There are so many that my mouth cannot speak of them all
And my tongue cannot search them out.
They have covered me from head to foot
So I cannot free them
From my trembling body,
And it frightens me greatly.

So I beg You for Your mercy,
For God does not desire that a sinner shall die a sinner,
Not until they have repented with all their heart
And have shown remorse for their sins
For You wish to be merciful and accept their repentance.

This reassures me
And so I beg You, God, to accept this prayer
From one who repents to You with all her heart,
And may You take into account
My good deeds with Your great mercy.
I beg You to accept this prayer that I offer You.

Lord of all the world,
I have sinned before You by day and by night,
When lying down and when I rise,
My body is full of sin.

I am ashamed to come before You
In my stained garments,
And my heart is embittered
For when I leave this world
And stand before You
I will remember that I corrupted my own body
With pleasures that lasted

No longer than the blink of an eye,
And now my soul is corrupted for ever,
And shall be bound in red because of the punishing
    angels[11]
Who were created because of the sin of man.

Almighty God, how was I so foolish?
How can the Blessed Name show me mercy
When He has chosen me to rule over cows
And over all animals,
And all things on the earth,
 And yet I, foolish woman that I am,
Cannot rule over my own body,
But have sinned and transgressed many times
And have been worse than a cow or an ox
Or a donkey.

I am a sinner who has chosen evil over good,
And have not thought about bitter death and how I must
    suffer,
Therefore I beg You, Almighty God,
Create in me a new heart,
Remove the stains from my tainted heart,
Banish the evil inclination,
And forgive my foolishness,
For my body is only ashes and earth.

When the Blessed Name takes my soul
And when my body is returned to the earth,
And my limbs are full of fear,
And my heart is consumed with weeping and shouting,
If I, Heaven forbid, do not repent
Of all the transgressions of my lifetime,
May the Blessed Name stand by me,
So I may serve His glorious Name.
And sin no more.

Part VIII

And so I beg You to be merciful

God on high in Heaven.
I beg You for mercy when You assess my service
And my deeds
Woe to me, woe to my soul,
How will it be
When You look to me for purity and find none.
I put my trust in Your mercy
And hope You will accept my wholehearted repentance
Which I shout out, weeping and fasting
And giving charity.

May my tears wash away my sins,
And may my fasting be accepted by You
In place of the Temple sacrifices,
And if the evil inclination threatens to take me over
And forces me to sin against my will,
I will do my utmost to protect myself.
And may You protect me from the evil inclination
And prevent him from leading me astray
So I never sin again.

Almighty God, Highest Lord,
You are one in the whole world.
There is no other God but You.
You, who gave me my body and soul,
May You turn my sins to merit,
And protect me from the evil inclination,
And may You instill in me the good inclination,
And remove all those things that hinder my repentance.
And may I pass before You into eternity.

Amen. Seloh.

 This tkhine should be said when fasting, with weeping and sighing

May my tears wash away
My worst troubles,
And may my repentance
Strike away Your anger

213

When You judge me.

Accept my table
As a substitute
For the holy sacrificial Altar.

And let the pot
That I have not placed
On the coal fire.[12]
Be the fire
On the sacrificial Altar.

And let the listlessness
Of my blood through fasting,
Be the sacrificial blood
That was dashed on the horns
Of the Altar.

And let my shrinking flesh
Be the fat
That was poured
Onto the Altar.

And let the sound
Of my weeping
Be the song
That the Levites sang
At the offering.

And let the taste of hunger
In my mouth
Be the scent
Of incense.

And let the weakness
Of my limbs
Be a substitute
For the gasping
Of the sacrifice.

And let my broken heart
Tear to shreds
All evil decrees,

And let my bath
That I avoid today [13]
Represent the washing of the Priests
In the Temple.

And in my turning to You,
May You turn to me,
And to all Israel.

Amen.

Notes

1. Appears at the end of verses in Psalms. Thought to be a musical direction.
2. These lines appear in Hebrew. The words for "God" are highly embellished by the scribe.
3. Despotic king, son of Hezekia, who ruled Judah for fifty-five years from 687 B.C.E. He lost his kingdom for ignoring God's words, but then humbled himself, repented, and was pardoned by God who restored his kingdom to him.
4. The word *gilgul* is used. According to Jewish folklore, this is the being into which the soul of a dead person passes to continue life and atone for sins committed in the previous incarnation.
5. Gen. (Breyshis) 49.18.
6. Ps. 31:6.
7. Ps. 17:15.
8. These are the first two lines of the *Shema* prayer, recited every morning as a requirement of the Torah. The prayer is an acceptance of God's absolute sovereignty.
9. This is the second line of the *Shema* prayer. The line is recited silently.
10. Ps. 139:14. This passage is in Hebrew.
11. Angels who inflict pain on those in their graves who are evil or have not repented.
12. No fire would be lit and no cooking carried out during the hours of the fast. Both are prohibited.
13. Bathing is prohibited during the hours of the fast.

Single Prayers and Songs in Tkhine Language

This section presents to the twenty-first-century reader, six women who are virtually unknown today, whose works were published around 350 years ago in Yiddish. I have included among them a male author, Yankev ben Elyohu, because of his vivid, though disparaging depiction of women as unredeemable corrupters.

Of the seven works that follow, two are entitled *Tkhine*, one *Tfile*, and four *Lid*. They share a common vocabulary and style in the Yiddish originals, though the *lider* are in rhyme and are instructed to be sung, while the *tkhines* are in prose and are to be spoken. The *tfile* is to be spoken but is composed in rhyme, crossing the boundaries of prayer and song. Even though these works bear the names of authors, they are not personal expressions in an individual voice, but rather communal hymns or devotions based on universal religious precepts.

 Sabbath prayer

From the booklet of Khane Kats

Both this and the next prayer appear in a booklet of four works printed under the name of Khane Kats.

Beloved God,
Creator of all souls,
I wish to praise You,
And thank You,
For choosing us
As Your beloved people.

You are our God,
Who created Heaven and earth,
And gave us the holy Sabbath.
Be merciful to us.

We observe and honor
This beloved, holy Sabbath,
With fine meats,
And good food to eat
That we have prepared,
And sweet drinks to drink,
And all delights
To perform.

May our husbands and children
Be worthy with us,
To live long
In honor and plenty.

On the beloved holy Sabbath,
We glimpse Paradise.
May we be worthy
To be in this world,
And in the next.

And may the beloved Messiah
Take us by the right hand
And lead us into the Holy Land.

Amen.

 Ma Toyvu (How good)

Ma Toyvu is a Hebrew prayer recited by individuals on entering the
synagogue as they stand and pray silently for a few moments. It is

composed of a number of different verses from Ps.5:8, 26:8, and 69:14 and appears at the beginning of the Hebrew *Sider* and also in Hebrew in many editions of the *Seyder Tkhines*. This is an adaptation of the prayer into *tkhine loshn* from Khane Kats's booklet.

I have provided a direct translation of the original Hebrew so that a comparison can be made between this and Khane's version which, although based on the original, has become something quite different and typical of its time.

A translation of the original Hebrew prayer

> How good are your tents, Jacob, your dwellings, Israel
> And through your great mercy, I may enter your house.
> And in awe of You, I will prostrate myself toward Your
>   Holy Sanctuary.
> God, I love the house where You dwell and the place
>   which is a shrine to Your glory
> May my prayer to You, God, be at an opportune time.
> God in Your great mercy answer me with the truth of Your
>   salvation.

Khane's adaptation

> How very good are Your tents, Jacob, Your resting place
>   Israel
> And God, with Your great mercy,
> Let the merit of Abraham our Father,
> May he rest in peace,
> Be of benefit to me.

> I come into Your house
> Wishing to bow down to the sanctuary of Your holiness.
> Beloved Father, let the merit of Isaac
> Who was bound with holiness on Mount Moriah,
> Be of benefit to me.

> God, in Your wonder,
> Let the merit of Jacob,
> And the way in which he spoke
> Of the great wonder of that place,
> Be of benefit to me.

219

Master of the Universe,
I enter Your house to pray to Your holiness.
I beg You to allow the merit of our Patriarchs
To benefit me.

May my prayer to You, God,
Come at an opportune time.
God in Your great mercy answer me
With the certainty of Your salvation.
Grant that through Your angels
My prayer shall be a crown on Your head.

I beseech You God,
Do not delay in answering my prayer,
And pay no heed to my guilt,
Or the evil thoughts that I have had,
So that my prayer may come
Before Your beloved, holy Name.

God my God,
Stretch out Your hand from under Your wing
So that Your angels,
Those who are called cherubim,
May receive my prayer.

In the shadow of your wing
May You shield and protect my prayer from all accusers
And give me strength to drive away the same.
And purify my body and my soul from all my sins
So I may straighten out all my crooked deeds,
And be worthy to come in purity
Before Your beloved Name.

Amen.

 Simkhes Toyre song

Rivke Tikiner

This next work is a joyous communal song to be sung in synagogue over the Torah scroll on the festival of Simkhes Toyre.[1] At the end of each line comes the exultant response of "Hallelujah!" Its intention for performance over the Torah scroll, which would be found in the main body of the synagogue, indicates that it might have been sung by the whole congregation, but it is also possible that it was sung only by women sitting in their own part of the synagogue[2] from where they could have glimpsed the Torah scroll. There were female prayer leaders, known as *firzogerins* (literally, speech leaders), who led women in prayer. The structure of this song suggests that each line could have been read out loud by the *firzogerin* followed by a response of "Hallelujah" from the rest of the women. There are two known extant editions of this song, both thought to have been published in Prague in the seventeenth century. One appears in a small book together with two other songs, written not by Rivke, but by a Yankev ben Elyohu whose own song is translated below.

References to God change back and forth from the second person, "You" to the third person "He," and some of the lines are written as the voice of God, in the first person, "I."

Our God is one. You are my God:	Hallelujah!
Who created me, body and soul:	Hallelujah!
You created Heaven and earth:	Hallelujah!
We will praise You forever:	Hallelujah!
You always were and always will be:	Hallelujah!
You created us all:	Hallelujah!
All things are of Your making:	Hallelujah!
We praise You day and night:	Hallelujah!
You can relieve our suffering and pain:	Hallelujah!
Therefore we praise You alone:	Hallelujah!
Your Commandments are pure and true:	Hallelujah!
For this, Oh God, we thank You:	Hallelujah!
You are always standing by:	Hallelujah!
You will save us from damnation:	Hallelujah!
You are our consolation:	Hallelujah!
You promised us life:	Hallelujah!
So our praise for You is endless:	Hallelujah!
Those who incur Your wrath:	Hallelujah!
Must languish in Hell forever:	Hallelujah!

221

Like wax in the flames:	Hallelujah!
For nothing can defeat You:	Hallelujah!
You live forever on Your heavenly throne:	Hallelujah!
You reward the pious with concealment:	Hallelujah!
You are mighty, our God alone:	Hallelujah!
You help all those who pray to You:	Hallelujah!
There is no other God but You:	Hallelujah!
Therefore Heaven and earth will go on forever:	Hallelujah!
The sparkle of precious gems is dull compared to Your light:	Hallelujah!
You conceal this light in eternity:	Hallelujah!
You illuminate Your friends in the Kingdom of Heaven:	Hallelujah!
Lead us to eternity:	Hallelujah!
Banish all our sadness:	Hallelujah!
He will bedeck us with His crown:	Hallelujah!
All those for whom Moses received the Torah:	Hallelujah!
He will come to our aid with His heavenly sword:	Hallelujah!
And all will come right:	Hallelujah!
He will call out in grim anger:	Hallelujah!
And Heaven and earth will tremble at His voice:	Hallelujah!
The blast of the *shofar* of the Messiah will be heard:	Hallelujah!
And all the righteous will awaken:	Hallelujah!
He will comfort His beloved servants:	Hallelujah!
All those who have served Him well:	Hallelujah!
He will judge their confession:	Hallelujah!
And He will bring here from all the four corners of the earth:	Hallelujah!
All those who are scattered in exile:	Hallelujah!

We will enter the house into which the
  Messiah will bring us: Hallelujah!
He will gather together His scattered sheep
  in Jerusalem: Hallelujah!
All those who have suffered cruel
  punishment in exile: Hallelujah!
This will all come true: Hallelujah!
As our prophets clearly wrote: Hallelujah!

It will become clear for all to see: Hallelujah!
Pregnant women, children and all others: Hallelujah!
That we will become one brotherhood: Hallelujah!
He will share out His great mercy among us: Hallelujah!
So we may fulfil all our days: Hallelujah!

God, blessed be His Name: Hallelujah!
Shall heal us completely and entirely: Hallelujah!
Girls and boys will rejoice in a dance: Hallelujah!
We will walk on the righteous path: Hallelujah!

And on the same day: Hallelujah!
Young and old will all be judged: Hallelujah!
They will quickly pay their accounts: Hallelujah!
We will multiply like holy sheep: Hallelujah!

Exile will seem like a sleeping dream: Hallelujah!
You will show us all what we possess: Hallelujah!
Lament will turn to happiness: Hallelujah!
Jewish children will walk the right path: Hallelujah!

I will lengthen your days: Hallelujah!
Pure gold I will bring you for brass: Hallelujah!
For iron, I will bring you silver: Hallelujah!
I will gather you together when the sun
  goes down: Hallelujah!

One good meal cannot last too long: Hallelujah!
Every last Jew will be supported: Hallelujah!
In Your light we shall go: Hallelujah!
We will praise the one God: Hallelujah!
Who created us all.   Hallelujah!

A tkhine to be said before Kedushe

Beyle Hurvits

Extracted from a booklet of penitential *tkhines* entitled *Tkhines* to be said in synagogue from the beginning of the month of Elul until the Day of Atonement (*Tkhines vos men zol zogn fun Rosh Khoydesh Elul to Yom Kipor*).[3]

As an introduction to Beyle's work, I have translated the title page, which reads like an advertisement and is a good example of how the Jewish printing industry of the time combined profit with prayer.

Title Page

Beloved women,
Hurry here and buy these beautiful *tkhines*.
I know that when you read them
They will gladden your hearts.

So beloved women,
Don't begrudge a tiny sum of money
When with this prayer and the *shofar*,
You will gain instant merit.

And may the son of David
Be sent in our days,
And let us say
Amen.

This tkhine is said before *Kedushe*[4]

Near You, God, there is no night,
And candles are not needed beside You,
For You light up the whole world with Your light.
And the morning speaks of Your mercy,
And the night speaks of Your truth,
And all creatures acknowledge Your wonder.
God, You help us every day.

Who can speak of the great wonder
That You might impart to the pious men on their day,
In the place where all the people of creation will sit
For Your one day is a thousand years
And Your day is longer than the whole of the world's
　　existence.
And You are forever in eternity,
You outlive all Your creation,
And You remain eternal,
And as You live eternally,
So, too, do Your servants
Live in eternal life.

And how holy You are.
Everyone sanctifies You
In Heaven three times a day
And on earth.
And not only do the angels say
"Holy, holy, holy"[5]
But so do Your holy people, Israel
Sanctify Your name by saying
"Holy, holy, holy."

You are sanctified, Lord,

Amen.

 # A song of the Ten Commandments

Sheyndele

This song about the giving of the Ten Commandments on Mount Sinai was published in 1686, most likely in Prague. Like Rivke's song, this too, seems likely to have been performed by a *firzogerin* for a group of women, as it possesses many of the devices found in oral literature. It is in rhyme and related by a narrator who links the verses with phrases such as "Yes, you will hear more," "I will tell you, so you will know," and "Only hear how it continued." The recitation of the Ten Commandments and the biblical account is interlaced with additional awesome tales and legends.

I will begin by praising God
Who created us all.
I will begin with the Ten Commandments
Which God, Blessed be He,
Gave to us by the hand of Moses.

All of us stood at Mount Sinai,
Each individual, young and old, big and small
Was terrified by His wonder
As the *Shkhine*[6] showed himself on the mountain.

Listen well, Israel, to what I say
Make yourself holy for three whole days
Do not approach Mount Sinai
If you wish to have sight of the Holy *Shkhine*.

Mount Sinai will rise high above the earth.
The *Shkhine* will be on high with Moses,
While all Israel remain on the ground below.
Only listen to the wonders that occurred.

Only listen to what happened to the pregnant women,
The babies called out from their mother's bodies,
"It will be done," so beautiful and fine,
"We will receive the beloved Torah."

How quickly our beloved Lord God began
The first word of the Ten Commandments
Anoki,[7] it is I,
I am your only God
Who brought you out of the land of Egypt.

In their terror they could not remain where they stood,
As their souls swiftly fled from them.
Just as swiftly, the beloved Torah commanded
That their souls be restored to their bodies.

God forbid you should turn to any other god.
"If you do not believe in Me, early and late,
Almighty God will judge you sternly,
And He will punish you to the fourth generation."

He will favor and reward for two thousand generations
Those who observe His beloved Holy Torah,

And lovingly keep His Ten Commandments
That He wrote in His Torah.

Yes, you shall hear more.
You shall swear no false oaths,
The Holy Name then commanded,
And do not make graven images,
Or you will for ever wander around the world.

Do not take My Name, the Name of God, in vain,
For it is certain that if you do,
It will be as if you have renounced God
Who created Heaven and earth.

Another thing I wish to say to you:
Observe the beloved *Shabbos*
And honor its great holiness
So you are certain to live for ever.

You shall ply your trade for six days
And then on the seventh day
You shall rest,
As shall your son and daughter
And your maid and servant
And all your animals.

God created Heaven and earth in six days,
And on the seventh day He rested.
Therefore on *Shabbos*
We must rejoice.

Set aside business matters,
And eat and drink and read the Torah with great joy,
For *Shabbos* is a foretaste of the world to come,
And how soon Elijah the prophet will come to you.

God issued His Commandments solemnly.
Honor your father and mother diligently,
And your days will be lengthened,
And you will live forever with God in Heaven.
And the Holy Name desires that you also respect
    and honor
Your elder brother and your stepmother.

227

You must spill no blood
Or the Holy Name will punish you
And you will be known as a murderer
Entirely shamed among men.

You must not commit adultery,
A strange man with a strange woman
For God considers this sin so great
That the souls of those who commit this sin
Will become evil spirits.

If you steal money or belongings from another,
God will pay you in the other world,
While in this world you will be dishonored,
For word travels to every land.

You must never speak false witness,
For it is as if, God forbid, you had hit your friend,
And taken away all his money and luck,
And you must never stand in your neighbor's blood.

It is in the beloved and holy Torah,
Which God has written himself,
That you shall not desire your neighbor's house or
     his wife.
Or anything else that belongs to him.

In words so solemn and profound,
Six hundred and thirteen commandments are
     commanded,
And are all written in the Ten Commandments,
Given to us by Almighty God.

I will tell you, so you will know,
How Moses, the holy man
Went up into the clouds
And soon came to the Heavenly Throne,
When a holy angel barred his way.

Yes, you will know, for I shall tell you.
Not everyone may approach His Name,
For twelve thousand angels guard him from below,
And this angel was eager to dismiss the pious Moses.

But the saintly Moses pronounced a holy name
That he had learned when he saw the burning bush
Which made the angel spring twelve thousand miles in a
    puff of smoke
And Moses knew that he could go on.

But his way was barred by another angel,
Who struck Moses' heart with terror,
But Moses pronounced a very great name
And thus overpowered the angel.

Only hear how it continued.
With the greatest joy, the angel
Led Moses up to the Seat of Mercy
Where he was addressed
By our beloved Lord God.

Listen, young and old,
And hear how it is written in our Holy Books,
How our beloved Lord God likened himself to a
    bridegroom,
Handsome and fine,
And all Israel became His bride.

This is how the *Kesube*[8] was written
And Moses was its scribe at God's command,
And as Moses received God's Commandments,
His face lit up like the shining sun.

Rich God in Heaven and on the earth,
You are the God we love.
You brought us out of the land of Egypt,
And gave us Your beloved Torah.

"Hear, Oh Israel," began the Eternal God,
"The Lord our God, the Lord is One,"
All Israel answered.
Moses immediately responded:
"Blessed is the name of his glorious kingdom forever
    and ever."[9]

That holy mountain, Sinai, was bedecked with fine jewels
And with rich vegetation and delicious food.

The blowing of the shofar was heard clear and strong
Just as Isaac once heard it.

God solemnly bestowed His Commandments
Because he created the world for the Torah.
Our beloved Lord God has helped us many times,
So take God's wonder to heart
And speak of it night and day.

The wonder of our Lord God
Will grow ever stronger,
And at the moment when we become worthy,
God, Blessed be He, will let us enter the Holy Land
In our days,
So let us say

Amen.

 Song (Lid)

Yankev ben Elyohu

An interloper in this section, because it is by a man rather than a woman, this song demonstrates that in spite of the new prestige women had gained in their prayer life, they were still viewed as irredeemable creatures who could never atone for the sin of Eve, and were the cause of all human death. The message, however, is ambiguous, as women are urged to fulfill their commandments and to pray and repent in order to be redeemed since certain pious and saintly women have made a successful transition to the next world. Therefore, redemption for women is portrayed confusingly as impossible, yet achievable. This song is typical of others of the period, one of which has the title: "A beautiful new song of death." This song was published in a booklet of three Yiddish *lider* that contains another by the same author and an edition of Rivke Tiktiner's *Lid* for *Simkhes Toyre*.

Let us begin to sing,
From the first word to the last,
Then we will part from here.

Wives, children, and maidens
Must all suffer a bitter death.
Even if you become the greatest hero
And become fabulously rich,
You still have to go to the next world.

You may shout and beat your breast,
And attempt to escape death,
But your stone houses and golden chains
Cannot protect you.

When the Angel of Death comes,
You must leave behind
All the money and possessions
That make you so brave,
All your silver and gold.

You take with you a sack of earth,
Nothing more.
You own nothing,
Even when you are rich,
For in one day you can be in need
Just like a skinny beggar who dies
With no more than two pieces of pottery,
Laid on your eyes.
Oy, oy, how can you free yourself?
Your heart and body will be afraid.
Remember how men are laid out on straw,
And covered with only a sprinkling of earth?

Wife and child begin to shout:
"*Oy vey,* where is my husband?
Who will support me now?
Oy vey, my very best friend is gone!"

In the ground you will not rest
For worms will slip in and out of you,
Like needles stabbing you,
Tearing your heart and body.

The gravity of your sins will be reckoned.
"God in Heaven," you will call out,

"What will the worms do to me?
They are living in me, big and small.
They are crawling in my liver.
They are eating my flesh to the bone."
Nothing can stop them.

When the Angel of Death arrives,
You will dread standing before your Master,
And you will begin to drip with sweat.
You need speak no word.
Your face will tell all.
Your eyes will stream.
You will receive a blessing.
And after that you will depart
Entirely from here.

When you are carried to the graveyard,
The living come to cry,
And beat their breasts,
Oy vey oy vey, oy vey!
A man is brought here
Along with his evil deeds,
And everyone speaks of what he did
In his lifetime.

What he did day by day,
Each transgression,
Every sin is considered one by one.
You will recognize them.
Oy vey, vey,!
How you will roast and burn.

Then will come those
Whose red hands
Will lash you with fire.
Why did you not try harder to do good service?
The flesh will be torn from your bones.

Dear one, you have not listened well enough
To discover how to avoid sin.
God your Master sees everything
And writes it all down.

So come, all of you,
I wish to advise you
So you may enter Abraham's garden.

Be pious and give alms.
With money and bread,
You can protect yourself in death.

When a poor man comes to you for help
In his prayer shawl or tunic,
Or his wife in her Sabbath hat,
Do not be impatient or irritable,
Or turn them away,
Or his tears will fall at your door.
The voice of a poor man is great.
God hears his cries.
Wives must become widows,
And children orphans.

God loves the poor man very much.
He gives him no silver or gold.
He does not wish to give him money
So he may attain eternal life.
Perhaps those who make much money
Are not so pious.

When a poverty-stricken friend
Comes to you for help,
You may look down on him
And not wish to listen,
But he wishes you no harm, poor thing.
Yet you shout at him
And refuse to help him.

You should not swear,
Yet the whole world ignores this.
God has forbidden it.
Yes, just hear how people swear,
Men, women, and children.
They shall linger in purgatory
Those who speak so in their lifetime.

Your tongue and mouth shall be burnt
If you use the Holy Name in vain.
Oy vey! How has man come to such behavior?
Sulfur and pitch pour from his throat,
And he is thrown into acrid flames.

You must speak no evil, no gossip.
This is the greatest of all sins,
The worst of all.
Women must be guided.
They have stemmed from Eve,
Who spoke falsely to her man,
And man was expelled
From the Garden of Eden,
And had his life span shortened.

Women can never atone for this sin.
They must therefore immerse themselves,
They must suffer in childbirth,
And must suffer at the hands of their husbands,
Who must beat them
To ensure their goodness.

God has said the same.
The sin of Eve must be atoned.
Therefore women go to the ritual bath,
And light two candles or more,
And separate the *khale* dough.
Because women have precipitated death,
They must be punished and suffer hardship.
But if a man makes a mistake,
Then women must punish the man among themselves.

The Angel of Death springs out
Before a woman,
And dances and laughs and sings.
He says, "Let me not leap and laugh,
Women have made me a slaughterer.
I must haunt them when they sleep or wake."

Have you remembered
That you must treat a maid or servant correctly?

You must not drive them from your table
To wash up or clean up
While something is still in their dish.

Also you must not plague them too much,
Then you will not need to beat them.
They must live happily with you,
Which is why you pay them good wages.

You should lock no food away from them,
But treat them like your own children,
So they suffer no hunger at your hands,
Or God may cut short your days.
They are your servants and maids.

Let us return to the first point.
No one should ascend too high,
Because he who rises high, will fall
And break his limbs,
And is not worthy of further help.

Therefore, dear one, take time to consider
And lay your pride to one side.
Remember whence you came
And that you will be laid in a very dark grave.

You should correct yourself at all times.
God the Lord stands before you
And will judge you.
When you remember this,
You will surely not wish to commit a sin,
And will just as surely enter the next world.

On that note I will now end.
May God the Lord bestow much good,
And may the Messiah come to us,
And lead us into the Holy Land,
So God may rebuild the Temple for us
With magnificence and glory.

Amen. Seloh.

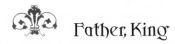 # Father, King

Toybe Pan

Toybe's *lid* is a communal plea for relief from the plague that devastated the community in Prague. At the Olsany cemeteries, Prague's largest, more than one million people are buried. The first bodies were buried there during the great plague epidemic in 1680, when small, parochial graveyards inside the city could no longer hold the thirty thousand dead that needed to be buried over a period of several weeks. Toybe refers to this crisis in her *lid*. She expresses not only the death and physical suffering of the Jewish community, but the fears and insecurities they felt at such times of crisis. They might easily be held responsible, accused of bringing bad luck to their neighbors and forced to leave their homes and move on. Like the other *lider* in this section, there is a response that indicates that the verses might have been sung by a *firzogerin* and then responded to by the rest of those present with the phrase "Father, King." With this response, Toybe echoes the phrase from the Hebrew *Ovinu Malkeynu* prayer (Our Father, Our King), which is recited throughout the Ten Days of Penitence, except on Sabbath, and also at the end of the morning service on the Jewish New Year (Rosh Hashone). This prayer is a confession of sins and concludes with a plea to God to accept the supplications of the community, making it an appropriate and familiar source for Toybe's pleas.

> Lord God, You are very merciful
> So incline Your ears toward us
> And remove Your anger from us
> For the great sins that we have committed.   Father, King
>
> Day and night we will pray to God
> To accept our pleas,
> And hear our prayers
> And all our petitions.   Father, King
>
> When You know how forlorn we are,
> And how we are suffering,
> May You, beloved Lord God,

Quickly answer our prayers,
And let no more harm come to us.   Father, King

Bring help to us soon,
Beloved Lord God, take up our cause.
Help to rid us of the plague.
Let us find mercy and grace.   Father, King

Help us out of our great predicament,
And let no one suffer such death.
And may we not encounter the
    Angel of Death,
So that none shall die.   Father, King

Merciful God, let the plague end.
We pray to You, young and old,
May we soon recover,
And may none be driven away.   Father, King

As soon as we fall ill,
We lie suffering inside our houses,
Afraid that we will die.
Beloved Lord God, be merciful.   Father, King

Five good men go around
And search everywhere,
So none will be neglected.
Blessed God, reward them well.   Father, King

Pious women also help the sick
Doing good at all times.
So many women carry out
So many *mitsves*
Without complaint.
May God protect them from all suffering.   Father, King

May God notice
All the good that has been done,
And may God lengthen the lives
Of all those who have given much charity.   Father, King

Some give charity and others go around
Doing good, all with Your help.

Beloved Lord God,
Leave us in pain no longer.   Father, King

Beloved God, You are gracious.
May you be merciful to us
As You sit on Your seat of mercy,
And may our troubles soon disperse.   Father, King

We pray, young and old,
So You will soon relieve us of our troubles,
May they soon disappear,
And may all our suffering, great and small
   be at an end.   Father, King

Beloved God, we call to You for support,
And we trust You will support and
   help us.
We build our hope on Your mercy,
And trust You will come to our aid.   Father, King

There is loud lament and wailing
When each person is carried out,
And our greatest pain and suffering
Is that they may not even be buried in
   our graveyard.
Beloved Lord God, help us out of all
   our pain.   Father, King

We pray day and night.
Give the greatest consideration to Your poor
   sheep,
For You are our strength and we are Your
   sheep.
Beloved Lord God, remove Your punishment
   from us.   Father, King

In Sodom when ten righteous men
   were found,
You would not allow a catastrophe to happen,
And here, thank God, there are
Very pious, righteous men and saintly men,
So beloved Lord God, save us, too, from ruin. Father, King

Beloved Lord God, accept our prayers
    at all times,
And be merciful to us today.
Acknowledge our charity and good deeds,
And accept our prayers on our merit.   Father, King

When we have sinned,
We repent to You on high.
We can never repent adequately.
Lord God, we fall at your feet.   Father, King

When just one observance is left undone,
    beloved Lord God,
It is like the sacrifice with incense that we
    are still unable to carry out.
Instead we must use pigeon dung.
Beloved Lord God, help us in our time of need.   Father, King

As it happened to King David
When the Angel of Death ran in the streets,
And You were merciful to him.
May You again allow no more to die.   Father, King

Both young and old repent now.
Only end the plague.
If we, Heaven forbid, are all full of sin,
May You reward us appropriately.   Father, King

Beloved Lord God, let our good deeds
From the Torah be acknowledged,
So we shall find grace and honor in the
    eyes of the king,
And may all the ill spoken of us not be
    believed.   Father, King

The heart of the king is in Your power.
Beloved Lord God, You must help at once
To fill his heart with mercy
For the poor common folk.   Father, King

God of Life, may our beloved king live
    one hundred years,
With his queen and with the young princes,

And with all who turn to him,
And all those who speak well of the poor
   common folk.
May no sickness come into their homes.   Father, King

We no longer have a Temple.
Nor the priests who once represented us
And prayed on our behalf.
Beloved Lord God, accept our prayers.   Father, King

When we neglect God,
He rewards no one.
May He remember His scattered sheep
And soon end our punishment.   Father, King

Beloved Lord God, though we are desperately
   in need
No days have been as bad as death.
Beloved God, may You have mercy on Your
   poor children
And let none of us die before our time.   Father, King

Beloved Lord God, remember Abraham, Isaac,
   and Jacob,
Our forefathers,
And keep Your promise,
That when Your people, Israel, are in great
   need,
You will help them out of their pain.   Father, King

You promised Abraham when Isaac was
   bound to the altar,
That you would protect us beneath Your
   hand,
Please do so now
As You promised Jacob our forefather.   Father, King

First there must be great trouble,
Followed by great joy.
Great happiness starts with small beginnings
So let all illness cease.   Father, King

We beg You, Merciful Father,
Relieve our troubles,
So our burdens become lighter.
Blessed Lord God, release us from this pain.   Father, King

Over the past year, our communal messenger
And our beloved rabbi have died.
We are almost, Heaven forbid, corrupted.
We are without natural justice.
May our luck soon change for the better.   Father, King

Just as our beloved rabbi was put into the
    world for our benefit
Before the troubles began,
May much good health come to us
In his going to God, who has taken him
    from us.   Father, King

When God wishes to punish Israel,
He excludes the righteous ones in Paradise
From all earthly troubles.
May God take the pain away from us.   Father, King

Our rabbi has spent his year away from
    life in joy,
And he gave much charity in his day,
And performed many good deeds.
May his merit benefit us at all times.   Father, King

May we benefit from his deeds.
May he plead on behalf of all Israel in the
    next world
And pray for us.
May his merit benefit us at all times.   Father, King

May the angel shout out loudly
For an end to the plague,
Especially for the children who die racked
    with blisters.
May You, beloved Lord God, be merciful
    to us.   Father, King

Young lads of two or three years old,
And also those who can read and pray,
Are all God's soldiers.
Remove us from all harm.   Father, King

Every gate is locked except the gate of tears.
Beloved Lord God, hear our prayers.
Collect our tears in Your vessel,
And rescue Your people, Israel.   Father, King

May our tears wash away our sins.
You are our Father and we Your children.
All that You are is beloved by us.
Beloved Father, do not abandon Your
    children.   Father, King

We are aware of all You have done for us
Through Your great mercy.
There is no other to whom we would turn.
Beloved Lord God, hear us soon.   Father, King

Beloved God, You sit in judgment.
May You give great consideration to Your
    poor sheep.
May Your severity give way to compassion,
So that we may soon be discharged.   Father, King

Beloved Lord God, no one can escape
    from You.
You can find everyone,
But he who has strayed can repent.
May God accept our prayer.   Father, King

You do not end the life of a sinner.
There is no need if he repents.
Even with the righteous You are strict.
Beloved Lord God, help us from our pain.   Father, King

Therefore we beg You with all our hearts,
Save us from this agony,
And remove the plague from us,
And go on protecting us from everything
    unclean.   Father, King

May all the angels in heaven pray on our
  behalf,
And may God accept the prayer.
May our prayer endure,
And may all illness end.   Father, King

Now I will end my pious song.
May Blessed God accept all our prayers,
And may He protect us from all pain,
And may we soon be led into the Holy Land.   Father, King

If ever You wish to know who wrote
  this song,
It was Toybe, wife of Jacob Pan who
  created it,
Daughter of Leyb Pitsker of beloved memory.
May God protect us all.   Father, King

 Daily tkhine

Rokhl Soyfer

The work that follows is an extract from a small booklet of daily *tkhines* entitled *Tkhine*. This was published under the name of Rokhl bas Mordkhe Soyfer, dated around 1700 and thought to be printed in Prague. The booklet is a patchwork of Yiddish translations and adaptations of paragraphs or phrases extracted from Psalms and various Hebrew prayers. They are mainly penitential in content. I have translated here only the final lines of Rokhl's *tkhine* that are based largely on a theme found in The Song of Songs[10] that describes the relationship between God and Israel, based on scriptural references. These lines stand alone as an attractive prayer of praise and they illustrate the work of another Jewish woman of the period. I have also reproduced the title page, which is not only another example of profit and prayer, but also shows that Rokhl's *tkhine* was intended to be read by women.

> *Title Page*
> This beautiful *tkhine* is to be said
> Every day with *kavone*.

Then God will shield us from all afflictions,
And the Blessed Name will forgive us our sins
And we will have eternal life,
For by our merit,
We will be worthy to enter *Erets Yisroel*.[11]

These beautiful *tkhines* were created
For pious women and girls,
For a sum that you will not consider
To be too high.
It is a fair price for you to pay
To pass through to the next world,
And this *tkhine* is well worth the money,
For it was brought into print
By a pious woman, Rokhl,
Daughter of Reb Mordkhe Soyfer, of blessed memory
Of the holy community of Fintshuv.[12]

Tkhine (an extract)

How can I praise Him adequately
When even a portion of the praise
That falls from my lips
Could fill the entire world.

He feeds everyone with His grace
And with His mercy.
He is righteous.
Blessed is the name of His glorious kingdom
Forever and ever.

He is the eternal King.
He is the highest,
And His heart is compassionate
As are His ways.

He is the first Father,
And He is the last Father,
Who is merciful to His beloved children.

He is our Master; we are His servants
We are His vineyard; He is our Keeper
We are His creation: He is our Creator
We are His loved ones; He is our God
We are His people; He is our King
We are full of sin; He is full of mercy
We and our days are as a passing shadow;
He and His years are unending.[13]

And Your Name is praised always and forever
And You are merciful and loved forever
We beg You to protect us from all who would envy us
And may You lock up the tongues
Of those who would do us harm
With Your heavenly locks
And deflect their blades so they will not harm us.

Here I swear by ten *sifrey toyre*[14]
And by ten mezuzes[15]
With a thousand good angels
So You, Beloved God, my Helper
Will send the Angel Michael
To be at my right hand
And at my left side
The Angel Gabriel
With Raphael behind me
And at my head
The *Shkhine* of God, Blessed by He
And may Elijah the prophet
Pave my path with good fortune.

Amen.

Notes

1. Hebrew for "rejoicing in the Law."
2. At this period in history it would have most likely been a heavily screened balcony or a separate room.
3. This is an annual period of intense penitence ending on the most solemn day of the Jewish calendar, the Day of Atonement.
4. A synagogue prayer in which the community of Israel, together with the heavenly hosts, proclaim God's holiness.
5. "*Kadoysh, kaydoysh, kadoysh*" (Holy, holy, holy) from the *Kedushe*. When these three words are recited in synagogue, it is customary for worshippers to lift their heels at each word.
6. Holy Divine Presence (God). It also means the female side of God, or God the bride, who must be united with God the bridegroom, for perfect harmony to ensue.
7. God addressed his first word, *Anoki*, to the people of Israel in the Egyptian language, because it was their vernacular. Then he continued in Hebrew.
8. Jewish marriage contract.
9. The opening lines of the *Shema* prayer, the oldest fixed daily prayer in Judaism, which consists of Deut. 6:4-9, Deut. 11:13-21, and Num. 15:37-41.
10. *Shir Hashirim*; Rabbah 2:1b12.
11. The Land of Israel, here meaning in its paradisal form.
12. Near Wolbrom, Poland, one of many Jewish communities destroyed by Stefan Tsharnietski in the wake of the Polish-Swedish wars. Rokhl's family must have fled to Prague.
13. The text here changes from referring to God in the third person to addressing Him directly.
14. Torah scrolls.
15. Mezuze (Lit. doorpost). A receptacle attached to the doorposts of houses, containing a scroll with passages of scripture written on it.

Glossary

Amide. (Standing prayer). Central prayer of the three daily synagogue services. It is also known as the *Shmoyne esrey*, which means "eighteen," denoting the eighteen blessings of which the original consisted; or simply *Tfile* meaning "prayer."

Ashkenazim. (Adj. Ashkenazic) The Jews (and their descendants) who began to settle in the German-speaking lands in the basins of the Rhine and Danube rivers about a thousand years ago. The term was applied retrospectively.

Av Harakhamim. Prayer usually said in Ashkenazic synagogue services on Sabbath mornings in memory of the martyrs of the Crusades. It was composed during the first Crusade and left on the reader's desk in the synagogue at Worms by its unknown author.

Bovo-bukh. Yiddish literary epic first printed in Isny in 1541. Composed by Elijah Levitah in ottava rima. The term *bobe-mayse*, which today is widely believed to mean "old wives tale" (lit. grandmother's story) stemming from the Slavic word *bobe* (grandmother), in fact stems from the title of this tale of adventure and romance.

Colophon. Words usually found at the end of the last printed page in a book. Early printed colophons included the date when printing began and/or ended, the number of copies printed, and the name of the ruler under whose protection the book was issued. The word "colophon" is derived from the Ionian city of Colophon. It was believed that the Colophonians could tip the scale of favor for whichever side of battle they fought, enabling the battle to end; hence the phrase of Erasmus, *Colophonem adidi*, "I have put the finishing touch to it," and its use to describe the words at the end of a book.

Firzogerin. Female prayer leader in a gathering of female worshippers.

Galkhes. Term used by Jews to describe Christian books or books in Latin characters rather than Hebrew characters, i.e., *galkhes sforim* (Christian books). Denotes "Christian priestly" and derives from the word *galekh* (a derogatory Jewish term for a Christian priest), which itself stems from the root of the Hebrew verb "to shave" and indicates the tonsure on the head of a monk or priest.

Gemore. The talmudic commentary on the Mishnah.

Hadlokes ha-ner. Kindling of candles on Sabbath and Festivals. One of the three women's commandments.

Halakhe. (1) The word *halakhah* is usually translated as "Jewish Law," although a more literal translation might be "the path that one walks." It is the set of rules and practices that affect every aspect of Jewish life, including the 613 commandments. (2) A specific ruling within Jewish law.

Hasidism. (Adj. Hasidic, n. Hasid, pl. Hasidim). Jewish mystical movement that originated in Podolia in the Ukraine, and has now spread across the world. It was founded by Israel Baal Shem Tov (1699–1761) in the eighteenth century in response to catastrophic social, religious, political, and economic conditions of the time; known for its intensification of traditional orthodoxy and its preservation of the traditions of Eastern European Jewish culture.

Haskole. The Jewish Age of Enlightenment or Berlin Enlightenment, which began in western Europe. It was a movement that strove for the assimilation and acceptance of Jews into the wider community. This was the beginning of modern, secular Judaism.

Kabbalah. (Hebrew for "tradition"). The mystical religious stream in Judaism that originally denoted the oral tradition transmitted alongside the Written Law, but was adopted in the twelfth century as text to denote the continuity of the mystical "tradition" from early times.

Kavone. Intention. Deep concentration. Spiritual intensity.

Khale. (1) Bread baked in honor of the Sabbath and Festivals. (2) One of the three women's commandments: the setting aside of a portion of the dough used for making Sabbath bread as a symbolic priestly offering, in the custom of the ancient Temple in Jerusalem.

Levite. (1) A descendant of the tribe of Levi. (2) the nonpriestly branches of the descendants of Levi who were employed in the Temple in Jerusalem as laborors, musicians, and choristers.

Lid, pl. *lider*. Song(s).

Loshn halb koydesh. (Semi-sacred tongue). Term that has been applied to the brand of Yiddish found in the *Seyder Tkhines* and other contemporary, related liturgical works.

Loshn koydesh. (Sacred tongue). Yiddish term for the Hebrew language.

Ma Toyvu. The Hebrew prayer that appears in both the *Sider* and many editions of the *Seyder Tkhines*, which is said on entering the synagogue.

Mame loshn. (Mother tongue). Yiddish term for the Yiddish language.

Marranos. Spanish and Portuguese Jews who were baptized at the time of the Inquisition, and their descendents, who often continued covertly to practice Judaism.

Mashket. The particular, cursive form of Hebrew lettering in which Yiddish was printed to differentiate it from the square Assyrian lettering used for Hebrew text.

Mayne Loshn. Yiddish book of graveyard prayers popular in the seventeenth and early eighteenth centuries.

Mayrev. Evening synagogue service.

Megile. (Lit."scroll"). Usually refers to the Book of Esther.

Menoyre. (1) Seven-branched candelabrum that stood in the Temple in Jerusalem. (2) A prayer printed in the shape of the menoyre that consists of Psalm 67.

Mezuze. (Lit. "doorpost"; pl. mezuzes). A receptacle attached to the doorposts of houses containing a parchment with passages of scripture written on it (Deut. 6:4-9; 11:13-21). Traditionally attached to the right doorpost of every door of a building.

Mikve. Bath for ritual purification.

Minkhe. Afternoon synagogue service.

Minyen. A group of ten adult males constituting a quorum for public prayer.

Mishnah. The Code of Jewish Law that dates mainly from the middle of the first century to the second decade of the third century C.E., codified under the direction of Rabbi Judah Ha-Nasi.

Mitsve. (1) Commandment. (2) A religious obligation. (3) A good deed.

Mitsves Noshim. (Lit."women's commandments"). Title of book first printed in the sixteenth century on the subject of the three women's commandments of *khale*, *nide*, and *hadlokes ha-ner*.

Nakdanim. Those who add the diacrytic vowels or points above and below the Hebrew letters on a manuscript.

Nide. (1) One of the three women's commandments, it relates to menstruation and purity. (2) The state of menstrual impurity. (3) A woman in this state.

Orthodox Judaism. This term designates adherence to accepted traditional Judaism. Its leaders in Central Europe in the nineteenth century (including Moses Sopher, Azriel Hildesheimer, and Samson Raphael Hirsch) separated themselves from Reform Judaism, which had gained ascendancy. Eastern European Orthodoxy, mostly in the form of Hasidism, uncompromisingly opposed all innovation, even in speech, dress, or manner of education. German and Western European Orthodoxy, however, adopted the policy of preserving traditional life, while accepting modern dress and use of the vernacular in everyday speech and general education.

Ottava rima. Poetic meter of the *Bovo-bukh*. A stanza of eight iambic lines, containing three rhymes (invariably arranged as: a b a b a b c c), is an Italian invention that dates back to the poetry of the fourteenth century. Boccaccio employed it for the *Teseide*, which he wrote in Florence in 1340, and for the *Filostrato*, which he wrote in Naples some seven years later.

Rashi script. The particular, cursive form of Hebrew lettering in which commentaries on the Bible and the Talmud by Rashi (Rabbi Shlomo Yitzchaki) (1040-1105) are printed.

Reform Judaism. A movement within Judaism with roots in the eighteenth century Haskole. As a reaction to the Napoleonic emancipation in striving to accommodate contemporary exigencies, Reform Judaism introduced modifications in traditional Jewish thought and practices, such as shortening the synagogue service, introducing vernacular prayer, integrating men and women in synagogue seating, etc.

Rubric. Instructional title.

Seyder Tkhines. The common prayer book for women in Yiddish first printed in Amsterdam in 1648. Many editions were printed and circulated until the 1720s.

Shabbos. The Sabbath. Saturday.

Shakris. Morning synagogue service.

Shkhine. (1) Divine presence of God. (2) The female side of God.

Shofar. (Lit. "trumpet"). Ram's horn blown like a musical wind instrument on the New Year and at the end of the Day of Atonement.

Shulḥan Arukh. Sixteenth-century legal code by Joseph Karo that serves as an authoritative guide to Jewish Law.

Sider, pl. *Sidorim*. Also known as *Seyder Tfile* (Order of prayer). The common Hebrew prayer book.

Simkhes Toyre. (Lit. "Joy of the Torah"). The annual celebration of the completion of the weekly readings of the Torah and the immediate recommencement of the first reading for the New Year.

Talmud. A compilation of the Mishnah and *Gemore* codified in two versions, the Babylonian Talmud c. 500 C.E., and the Palestinian Talmud (the Jerusalem Talmud) in 400 C.E.

Tallis. Prayer shawl to which fringes (*tsitsis*) are attached at each corner.

Targum. Five Books of Moses translated into Aramaic at the beginning of the Christian era by Onkelos, a convert to Judaism, at a time when Hebrew had ceased to be the spoken language of the Jewish people and Aramaic took its place.

Tefillin. Phylacteries. Two small black boxes containing portions of the Torah inscribed on parchment that men strap to their head and left arm during morning synagogue prayers, except on Sabbath and Festivals. (Deut. 6:8).

Temple. The ancient building in Jerusalem that was thought to house the Divine Presence of God. The First Temple was destroyed 586 B.C.E.; the Second Temple 349-69 B.C.E.

Tfile. Prayer. Also a title given to the *Amide*.

Glossary

Tkhine. pl. *tkhines*. Prayer or supplication. From the Hebrew *tehinnah* (pl. *tehinnoth*).

Tkhine loshn. (Lit. *tkhine* language). Style and language in which Yiddish *tkhines* and other seventeenth-century Yiddish prayers and songs are written.

Torah. (Hebrew for "understanding") and TANAKH (derived from the initial letters of Torah in Hebrew). *Torah, Neviim, Ketuvim* (Pentateuch, Prophets, Hagiographa) are synonyms for the Hebrew Bible that includes, in its largest definition, both the Oral Law and Written Law. The Pentateuch in the Torah consists of the Five Books of Moses.

Tsadik. (Lit. "righteous one," pl. *tsadikim*.) The term refers to a wholly righteous or saintly individual and generally indicates that the person has spiritual or mystical power.

Tsene-Rene. Book by Yankev ben Yitskhok Ashkenazi of Yanov that first appeared in early seventeenth century. Also known as the *Taytsh Khumesh* (Yiddish Bible or Women's Bible). It is a free-flowing Yiddish translation of and exegesis upon the Pentateuch, together with weekly and festival readings from the Prophets, interlaced with homiletic material. Its name derives from a passage in The Song of Songs: "Come out you women, and see" (3:11).

Tsitsis. Ritual fringes attached to the tallis as a reminder of the commandments in Num. 15:37–40 and Deut. 22:11).

Yeshive. Talmudic seminary.

Yiddish. The everyday language of Ashkenazic Jewry across Europe at the time of the *Seyder Tkhines*. It spread across the world with the migration of Jews from Eastern Europe in the twentieth century, but has been replaced by national languages, and remains an everyday language only in parts of the Hasidic community.

Zohar. (Book of Radiance). The central work of Jewish mysticism, written in Aramaic and purported to be the teachings of the second-century Palestinian Rabbi Shimon ben Yohai. In the thirteenth century, a Spanish Jew, Moshe de Leon, claimed to have discovered the text that was subsequently circulated throughout the Jewish world and is believed by some to have been its author. Most of the Zohar is in the form of a mystical commentary on sections of the Pentateuch and parts of the *Hagiographa* (from the Greek for "Holy Writings"; Heb. *ketuvim* or "writings"), the third and final section of the Bible (after the Pentateuch and Prophets) containing 13 books: Psalms, Proverbs, Job, The Song of Songs, Ruth, Lamentations, Ecclesiastes, Esther, Daniel, Ezra, Nehemiah, 1 Chronicles, and 2 Chronicles.

Bibliography

General Reference

Adler, R. 1983. "The Jew Who Wasn't There: *Halakhah* and the Jewish Woman." In *On Being a Jewish Feminist*. Ed. D. Heschel, New York: Schocken Books, 12. First published in *Response* 7, no. 22 (summer 1973): 77–82.

Æmilius, Paulus. 1544. *Khamishey khumshey toyre im khomesh megiles vehaftoyres*. Augsburg.

Agnon, S.Y. 1965. *Days of Awe*. New York: Schocken Books (original edition), 1848.

Amittai. 780–850. *Tkhine*.

Anshl, Rebi. [1530–1536]. *Merkeves hamishne (Seyfer Rebi Anshl)*. Krakow: Shmuel, Osher & Elyokim Helic.

Aren ben Shmuel. [1709]. *Liblikhe tfile toder kreftige kartsney afar guf gun neshomen* [Hergeshausen].

Asaf, S. 1925. *Mekhorot letoledot hahinukh beyisrael*. Vol. 1. Tel Aviv.

Ave-Lalleman, F.C.B. 1858–1864. *Das deutsche Gaunertum*.

Avrom Gumbiner ben Khayim Kalish, 1692. *Mogeyn Avrom*. Bahya ibn Pakuda [1161]. *Khovat Halevavot* (in Arabic). Translated into Hebrew by Yehuda ibn Tibbon [1167], Spain

Banetn, D. H., and S. D. Goiten. 1864. *A Tentative Bibliography of Geniza Documents*. Paris: Mouton & Co.

Bas, Shapse. 1680. *Shifsey Yesheynim*. Amsterdam: D.Tartaz.

Beddoe, D. 1983. *Discovering Women's History: A Practical Manual*. London: Pandora Press.

Ben-Yankev, I.A. 1880. *Bibliographie der gesammten Hebræischen Literatur mit Einschluss der Handschriften (bis 1863)*. *Oytsar haseforim*.Vilna

Benyomin ben Avrom. 1577. *Mitsves hanoshim*. Krakow.

Benyomin of Ordona. 1552. *Mitsves noshim*. Venice.

Berkovits, E. 1990. *Jewish Women in Time and Torah*. Hoboken, N.J.: Ktav Publishing House.

Biale, R. 1984. *Women and Jewish Law: An Exploration of Women's Issues in Halakhic Sources*. New York: Schocken Books.

Birnbaum, S.A. 1979. *Yiddish: A Survey and a Grammar*. Toronto: University of Toronto Press; Manchester: Manchester University Press.

Blitz, Yekusiel ben Yitskhok. 1678. *Toyre veneviim ukesuvim*. Amsterdam: Uri Faybesh.

Blumenthal, D. R. 1978, 1982. *Understanding Jewish Mysticism: A Source Reader*. 2 vols. New York: Ktav Publishing House.

Bibliography

Boekh, J. G., G. Albrecht, K. Böttcher, K. Gysi, P. G. Krohn, and H. Strobach, eds. 1963. *Geschichte der deutschen Literatur 1600 bis 1700*. Berlin:Volk und Wissen Volkseigener Verlag.

Borokhov, B. 1913. "Di biblyotek funem yidishn filolog" In *Der pinkes Yorbukh far der geshikhte fun der yidisher literatur un shprakh, far folklor, kritik un bibloyografe*, edited by Sh. Niger, 1–68 [separate pagination at end of volume]. Vilna:Vilner farlag fun B. A. Kletskin.

———. 1966. *Shprakh-forshung un literatur geshikhte*.Tel Aviv: Farlag Y.L. Perets.

Brayer, M. M. 1986. *The Jewish Woman in Rabbinic Literature: A Psychological Perspective*. Hoboken, N.J.: Ktav Publishing House.

Buxtorf, J. 1603. *Synagog Judaica. Das ist Jüden Schul*. Basel: S. Henricpetrus.

Cantor, A. 1983. "The Lilith Question." In *On being a Jewish feminist.* ed. D. Heschel, 40–50. NewYork: Schocken Books. First published in *Lilith* 1 (fall 1976).

Clarke, S. L. "Sibylle Schwarz: Prodigy and Feminist." In *Women Writers of the Seventeenth Century*, eds. Katharine M.Wilson and Frank J.Warnke. Athens: University of Georgia Press, 1989.

Cohen, A. 1965. *The Psalms: Hebrew Text and English Translation with an Introduction and Commentary*. London: Soncino Press. Original edition 1945.

Cohen, J. 1973. *The History of Jewish Prayer*. London: United Synagogue.

———. 1986. *Horizons of Jewish Prayer*. London: United Synagogue.

Copeland, R. M. and N. Süsskind. 1976. *The Language of Herz's Esther: A Study in Judeo-German Dialectology*. Alabama: University of Alabama Press.

Cowley, A. E. 1929. *A Concise Catalogue of the Hebrew Printed Books in the Bodleian Library*. Oxford: Clarendon.

Dan, R. 1979. *Accumulated Index of Jewish Bibliographical Periodicals*. Budapest: Akadémiai Kiadó.

De Boor, H., and R. Newald. 1964. *Deutsche Gedichte von Hildegard von Bingen bis Ingebor Bachmann*. Frankfurt am Main: Suhrkamp Verlag.

de Lange, N. 1984. *Atlas of the Jewish World*. Oxford: Phaidon.

Eidelberg, Shlomo 1962. *Jewish Life in Austria in the Fifteenth Century*. Philadelphia: The Dropsie College for Hebrew and Cognate Learning.

Elieyzer Soyfer ben Leyb. c. 1688. *Mayne loshn*. Frankfurt an der Oder.

Elye Bokher (Elijah Levita). 1541. *Bovo de Antona*. Isny: [Paul Fagius].

———. 1545. *Seyfer Tilim*. Venice: Corneleo Adelkind and Meyer bar Yitskhok.

Enelow, H. G. 1913. "Kawwana: The Struggle for Inwardness in Judaism." In *Studies in Jewish Literature: Issued in Honor of Professor Kaufmann Kohler on the Occasion of His Seventieth Birthday*. Berlin: Georg Reimer.

Epshteyn,Y. M. 1683. *Seyfer kitser shney lukhes habris (Kitser shelo)*. Fürth

———. 1697. *Seyder tfile derekh yeshore*. Frankfurt am Main.

———. 1707. *Seyfer derekh hayosher looylem habe*. Frankfurt am Main.

Erik, M. 1926. "Bletlekh tsu der geshikhte fun der elterer yidisher literatur un kultur." *Tsaytshrift*, 1:173–78.

——— 1928a. *Di geshikhte fun der yidisher literatur fun di eltste tsaytn biz der haskole-tkufe*. NewYork: Congress for Jewish Culture. Original edition 1927.

——— 1928b. "Inventar fun der yidisher sphilman-dikhtung," *Tsaytshrift* 2-3:545–87.

Fagius, P., [1543]. *Prima quatuor capital geneseos Hebraice, cum versione Germanica....* Constance: Paulus Fagius.

Falk, F. 1961. *Das Shmuelbuch des Mosche Esrim Wearba*. Assen.

Bibliography

Feldman, D. "Women's Role and Jewish Law." In *Conservative Judaism*, no. 4: 26:29-39. Summer 1972.

Finkelstein, L. 1924. *Jewish Self-Government in the Middle Ages*. New York: Jewish Theological Seminary of America.

Fishls, R. 1586. Introduction to *Tilim bukh*, translated by M. Shtendl. Krakow: Yitskhok ben Aren Prostits.

Fishman, I. 1944. *Jewish Education in Central Europe XVI–XVIII Centuries*. London: Edward Goldston.

Fleischer, E. 1975. *Hebrew Liturgical Poetry in the Middle Ages*. Jerusalem: Keter Publishing House.

Frakes, J. 1989. *The Politics of Interpretation: Alterity and Ideology in Old Yiddish Studies*. Albany: State University of New York Press.

Frankfurter, Akiva ben Elieyzer [1599]. *Tkhines*. Edited by Elie Loants. N.p.

Freehof, S. B. 1923. "Devotional Literature in the Vernacular." In *Yearbook of the Central Conference of American Rabbis*. Chicago: Central Conference of American Rabbis.

Fuks, L. 1957. *The Oldest Known Literary Documents of Yiddish Literature (c. 1382)*. Leiden: E. J. Brill.

———. 1965. *Das altjiddische Epos Melochimbuch*. Publ. Bibl. Rosenthaliana, no. 2. Assen: Van Gorcum.

Fürst, A. 1849–1863. *Bibliothecha Judaica: Hanbuch umfassend die Druckwerke der jüdischen Literatur, I–III*. Leipzig.

Gaster, M. 1981. *Ma'aseh Book: Book of Jewish Tales and Legends*, translated from the Judeo-German by Moses Gaster. Philadelphia: The Jewish Publication Society of America. Original edition 1934, 2 vols.

Gilbert, M. 1976. *Atlas of Jewish History*. U.S.A.: Dorset Press. Original edition 1969.

Goldshmid, D. 1970. *Makhzor leyamim moraim lefi minhage bene ashkenaz lekhol anfehem*. Jerusalem: Koren.

Gombiner, Avraham Abele vben Hayim Halevi. 1692. *Mogeyn Avraham*. Dyhernfurth.

Grayzel, S. 1969. *A History of the Jews*. New York: The New American Library Inc. Original edition 1947.

Grünbaum, M. 1882. *Jüdischdeutsche Chrestomathie. Zugleich ein Beitrag zur Kunde der hebräischen Literatur*. Leipzig: F. A. Brockhaus.

Güdemann, M. 1880–1888. *Geschichte des Erziehungswesens und der Cultur der Juden in Frankreich und Deutschland von der Begründung der jüdischen Wissenschaft in diesen Ländern bis zur Vertreibung der Juden aus Frankreich. I–III*. Vienna: Alfred Hölder.

Habermann, A. M. 1978. *Perakim be-Toldoth ha-Madpissim ha-Ivrim we-Inyene Sefarim*. Jerusalem: Rubin Mass.

———. 1980. *Hamadpiss Cornelio Adelkind ubeno Daniel*. Jerusalem: Rubin Mass.

Hagode. 1526. Prague.

Hakoyen, Dovid. 1535–1538. *Azhoras noshim*. Krakow: Shmuel and Elyokim Helic.

Hanover, N. 1662. *Sha'arey tsiyon*. Prague.

Hershl ben Yehude Toytek, seventeenth century. *Eyn hipsh lid fun Reb Lipman khazn*. N.p.

Hokh-Koyfman. 1892. *Mishpokhes kehile kedoyshe Prog*. Prague.

Bibliography

Hosofer, D. 1989. *Devorah: An Album for Women and Girls*. Melbourne: privately issued. Audiocassette.
Hurvits, Y. 1649. *Shney lukhes habris (Shelo hakoydesh)*. Edited by Shapse ben Yeshaye Hurvits. Amsterdam.
_____. 1717. *Shaar hashomayim*. Amsterdam.
Hymes, D. H. 1971. *On Communicative Competence*. Philadelphia: University of Pennsylvania Press.
Israel, J. I. 1989. *European Jewry in the Age of Mercantilism: 1550-1750*. Oxford: Clarendon Press. Original edition 1985.
Jacobs, L. 1964. *Principles of the Jewish Faith*. London: Vallentine-Mitchel.
Judaica Bohemia 1965-1988. Prague: Statni Zidovské Muzeum.
Kahan Newman, Z. 1986. "Kabbalistic ideas in the women's yiddish prayer book, 'Tkheenes.'" In *A Festschrift for Sol Liptzin on the Occasion of His Eighty-Fifth Birthday*, edited by Mark H. Gelber. New York: Peter Lang Publishing Inc.
Kay, D. 1988. "Words for 'God' in seventeenth-century women's poetry in Yiddish." In *Dialects of the Yiddish language. Winter Studies in Yiddish 2*. Edited by D. Katz. *Language and Communication* 8:57-67. Oxford: Pergamon Press.
_____. 1991. *Women and the Vernacular: The Yiddish Tkhine of Ashkenaz*. Thesis for the degree of Doctor of Philosophy, University of Oxford.
_____. 1993. "An Alternative Prayer Canon for Women: The Yiddish *Seyder Tkhines*." In *Zur Geschichte der jüdischen Frau in Deutschland*, edited by J. Carlebach. Berlin: Metropol-Verlag.
King, U. 1989. *Women and Spirituality*. Basingstoke and London: Macmillan Education.
Kliers, T. G. 1984. *Bizkhus fun Sore, Rivke, Rokhl un Leye*. Thesis for ordination. Hebrew Union College: New York.
Korman, E. 1928. *Yidishe dikhterins: Antologye*. Chicago: Farlag L. M. Stein.
Lacks, R. 1980. *Women and Judaism: Myth, History and Struggle*. New York: Doubleday & Company.
Landau, A., B. Wachstein. 1911. *Jüdische Privatbriefe aus dem Jahre 1619 (Quellen und Forschungen zur Geschichte der Juden in Deutsh-Österrsich, III)*. Wien and Leipzig: Wilhelm Bramüller.
Landau, L. 1912. "Arthurian Romances or the Hebrew-German Rhymed Version of the Legend of King Arthur." in Uhl, W. T. (ed.) *Arbeiten zur germanischen Philologie*, 21. Leipzig: Eduard Avenarius.
Lexers, M. 1986. *Mittelhochdeutsches Taschchenwörterbuch*. Stuttgart: S. Hirzel Verlag.
Liberman, Kh. 1952. "Barmerkungen tsu Shloyme Nobls artikl: R[eb] Yekhiel Mikhl Epshteyn—a dertsiyer un kempfer far yidish in 17tn yorhundert." *Yivo Bleter* 36:305-19.
Liebowitz, N. 1931. "Die Übersetzungstechnik der judish-deutschen Bibeluberset-zungen des XV. Und XVI. Jarhunderst dargestellt an den Psalmen." In *Beiträge zur Geschichte der deutschen Sprache und Literatur* 55:377-463. Halle.
Liptsin, S. 1972. *A History of Yiddish Literature*. New York: Jonathan David Publishers.
Lockwood, W. Ben 1963. "Die Textgestalt des jüdisch-deutscher Sprache." *Beiträge zur Geschichte der deutschen Sprache und Literatur* 85:433-47.
Loewe, H. 1926. *Catalogue of the Manuscripts in the Hebrew Character Collected and Bequeathed to Trinity College Library by the Late William Aldis Wright*. Cambridge: Cambridge at the University Press.

Bibliography

Löwenstein, L. 1893. "Jüdische un jüdisch-deutsche Lieder." *Monatsschrift für Geschichte und Wissenschaftes Judenthums* 38:184-92.

Lowenthall, M. 1977. *The Memoirs of Glückel of Hameln* (in English). With introduction by Robert Rosen. New York: Schocken Books. Reprint of 1932 edition, New York: Harper.

Luther, M. 1543. "Von den Juden und ihren Lügen." In *Luthers Werke, Kritische Gesammtausgabe*, 53:522-27, edited by D. Martin. Weimar, 1920.

_____. 1545. *Biblia: das is: Die gantze Heilige Schrift: Deudsh Auffs New zugericht.* Wittemberg: Hans Lufft.

Lyons, J. 1986. *Semantics.* 2 vols. Cambridge: Cambridge University Press. Original edition 1977.

Maimonides (Moses) c.1200. *Guide for the Perplexed (Moreh Nevukhim).*

Margoliouth, G. 1893. *Descriptive List of the Hebrew and Samaritan Manuscripts in the British Library.* London: Trustees of the British Museum.

_____. 1965. *Catalogue of the Hebrew and Samaritan Manuscripts in the British Museum.* London: Trustees of the British Museum. Original edition 1899.

McLaughlin, E. 1979. "Women, Power and the Pursuit of Holiness." In *Women of Spirit: Female Leadership in the Jewish and Christian Traditions*, edited by R. Ruether and E. McLaughlin, 100-30. New York: Simon & Schuster.

Meiselman, M. 1978. *Jewish Women in Jewish Law.* New York: Ktav Publishing House.

Menakhem ben Makhir. Eleventh century. *Kehoyshato Odom.* Germany.

Mendele Moykher Sforim. 1896. *Fishke der krumer.* Berditchev.

Mennasseh ben Israel. 1636. *De Resurrectione Mortuorum, Libri III.* Amsterdam: by author. 2nd edition, Groningen, 1676. In Spanish: *De la Resurrection de los Muertos, libros III.* 1636, Amsterdam, by author.

_____. 1650. *Esperança de Israel.* Amsterdam: by author.

_____. [1651] "To his Highnesse The Lord Protector of the Commonwealth of England, Scotland and Ireland." (A letter). Amsterdam: by author.

Milligram, A. E. 1971. *Jewish Worship.* Philadelphia: The Jewish Publication Society of America.

Minkoff, N. B. 1952. *Glickel Hamel (1645-1724).* M. Vaxer: New York.

Minkov and Joffe. 1942. "Alt-yidishe literatur." In *Algemeyne entsiklopedye* (Supplementary volume: *Yidn* 3:5-63). Paris: Dubnov fond.

Mitsves hanoshim. 1552. Venice: Daniel Adelkind. 2nd ed. 1588.

Mlokhim-bukh. 1543. [Moyshe Esrim-vearbe (trans.)]. [Augsburg: Paulus Æmilius]. 2nd ed. 1582.

Mordkhe ben Yankev Toplits. 1582. *Seyfer Mishley.* Krakow.

Moyshe Henokhs Yerushalmi. 1596. *Brantshpigl.* Krakow.

Munk, E. 1951. *The World of Prayer.* 2 vols. New York: Feldheim.

Neubauer, A. 1886. *Catalogue of the Hebrew Manuscripts in the Bodleian Library and in the College Libraries of Oxford.* Oxford: Clarendon Press.

Newman, E. 1972. *Life and Teachings of Isaiah Horowitz.* London: G. J. George.

Niger, S. 1913. "Di yidishe literatur un di lezerin." In *Der Pinkes: Yorbukh far der geshikhte fun der yidisher literatur un shprakh, far folklor, kritik un biblyografye.* Vilna: Vilner farlag fun ben A. Kletskin.

Noble, S. 1943. *Khumesh-taytsh: An oysforshung vegn der traditsye fun taytshn khumesh in di Khadorim.* New York: Yivo.

_____. 1946. "Sacred and Secular in the Language of the Yiddish Bible Translation." In *Yivo Annual of Jewish Social Science* 1:274-82. New York: Yivo.

Bibliography

_____. 1951. "R[eb] Yekhiel Mikhl Epshteyn—a dertsier un kempfer far yidish in 17tn yorhundert." *Yivo Bleter* 35:121-38.

_____. 1952. "A tshuve Khayim Libermanen." *Yivo Bleter* 36:319-21.

Odem, Mikhl. 1544. *Khamishey khumshey toyre in khomesh kmegiles vehaftoyres.*Constance: Paulus Fagius.

Ozick, C. 1983. "Notes towards Finding the Right Question." In *On Being a Jewish Feminist,* edited by D. Heschel. New York: Schocken Books. First published in *Lilith* 6 (1979).

Perles, J. 1876. "Bibliographische Mittheilungen aus München." *MGWJ* 25:351-61.

_____. 1884. *Beiträge zur Geshichte der hebraïschen und aramäischen Studien.* Munich.

Piekarz, M. 1964. "Vegn 'yidishizm' in sof fun 17tn yorhundert un der ershter helft fun 18tn yorhundert." *Di Goldene Keyt* 46:168-80.

Popkin, Richard H. "Jewish Messianism and Christian Millenarianism." In Perez Zagorin (ed.) *Culture and Politics from Puritanism to the Englightenment.* Berkeley and Los Angeles, 1990: 67-90.

Posner, R., and I.Ta-Shema. 1975. *The Hebrew Book.* Jerusalem: Keter Publishing House.

Prijs, J. 1964. *Die Baselr Hebräischen Drucke (1516-1828).* Olten und Freiburgim Breisgau: Urs Graf Verlag.

Prilutski, N. 1938. "Di umbakante altyidishe dikhterin Yente bas Yitskhok." *Yivo Bleter: Khoydesh-shrift fun yidishn visnshaftlekhn institut* 13 (3-4): 36-54.

Rabinowitz, L. I. 1944. "The Psalms in Jewish Liturgy." *Historia Judaica* 6:109-22.

Romer-Segal, A. 1986. "Yiddish Works on Women's Commandments in the Sixteenth Century." In *Studies in Yiddish Literature and Folklore: Research Projects of the Institute of Jewish Studies.* Monograph Series 7. Jerusalem: The Hebrew University.

Rose, E. 1960. *A History of German Literature.* New York: New York University Press.

Rosenberg, F. 1888. "Über eine Sammlung deutscher Volks-und Gesellschaftslieder in hebräischen Lettern." *Zeitschrift für die Geschichte der Juden in Deutschland* 2:291-2.

Rosenfeld, A., ed. and trans. 1983. *Seyder hayom litisha b'av.* New York: The Judaica Press.

_____. 1984. *The Authorised Selichot for the Whole Year.* New York: The Judaica Press. Original edition 1956.

Rosenfeld, M. 1984. *The Book of Cows: A Facsimile Edition of the Famed Kuhbukh.* London: Hebraica Books.

_____. 1987. "The Origins of Yiddish Printing." In *Origins of the Yiddish Language,* edited by D. Katz. *Winter Studies in Yiddish 1. Language and Communication* 7:111-26. Oxford: Pergamon Press.

Roth, C. 1977. *The Jews in the Renaissance.* Philadelphia: The Jewish Publication Society of America. Original edition 1959.

Roth, E., and H. Striedl. 1984. *Hebräische Handschriften.* Teil 3. Wiesbaden: Franz Steiner Verlag.

Salkind, S. M. 1953. *Bergonzi and the Yiddish Lid.* Tempo:Venice.

Satz, Y. 1977. *She'elot uteshuvot Maharil hakhadoshot.* Jerusalem: Makhon Yerushalayim.

Scherman, N., and M. Zlotowitz M (ed.). 1984. *The Complete ArtScroll Siddur.* The Artscroll Mesorah Series. New York: Mesorah Publications.

Scholem, G. 1946. *Major Trends in Jewish Mysticism*. London: Thames & Hudson.
_____. 1965. *On the Kabbalah and Its Symbolism* London: Routledge & Kegan Paul.
_____. 1971. *The Messianic Idea in Judaism*. New York: Schocken Books.
_____. 1973. *Sabbatai Sevi: The Mystical Messiah, 1626-1676*. Princeton: Princeton University Press.
Schröder, W. J. 1967. *Spielmannsepik*, 2nd ed. Stuttgart: Metzler
Segal, Agnew Romer, "Yiddish Works on Women's Commandments in the Sixteenth Century." In *Studies in Yiddish Literature and Folklore*, Research Project of the Institute of Jewish Studies, Monograph Series 7, The Hebrew University, Jerusalem, 1986.
Seyfer mides. 1542. Isny: Paulus Fagius or Paulus Æmilius.
Shatski, Y. 1927. "Naye arbetn tsu der geshikhte fun der Yidisher literature: A kritisher iberzikht." In *Pinkes: A ferlioriker zhornal far yidisher literaturgeshikhte, shprakhforshung, folklor un bibliografie*. Vol. 1(1-2):171-76. Edited by M. Weinreich, Y. Joffe, L. Cohen, S. Higer, Y. Rivkind, and Y. Shatski. New York: Yivo.
Shmelke ben Khayim. 1602. *A sheyn froyen bikhlayn*. Hanau.
Shmeruk, C. 1964. "Di misrekh-eyropeyishe nuskhoes fun der 'Tsene-rene.'" In *For Max Weinreich on His Seventieth Birthday*, 195-211. The Hague: Mouton.
_____, 1967. "Di naye editsye funem altyidishn 'Mlokhim-bukh.'" *Di Goldene Keyt* 59: 209-11.
_____. 1972. "Yiddish literature." In *Encyclopedia Judaica* 16:783-833.
_____. 1978. *Sifrut yidish. Perakim letoldoteha*. Tel Aviv: The Porter Institute for Poetics and Semiotics, Tel Aviv University.
_____. 1981. *Sifrut yidish bepolin*. Jerusalem: Magnes Press.
_____. 1986. "Can the Cambridge Manuscript Support the Spielmann Theory in Yiddish literature?" In *Studies in Yiddish Literature and Folklore: Research Projects of the Institute of Jewish Studies*. Monograph Series 7. Jerusalem: The Hebrew University.
_____. 1988. *Prokim fun der yidisher literatur-geshikhte*. Tel Aviv: Y. L. Perets farlag un Yidish opteylung, der hebreyisher universitet in Yerusholayim.
Shmuel-bukh. 1544. [Translated by Moyshe Esrim vearbe]. Augsburg: [Paulus Æmilius].
Shtendl, M. 1586. *Dos tilim bukh*. Edited by Royzl Fishls. Krakow: Yitskhok ben Aren Prostits.
Shtif, N. 1926-1928. "A geshribene yidishe biblyotek in a yidish hoyz in Venetsye in mitn zekhtsntn yorhundert." In *Tsaytshrift* 1:141-50 (1926); 2-3:525-42 (1928).
Shulman, E. 1913. *Sfas yehudis-ashkenozis vesifruso: mikeyts hameyo hates-vov vead shnoys hayud-khes*. Riga: Levin.
Shunami, S. 1965. *Mafteakh Maftekhot: Bibliography of Jewish Bibliographies*. Jerusalem: The Magnes Press, The Hebrew University. Original edition 1936.
Slonik, Ben A. 1577. *Seyder Mitsves hanoshim*. Krakow.
Smith, J. C. 1968. "Elye Levita's *Bovo-bukh*: A Yiddish Romance of the Early Sixteenth Century." Ph.D. diss., Cornell University.
Stark Zakon, M., ed. 1983-1984. *Tz'enah ur'enah*. With introduction by Meir Holder. 3 vols. Jerusalem: Mesorah Publications & Hillel Press.
Steiman, S. 1963. *Custom and Survival: A Study of the Life and Work of Rabbi Jacob Molin (Moelin) Known As the Maharil (c. 1360-1427) and Influence*

in Establishing the Ashkenazic Minhag (Customs of German Jewry). New York: Bloch Publishing Company.

Steinmeyer, E., and E. Sievers. 1879–1895. *Die althochdeutschen Glossen*. 5 vols. Berlin: Weidmann.

Steinschneider, M. 1848–1869. "Jüdisch-deutsche Literatur (Fortsetzung)." In *Serapeum: Zeitschrift für Bibliothekwissenschaft, Handschriftenkunde und ältere Litteratur*. Leipzig: C. P. Melzer.

_____. 1852–1860. *Catalogus librorum Hebraerum in Bibliotheca Bodleiana*. Berlin.

Sulks, Y. 1579. *Shir Hashirim*. Krakow: Yitskhok ben Aren Prostits.

Taz, Dovid ben Schmuel Haleyvi. 1586–1667. *Orach Chaim*, seventeenth century.

Tsinberg, Y. 1928. "Der kamf far yidish in der altyidisher literatur." In *Filologishe Shriftn* 2:69–106. Vilna: Yivo.

_____. 1943. *Di Geshikhte fun der Literatur ba Yidn* Vol. 6. New York: Farlag Morris S. Sklarsky. Original edition 1935 (Vilna).

Van Straalen, S. 1894. *Catalogue of the Hebrew Books in the Library of the British Museum Acquired during the Years 1868–1892*. London: The British Museum.

Wagenseil, J. C. 1674 ... *Sota* ... *una cum libri En Jacob excertis Gemarae, versione Latina, et commentario* .... Altdorf.

_____. 1699. *Belehrung der Jüdisch-Teutschen Red-und Schreibart*. Königsberg.

Waxman, Meyer. 1960. *A History of Jewish Literature*. Vol. 2. *From the Twelfth Century to the Middle of the Eighteenth Century*. New York and London: Thomas Yoseloff. Original edition 1933.

Weinreich, M. 1923. *Shtaplen. Fir etyudn tsu der yidisher shprakhvisnshaft un literaturgeshikhte*. Berlin: Wostok.

_____. 1928. *Bilder fun der Yidisher Literatur-Geshikhte fun di Onheybn biz Merndele Moykher-Sforim*. Vilna: Tomor.

_____. 1951. "Ashkenaz: Di yidish-tkufe in der yidisher geshikhte." *Yivo Bleter* 35:7–17.

_____. 1954. "Prehistory and Early History of Yiddish." In *The Field of Yiddish: Studies in Yiddish Language, Folklore and Literature*, edited by U. Weinreich, 73–101. New York: Linguistic Circle of New York.

_____. 1964. "Ashkenaz in algemeyn yidishn gerem." *Di Goldene keytt* 50:172–82.

_____. 1973. *Geshikhte fun der yidisher shprakh. Bagrifn, faktn, metodn*. Vols. 1–4. New York: Yivo.

Weissler, Chava. 1987. "Women in Paradise." *Tikkun* 2:2, 43–46, 117–20.

_____. 1989. "The Traditional Piety of Ashkenazic Women." In *Jewish Spirituality from the Sixteenth-Century Revival to the Present* 2:245–75, edited by A. Green. New York: The Crossroad Publishing Company.

_____. 1998. *Voices of the Matriarchs: Listening to the Prayers of the Early Modern Jewish Women*. Boston: Beacon Press.

Witzenhausen, Yoysef ben Aleksandr. 1679. *Toyre Veneviim Veksuvim*. Amsterdam: Josef Athias. Private collection.

Wolf, J. C. 1715–1733. *Bibliotheca Hebraica*. 4 parts. Hamburg: Leipzig.

Yankev ben Avrom Shloyme. 1615. *Mayne loshn*. Prague.

Yankev ben Shmuel. 1584. *Targum*. Breisgau.

Yankev ben Yitskhok Ashkenazi of Yanov. Early seventeenth century. *Tsene-rene*.

Yehude Khosid ben Shmuel. [1542]. *Shir hayikhud*. Isny: Paulus Fagius.

Yehude Leyb ben Moyshe Naftali Bresh. 1560. *Khamishe Khumshey Toyre*. Cremona.

Yehude Moscato of Mantua. c.1572. *Tkhine*. Mantua.

Yente bas Yitskhok. Nineteenth century. *Aseres hadibres bikhl*. N.p. See N. Prilutski, 1938, above.

Yitskhok ben Eliakum of Posen.1620. *Seyfer Lev-tov*. Prague: Bak.

Yitskhok ben Eliezer. [1579]. *Seyfer Hagan*. [Krakow] [Yitskhok ben Aren Prostits]

Yoysef ben Yokor. 1544. [Prayer Book]. Ichenhausen: Chaim ben Dovid Shakhor.

Zalmen of St. Goar. 1556. *Sefer Maharil*. Sabionetta: Tobias ben Eliezer Foa.

Zedner, J. 1867. *Catalogue of the Hebrew Books in the Library of the British Museum*. British Museum Trustees: London.

Zeligman, Ulma. 1610. *Tsukhtshpigl*. Hanau: Jans Yankev [Hena].

Zfatman, S. 1985. *Yiddish Narrative Prose*. Jerusalem: The Hebrew University.

ZfHB. n.d. *Zeitschrift für hebräische Bibliographie*. N.p.

Zim, R. 1987. *English Metrical Psalms: Poetry As Praise and Prayer*. Cambridge: Cambridge University Press.

Zunz, L. 1832. *Die gottesdienstlichen Vorträge der Juden, historisch entwickelt. Ein Beitrag zur Alterthumskunde und biblischen Kritik, zur Literatur und Religionsgeschichte*. Berlin: A. Asher.

_____. 1859. *Die Ritus des synagogalen Gottesdienstes*. Berlin: Julius Springer.

_____. 1865. *Literaturgeschichte der synagogalen Poesie*. Louis Gerschel Verlagsbuchhandlung. Berlin.

_____. 1920. *Die syngogale Poesie des Mittelalters*. Frankfurt am Main: J. Kauffman Verlag.

Printings of the Seyder Tkhines

1648. Amsterdam.* *Tkhines*.

1649. Amsterdam. *Taytshe Tkhines*. In German rite *Sider*.

1650. Amsterdam. *Seyder Tkhines*.

[1661-1671].** Frankfurt am Main. *Seyder Tkhines*.

[1666-1686]. Amsterdam. *Seyder Tkhines*.

1667. Amsterdam. *Seyder Tkhines*. In Polish rite *Sider*.

1667. Amsterdam. *Taytshe Tkhines*. In German rite *Sider*.

[1676]. Amsterdam. *Seyder Tkhines*. In German/Polish rite *Sider*.

1680. Amsterdam. *Tkhines*.

1686. Amsterdam. *Seyder Tkhines*. In German/Polish rite *Sider*.

1687. Frankfurt am Main. *Seyder Tkhines*. In German/Polish rite *Sider* with Yiddish translation.

1688. Prague. *Tkhines*.

1689. Amsterdam. *Seyder Tkhines*.

1696. Amsterdam. *Tkhines*. In German/Polish rite *Sider* with Yiddish translation.

1696. Frankfurt am Main. *Tkhines*. In German/Polish rite *Sider*.

1696. Frankfurt am Main. *Seyder Tkhines*. In German/Polish rite *Sider* with Yiddish translation.

c.1700. [Germany]. *Naye Tkhines*.

1701. Sulzbach. *Seyder Tkhines*. In German rite *Sider*.

c.1703-1704. Amsterdam. *Seyder Tkhines*. In German rite *Sider* with Yiddish translation.

1704. Amsterdam. *Naye Taytshe Tkhines*. In German rite *Sider*.

1705. Dyhernfurth. *Tkhines*. In German/Polish rite *Sider* with Yiddish translation.
1707. Frankfurt am Main. *Seyder Tkhines*. In *Seyder tfile derekh yeshore* by Yekhiel Mikhl Epshteyn.
1708. [Frankfurt am Main]. *Tkhines*
1710. Halle. *Tkhines*. In Polish rite *Sider* with Yiddish translation by Moyshe ben Avrom Ovinu.
1710. [Prague]. *Seyder Tkhines*. Further edition: c. 1710.
1711. Amsterdam. *Taytshe Tkhines*. In German rite *Sider* with Yiddish translation.
1712. Sulzbach. No title. In German rite *Sider*.
1713. Amsterdam. *Seyder Tkhines*. In German/Polish rite *Sider* with Yiddish translation.
1714. Amsterdam. *Seyder Tkhines*. In German rite *Sider* with Yiddish translation by Eliakim ben Yankev.
1714. Frankfurt am Main. *Seyder Tkhines*. In *Seyder tfile derekh yeshore* by Yekhiel Mikhl Epshteyn.
1715. Amsterdam. *Seyder Tkhines*. In German rite *Sider* with Yiddish translation.
1715. Amsterdam. *Seyder Tkhines*. In unspecified rite *Sider* with Yiddish translation.
1715. Frankfurt am Main. *Seyder Tkhines*. In German/Polish rite *Sider*.
1718. Prague. *Seyder Tkhines*.
1721. Wilmersdorf. *Tkhine*. In German/Polish rite *Sider*. (Not seen by author).
1723. Frankfurt am Main. *Seyder Tkhines*. In *Seyder tfile derekh yeshore* by Yekhiel Mikhl Epshteyn.

Other Tkhines and Related Yiddish Works

1586. Krakow. Moyshe Shtendl, trans. *Dos tilim bukh*. (Yiddish rendition of the Book of Psalms). Preface by Royzl Fishls, ed. Published by Yitskhok ben Aren Prostits.
[1590]. Prague. *Tkhine Zu* (in Hebrew and Yiddish). Prague.
Seventeenth century. [Prague]. Rivke bas Meyer of Tiktin. *Dos zingt men on simkhes toyre iber der seyfer toyre*.
Seventeenth century. [Prague]. Yankev ben Elyohu. *Lid*.
1605–1623. Yankev ben Eliohu of Tiplits. "Eyn sheyn nayen toyre lid." Another edition: [1620, Prague].
1609. Basel. *Tkhines Vegam Bakoshes* (in Hebrew and Yiddish).
1615. Prague. Yankev ben Avrom Shloyme. "Tkhines." In *Mayne Loshn*. Further editions: 1668, n.p.; 1678, Prague.
1650. Prague. *Eyn sheyn nay lid fun dray vayber*.
1650. Prague. *Menoyre*.
c. 1650. Amsterdam. Efrayim bar Yehude Haleyvi. *Eyn nay lid af der megile*.
c. 1650–1655. Amsterdam. Khane bas Yehude-Leyb Kats almones Yitskhok Ashkenaz. *Eyn hipshe droshe*.
c. 1650. Prague. Yoysef ben Yehude Heylbron. *Eyn sheyn getlekh lid*.
1657. Amsterdam. "Dos iz eyn hipshe tkhine . . . ." In *Mishley Khokhimim Vekhidushim* by Yehude ben Shloymne Kharitsi. [1680]. [Prague]. Toybe bas Leyb. *Pitsker eyshes Yankev Pan*. *Eyn sheyn lid nay gemakht b'loshn tkhine iz vorden oysgetrakht benign adir iyum benoyro*. Another edition: N.d., n.p.

Bibliography

[1661-1688]. [Prague]. *Tkhines.*

1686. [Prague]. Sheyndele eyshes Gershen ben Shmuel. *Eyn nay sheyn lid af aseres hadibres gemakht vorn benign khoydesh sesoyney.* Further editions: c. 1685, Prague; 1686, [Prague]; [1700, Fürth] under the title: *Eyn sheyn heylig lid.*

c. 1688. Frankfurt an der Order. Elieyezer Soyfer ben Leyben. *"Tkhines."* In *Mayne Loshn.*

c. 1688. Prague. Meyer ben Shimshen Verter. *Dos getleckh lid tut redn.*

1689-1701. Dyhernfurth Shapse Bas, ed. *Tkhines.*

c.1690. Prague. *Tkhines.*

c. 1691. Fürth. Meyer ben Shimshen. *Tfile loni* with *"Tkhine."* First edition without *"Tkhine"*: 1688, Prague.

[1692-1694]. Zolkiev. [Yeshaye Hurvits]. *Eyne sheyne naye tkhine.*

1697. Frankfurt am Main. *"Taytshe tkhines."* In *Seyder Tfile Derekh Yeshore.* Edited and translated by Yekhiel Mikhl Epshteyn.

1699. *Tkhine Yerakh Yankev.* Amsterdam.

c. 1700. [Prague]. Rokhl bas Mordkhe Soyfer, ed. *Tkhine.*

c. 1700. Frankfurt am Main. *Tkhines.*

c. 1700. [Frankfurt am Main]. *Tkhines.* (Different from the previous entry.) Another edition: 1713.

Eighteenth century. [Fürth]. *Tkhines*

c. 1700. N.p. Eliezer ben Arakh. *Tfile.*

[1701-14]. Frankfurt am Main. *"Tkhines."* In German rite *Sider.*

[1705]. Prague. Beyle bas Ber Hurvits eyshes Yoysef khazn. *Tkhines vos men zol zogn fun roysh koydesh Elul....* Further editions: 1718, Prague (two editions); [c. 1700, Frankfurt an der Oder].

1707. Frankfurt am Main. *"Seyder Tkhines* and additional *Tkhines."* In *Seyder Tfile Derekh Yeshore* by Yekhiel Mikhl Epshteyn. Further editions: 1714, 1723; both in Frankfurt am Main.

1707. Frankfurt am Main. "Menoyre." In *Seyder Tfile Derekh Yeshore* by Yekhiel Mikhl Epshteyn.

1708. Prague. Yitskhok ben Leyb Yudis Kats, ed.; Moyshe Tshuve, trans. *Tkhines.*

1708. Prague. [Yitskhok ben Shloyme Luria]. *Tkhines Khadoshoys.*

[1709]. [Hergeshaugen]. Arn ben Shmuel of Hergershausen. *"Tkhines."* In *Liblikhe tfile oder greftige artsney far guf un neshome.*

1710. Halle. Gele bas Moyshe hamadpis. "Colophon." In *Sider* with Yiddish translation.

1712. Sulzbach. "Menoyre." In German rite *Sider* with no Yiddish translation, together with a Yiddish *Seyder Tkhines.*

[1713]. [Frankfurt am Main]. *Dize tkhine zol men zogn....*

1715. Amsterdam. "Naye Taytshe *Tkhines."* In German rite *Sider.*

1718. Wilmersdorf. *Taytshe Tkhines.* In German/Polish rite *Sider* with interlinear Yiddish translation by Mikhl ben Avrom Kats.

1719. Prague. Matesyohu ben Meyer Sobatski. *Eyn naye tkhine fun di layt di do zaynen geshtorbn in der mageyfe.*

1720. Wilmersdorf. *Tkhines.* In German rite *Sider.*

1720. Vienna. Menoyre entitled *"Tkhine."* In a manuscript edition of a Yiddish translation of the *Sider.*

1728. Prague. *Tkhines.*

1732. Wandsbek. *"Tkhines"* (two). In *Seyder tkhines u-Vakoshes.*

1733. Sulzbach. *Naye Tkhines u-Vakoshes* (not seen by the author, but mentioned in Grünbaum 1882, 329–30).
1747. Fürth. *Seyder Tkhines*.
1769. Fürth. *Seyder Tkhines u-Vakoshes*. 1776. London. *Tkhines*. In German rite *Sider* with Yiddish translation.
1795. Sulzbach. Menoyre. In *Seyder Tkhines u-Vakoshes*.
1797. Lemberg. *Tkhine tshuve ve-tfile ve-tsadoke*.
1813. Brod. *Tkhine kol bakhies*.
1816. Vienna. *Seyder Tkhines u-Vakoshes*.
1828. Sulzbach. *Seyder Tkhines u-Vakoshes*.
1830. Lemberg. *Tkhine amoes*.
Twentieth century. Tel Aviv. *Tkhine Rav Peninim*.
1903. Vilna. *A Naye Shas Tkhines*.

Undated Tkhines

N.p. *Seyder Tkhines* in German rite *Sider*. Same edition without *tkhines*: 1701, Sulzbach.
N.p. *Di sheyne tkhine oys erets yisroel*.

*All works listed without the name of an author are anonymous.

**Square brackets appearing in these reference lists contain information, such as a date or publisher's name, that is ascertainable but not printed in the source's text. If there is a question mark inside the brackets, the information is uncertain.

Index